$13.00

6/14

Taking Sides

Taking Sides: the fiction of John le Carré

Tony Barley

Open University Press

Milton Keynes · Philadelphia

Open University Press
Open University Educational Enterprises Limited
12 Cofferidge Close
Stony Stratford
Milton Keynes MK11 1BY, England

and

242 Cherry Street
Philadelphia, PA 19106, USA

First published 1986

British Library Cataloguing in Publication Data

Barley, Tony
 Taking sides: the fiction of John le Carré.
 1. le Carré, John – Criticism and interpretation
 I. Title
 823'.914   PR6053.074Z/

ISBN 0-335-15251-1
ISBN 0-335-15252-X [pbk]

Library of Congress Cataloging in Publication Data

Barley, Tony
 Taking Sides
 Bibliography: P.
 Includes index
 1. le Carré, John, 1931–   – Criticism and Interpretation –
 Addresses, Essays, Lectures. I. Title.
 PR6062. E33Z59 1985 823'.914   85–28434

ISBN 0-335-15251-1

ISBN 0-335-15252-X [pbk]

Text design by Clarke Williams

Phototypeset by Dobbie Typesetting Service, Plymouth
Printed in Great Britain by J. W. Arrowsmith Ltd., Bristol BS3 2NT

Contents

Acknowledgements

Substantial extracts from the novels, articles and interviews of John le Carré are reproduced by kind permission of the author and his publishers as follows: from *The Spy Who Came in from the Cold* (© 1963 Victor Gollancz Ltd) by permission of Victor Gollancz Ltd and the Putnam Publishing Group; from *The Looking-Glass War* (© 1965 D. J. M. Cornwell) and *A Small Town in Germany* (© 1968 le Carré Productions Ltd) by permission of William Heinemann Ltd and The Putnam Publishing Group; from *Tinker Tailor Soldier Spy* (© 1974 le Carré Productions), *The Honourable Schoolboy* (© 1977 Authors Workshop AG), *Smiley's People* (© 1979 Authors Workshop AG), and *The Little Drummer Girl* (© 1983 Authors Workshop AG) by permission of Hodder & Stoughton Ltd and Alfred A. Knopf Ltd. For their encouragement and practical assistance I am very grateful to George Greenfield of John Farquharson Ltd, Eric Major of Hodder & Stoughton Ltd and particularly to John Skelton of The Open University Press. Many thanks are due also to friends and colleagues who directed me towards valuable material and often went to considerable trouble on my behalf: Bernard Beatty, Edward Burns, John Corner, Alison Cumpsty, Kevin Donovan, Jerry Hall, Clare Lees, Dick Leith, Steve Newman, John O'Brien, Jeffrey Peacock, Bob Ramsey, Nigel Relph, Vanessa Scully and David Seed. Most of all, my thanks to Jane Jameson for giving me continuous support and clear-headedly guiding my efforts throughout, and to Josie Skelton for her great help in sharpening blunt ideas and suggesting many improvements. I should add that although their work is not specifically cited in the main text, I am grateful to credit the personnel associated with Spartacist Publications as their meticulously researched historical material provided me with an invaluable resource in writing chapters 3, 4, 5 and 8. If I have been free with their interpretations of recent history the responsibility is mine alone.

Note on references

I have kept references in the main body of this book as brief as possible. Extracts from the novels of John le Carré and Graham Greene are given citing chapter not page to allow the reader to consult any of their numerous editions. Other quotations are identified by author, date and page number except for short (mainly review) articles in newspapers, weekly journals and magazines where author and date only are given. Quotations from le Carré's remarks in interviews are indicated by I at the end of a reference: thus 'Cameron, 8 September 1980. I.' refers to comments by le Carré in conversation with James Cameron. Further details of all cited materials may be found in the List of References.

Italics within quotations are always those of the original author.

1 Contexts: Genre and Ideology, Persons and Politics

Since the external disorder, and extravagant lies,
The baroque frontiers, the surrealist police;
What can truth treasure, or heart bless,
But a narrow strictness?   (Auden, 1977, p. 111)

It is clear that there are many John le Carrés; or perhaps it would be closer to the truth to say that le Carré's fiction has many faces and voices, and that they compete with one another, appealing variously to different kinds of reader. There is, to take one example, the le Carré who pays homage to the poet W. H. Auden by quoting from his early work from time to time, and by appropriating his mythology. Auden's abandoned agents, arbitrary borders, indistinguishable enemies, malign authorities and false guides figure in le Carré too and, like Auden's solitaries, le Carré's isolates are prompted into stark reflections on motive, value and allegiance, anxiously seeking solace in dreams of imaginary companions or in purely private moralities. Just a step away from Auden is the presence of his near contemporary – Graham Greene – the writer with whom le Carré is most often compared and with whose novels of conscience le Carré's debate. In fact, the later author's consciousness of 'literary' traditions is far broader than these comparisons suggest but it is likely that the immense commercial success of his fiction lies elsewhere than in its literary continuities. Undoubtedly, that success has more to do with le Carré's voice as the knowing insider, familiar to a fault with the secret life of the Security, Intelligence and Diplomatic Services. This le Carré is the pseudonymous, tantalizing source who leaks privileged information from what his readers are delighted to believe is the hidden heart of society. With mysteriously topical foresight, this le Carré seems to predict the next astounding exposure of yet another real-life spy and, equally engagingly, this le Carré records in careful detail the mundanities and inefficiencies of the secret world. Close at hand is le Carré the amused ironist and comedian of manners, fluently

1

mimicking the language of the old boy network and discreetly observing the sad absurdities of its bureaucracies. Alongside, is le Carré the harsh moral satirist, condemning the criminal excesses and dangerous fantasies of society's ostensible guardians.

And then there is le Carré the myth-maker, the creator of an almost entirely fictional Intelligence jargon, the awed narrator of the exploits of Smiley and Karla, and the elegist of declining Imperial power and lost national purpose. Equally, there is le Carré the 'social realist', the hard-nosed, vernacular reporter of the squalid and sordid. While on an altogether different plane, there is le Carré the political novelist, dramatizer and analyst of opponent positions, commentator on the practices of the Cold War, and historian of diverse crises – the Berlin Wall, rising Neo-Nazism in West Germany, the defeat of American Imperialism in South-East Asia, the Israeli invasion of the Lebanon. And from the political to the personal, there is le Carré the psychologist, attuned to domestic, marital transactions, and the projections and transferences which characterize relationships under stress. Somewhere or other, there is also the le Carré who may be the biographer (or autobiographer) of David John Moore Cornwell, but he is not the subject of this book. Most strikingly and obviously, there is le Carré the story-teller, the popular writer, the armchair and train journey entertainer, the master of the spy-thriller. All these aspects and identities offer themselves as legitimate starting-points for a description of le Carré's fiction.

For the most part this book will concentrate on le Carré's *political* and *psychological* materials and their specific intersections, as it is in these areas that le Carré's own preferred interests (and most distinctive achievements) seem mainly located. Nevertheless it would certainly beg too many questions to ignore entirely le Carré's role and reputation as perhaps the foremost exponent of the modern spy-thriller. So in this introductory chapter I look first at his relationship to genre, discussing his selective use of thriller patterns and his divergences from the generic norms; secondly, I turn to some of the typical critical responses to him as a writer of popular fiction. In particular, I begin to explore le Carré's novels as other than unproblematic props for Western ideology and examine briefly their general dealings with West versus East, including their approaches to the State, nationality, social class and gender. Finally, paving the way for a more detailed consideration of his 'mature' thrillers, I introduce some notions of how far and in what respects le Carré writes both a 'personal' and 'political' fiction. I argue that his idiosyncratic formal structures arise as the direct expression of his political and psychological subject matter – his repetitions, debate or interrogation structures and political/personal montage effects all stem from the apparently intractable political/personal confusions he so pointedly dramatizes.

The spy-thriller and John le Carré

Notwithstanding the presence there of a Secret Service hero, le Carré's first two novels, *Call for the Dead* (1961) and *A Murder of Quality* (1962) are more akin to the classic English detective story than to the spy-thriller. Although *Call for the Dead* charts George Smiley's investigations into the death of a suspected spy, its political dimension is downplayed in favour of the narrow 'psychological' approach required by detective fiction in which the tactics and deductions of the hero earn pride of place. In similar vein, *A Murder of Quality* eschews the extensive range of action expected of the spy-thriller and le Carré confines himself to the exclusive world of the British public school, always focusing attention inwards rather than looking out towards the larger political sphere. Smiley's Espionage and Security Service experience in this novel is merely a convention – it serves solely to suggest his expertise and ability in tracking down the guilty. As John Halperin has shown (1980, pp. 17–37), the thematic preoccupations of these early novels were to be reworked, developed and extended in *Tinker Tailor Soldier Spy*.

But by 1974 – the publication date of *Tinker Tailor Soldier Spy* – le Carré's identity as *the* writer of spy-thrillers was well established, and with the exception of those first two novels and *The Naive and Sentimental Lover* (a sabbatical excursion from the world of espionage into the private fantasies of its small cast of non-political characters), all his remaining novels to date have attracted to themselves the spy-thriller label. Because it is on these that the extent of his achievement has been (judiciously) gauged, his seven spy-thrillers furnish the primary material for the present study. At once, however, they come up against problems of category which irritatingly refuse to disappear. Ever since the publication of *The Spy Who Came in from the Cold* in 1963, his reviewers have seen le Carré as standing with one foot inside the genre boundaries and with the other outside, and consistently and predictably their commentaries have been concerned with evaluating his capacity to 'write something more than a thriller' (Hicks, 24 July 1965). Evidently the sense of le Carré's generic incongruity is more of an issue for literary criticism than it is for the author himself, and where the author characteristically dismisses the subject in his interviews, the genre analysts feel obliged to negotiate le Carré's 'difference' as best they can. In his *Anatomy of the Spy Thriller* for example, Bruce Merry disparages le Carré's ungeneric narrative structures and his self-conscious, 'highbrow' quest in search of the 'Great Novel' (1977, pp. 51, 214). John Atkins, on the other hand, simply reverses this judgement, insisting that le Carré's 'best spy novels are also mainstream novels' (1984, p. 170). Unfortunately, the conflation of a language of category with a language of evaluation raises more difficulties than it solves and consequently it is not my aim to pursue its implications. Nor am I interested to advance some revamped definition of the thriller so as to accommodate le Carré to the genre in some more comfortable way, nor even to speculate on the possibility that his work may somehow transform and redirect the thriller tradition. Those are areas for other projects. Nonetheless, an initial perspective on le Carré's relationship to the spy-thriller in terms of form and function is genuinely helpful in pointing towards what is distinctive in his fiction, and Bruce Merry's cogent analysis of the genre provides a solid framework against which to place le Carré's idiosyncrasies.

Merry abstracts the formal aspects of the thriller and considers too the system of values it habitually displays. The spy-thriller offers a non-mimetic, causal action, with an accelerating, narrowing storyline. It is divided into separate narrative sections and incorporates a decreasing quantity of episodic or recapitulated material. The narrative progresses in an increasingly suspense-laden and focused movement which culminates in a single moment of 'pay-off', usually a 'reversal of fortune' (Merry, p. 5). Both characterization and morality tend to serve formal ends but they also inscribe established social assumptions. The conventional hero – invariably 'different', 'hard-boiled' and 'tough' – is a man who has rejected the mundane and has open to him a range of 'romantic roles': 'bandit, detective, criminal, hunted man, sheriff, lone ranger, explorer or *parfit gentil* knight' (pp. 7–8). He acts within a context Merry defines as assembling 'an elemental theology of right and wrong, home country versus enemy state' (p. 4). Merry argues that spy-thrillers permit a passive readership to witness a manifest (and elementary) Virtue triumph over an equally elementary Evil, and that in most cases, this is achieved through the 'clear action' and 'fast thinking' of a character forced to run counter to the various incapacities of the authorities. With its pretensions to realism and its celebration of vigilante-like figures achieving eventual moral supremacy in the public interest, Merry concludes that the genre is 'a form of readable evasion' (p. 5). This 'ideological' function will be considered later in this chapter.

Any but the most cursory readings of le Carré's thrillers must find that they fail to tally with the formal rules Merry identifies. Frequently le Carré sets himself a succession of short generic tasks but they remain localized, as provisional functions rather than as determining principles of his stories. When, for instance, Guillam purloins information from a Circus safe in *Tinker Tailor Soldier Spy*, or Westerby 'burns' Frost in *The Honourable Schoolboy*, or Charlie delivers her briefcase bomb in *The Little Drummer Girl*, such sequences behave conventionally enough in furthering plot and creating suspense, but the narrative interest, even here, refuses to focus in a sustained and single-minded way on action alone. The treatment of Guillam's theft is a particular case in point. Just as he opens the safe-door Guillam hears a sound like a note from a flute – perhaps it has come from a car outside the building or perhaps it is the noise of a squeaking trolley in the corridor. Momentarily the task in hand is suspended:

> . . . for that moment it was one of those long, mournful notes which made up Camilla's practice scales. She played exactly when she felt like it. At

midnight, in the early morning or whenever. She didn't give a damn about the neighbours; she seemed quite nerveless altogether. He remembered her that first evening: 'Which is your side of the bed? Where shall I put my clothes?' He prided himself on his delicate touch in such things but Camilla had no use for it, technique was already a compromise, a compromise with reality, she would say an escape from it. All right, so get me out of this lot. (le Carré, 1974, ch. 11)

This is typical le Carré. Action is subordinated to character as linear thriller-plot expectations are displaced in oblique, generically extraneous diversions. What Guillam has to find in the safe recedes in importance and so too, to some extent, does his fear of being discovered; the theft feeds into his more general insecurity with Camilla, material which competes successfully with the comparatively limited concerns of the thriller-plot.

With the single exception of *The Spy Who Came in from the Cold*, which assiduously omits generically peripheral material, all of the succeeding 'thrillers' delight in the careful inclusion of expansive and dispersing information which decelerates the movement of the thriller action and draws the reader away from the standard expectations of what will happen next, and how. These excursive features are not the episodes and digressions which complement the core-story of thrillers because, simply, they comprise the primary narrative concern in le Carré's novels. The business involving surveillance, quest, chase, interrogation, violence, discovery, reversal and the like – the thriller's formal devices and motifs – is normally the object of wayward treatment on le Carré's part and is invariably used as part of the means of exploring a complex of psychological, moral and political concerns. And however finely-worked le Carré's thriller-plots prove, they act as scaffolding for other constructions. None of the novels employs Merry's 'funnel' structure, whereby the thriller narrative, merely *punctuated* 'with pauses and digressions' in its early and middle sections (p. 7), becomes rigorously channelled into the narrowing point of climax. (Merry himself criticizes *The Looking-Glass War* for its failure to 'funnel' pp. 50–3.) On the contrary, le Carré's climaxes are more often than not carefully separated from the general body of the story, appearing as heightened and comparatively stylized set-pieces. The climactic ending of *A Small Town in Germany* occupies a final chapter significantly entitled 'Epilogue', and le Carré has himself described both this conclusion and that of *The Spy Who Came in from the Cold* as 'theatrical' and 'operatic' (1968. I.). The same adjectives could well describe the tableau ending of the *The Looking-Glass War* where the Vopos enter a Kalstadt flat to arrest the cornered agent Leiser, or the explicitly theatrical assassination of Khalil which provides *The Little Drummer Girl*'s climax; these too have a self-contained effect and are prepared for with an anti-generic swiftness. 'False' or alternative endings, surrounding the climax, and competing with it, are also common to le Carré's thrillers in contrast to Merry's normative model (p. 7). Thus *Tinker Tailor Soldier Spy* locates its two climaxes (Haydon's unmasking and his murder) within a patterned series of endings, each independent of the others. The Guillam-Camilla plot achieves its own resolution while, as the finale of a quite separate action, Smiley takes the train to Immingham to meet Ann again. As a kind of coda, the novel closes with the rebuilt relationship between Prideaux and his pupil and protector, Roach.

Sometimes, it is true, le Carré's heroes enjoy a generic brashness – Leamas and Turner *look* like formula characters but they receive a treatment by which the conventional 'difference' of the thriller hero is denied. In novel after novel, what appears (conventionally) extraordinary in leading characters either becomes secondary or is revealed as a sham – normally le Carré's people are shown to embody and project socially typical behaviour and attitudes, however much they seek to assert the opposite. The extraordinariness of the generic situations in which they are placed, over and again forces them to become conscious of what is normal and typical in themselves, and the results are then offered for judgement. George Smiley's generic eccentricities combine to form a persona which covers a personality caught in political contradiction and emotional confusion. His generic 'brilliance' in spy-catching and interrogation is presented for admiration but it actually plays a subsidiary role in his portrayal. Jerry Westerby, the writer, journalist, part-time agent and 'honourable schoolboy' rebel is a John Buchan composite transported into a more complex world than his generic antecedents. Whenever the givens of the thriller tradition are employed, they are set up to be challenged and also to serve le Carré's individual and ulterior purposes.

For every leading character the morality of political deception and of loyalty to the West's democratic cause and way of life is encountered as acutely problematic and potentially debilitating. The tension between personal and corporate loyalties is accorded a similar highlight. That 'elementary' conflict of Virtue and Evil which Merry describes, surfaces in le Carré in radically altered forms. The notion of Western virtue, of good residing in a humanitarian liberalism (itself serving a hard, unpalatable, anti-communist Authority) is subjected to a continued and emphatic questioning. The Stalinist East certainly signifies a far cruder, elemental evil but le Carré does not ignore communism's worryingly incomprehensible attraction and the East's capacity to exact a terrifyingly clear commitment from its adherents. *The Quest for Karla* trilogy attends to this theme with an anxious persistence. Outside the overt Cold War clashes, le Carré also refuses to take the simplicities of thriller morality for granted. The indiscriminate violence of terrorism, an ideally-given basic Evil for the thriller writer, is treated in *The Little Drummer Girl* to a many-angled analytical process which subverts the genre's moral norm. Of course, it is every reader's prerogative to suppress such issues and concentrate on the thriller action alone, but le Carré makes that option difficult in the extreme by his sheer concentration on issue. If his novels comprise, in Merry's words, 'a form of readable evasion', they must do so in a more insidious and sophisticated form than their generic counterparts.

Reading for ideology in John le Carré

The ideology of popular fiction

The curious marriage of Structuralist and Marxist literary criticism that took place in the early 1970s – a marriage to which Marxism eloped – produced a new body of work intent on uncovering literature's ideological functions. The overriding concern to delineate and analyse literature's largely unwitting transmissions of society's dominant ideology combined here with a growing interest in the various genres of popular literature. Naturally the thriller became a prime subject for investigation:

> The focal point of the thriller, its central contribution to ideology, is the delineation of a personality that is isolated and competitive and who wins because he is better adapted to the world than anyone else. This superiority is incarnated in acts that are deliberately and explicitly deviant, and yet justified. The individuality, the personal worth of the hero is presented as inseparable from the performance of actions that in any other circumstances would be reprehensible; yet at the same time the 'circumstances' are a fictional construct, designed to justify the pleasure that the reader derives from the representation of such acts. (Palmer, 1973, p. 141)

In his book *Thrillers*, Jerry Palmer amplifies this argument to suggest that the ruling class's 'fear of conspiracy' and its desire to 'present society as . . . in the normal run of events, devoid of conflict' are 'incarnate' in the thriller (1978, p. 66). Here, 'ideology' is not used in its conventional, parliamentary (and usually dismissive) meaning as a consciously-held abstract system of beliefs; it denotes instead those ideas embedded in the practice of routine social existence which maintain and defend the status quo through the false cognition they habitually reproduce. For Palmer then, the thriller, in its own unique way, encodes, embodies, transmits and recommends those false notions about the world that the ruling order requires for its preservation, and which are 'incarnate' in other forms in the general life of a particular society.

The following example offered by Palmer is pertinent to le Carré's fiction:

> In fact, the contradiction between individuality and sociality is as fundamental a contradiction as there is to be found within the ideology of our society, and the thriller is devoted to resolving it, fictitiously of course, to the benefit of individuality. The fact that the dichotomy is false, that individuality and sociality are not in any sense necessarily opposed to each other, only strengthens the case: the essence of ideology is not to give false answers to real problems, but to pose problems in such a (false) way that the recommendations one wished to make in the first place appear to correspond to a real problem. Insofar as individuality and sociality are seen to have conflicting claims, no-one will perceive the reality of the case: that the individuality that makes these claims is an entirely social creation. (1978, p. 204)

Although it does not function in the standard (Bond-type) generic manner of reconciling the agent's 'individuality' with the society whose normal rules he breaks, *The Spy Who Came in from the Cold* may be seen as offering a more sophisticated variant on the above. The 'problem' of the novel indeed dramatizes a 'dichotomy' between individual and society and ends with a resolution favouring 'individuality'. Realizing that the British Secret Service (the 'Circus') has set him up and killed his lover, the agent Leamas chooses suicide in preference to returning to his controllers and safety. But by this act he acknowledges his own humanity and is morally saved. He dies for love and his martyrdom brings him into line with the larger social value his bosses pretend to endorse and protect yet, through their evil methods, actually deny. Taking such a reading as paramount, le Carré's condemnations of the West's espionage excesses recede in importance, the deeper ideology of humanism – the essential decency of the ordinary man – surfaces to over-ride and obfuscate former contradictions. A comparable reading of *The Spy Who Came in from the Cold* appears in an article by Roger Bromley subtitled 'the Social Function of Popular Literature' and published in the literature journal of the Communist Party of Great Britain. Bromley argues that popular literature is 'dominated by "feeling", "personal experience", and immediate empirical perception' which 'fails to grasp or acknowledge, by omission, the *political* as the crucial level of the social formation':

> The evacuation from the novel *The Spy Who Came in from the Cold* of the political (or, more precisely, what is offered as the political) by a constant personal/political antithesis which is resolved in terms of the 'personal' is a critical instance . . . (1978, pp. 39–40)

While the related approaches of Palmer and Bromley are undoubtedly instructive in advocating the search for ideology, they also pose significant problems, especially with regard to le Carré's writing. Bromley's insistence that *The Spy Who Came in from the Cold* evacuates 'the political' by privileging 'the personal' seeks, understandably, to deny the autonomy of 'the personal' but seems to neglect, *en route*, that it is only through human subjects that politics are enacted at all. Where an ideological humanism indeed appears in the novel's conclusion, it is a reductive distortion to count as simply ideological those tensions in characters' attempts to negotiate between personal and political concerns. In fact, those tensions are manifestly present in the real world, ideology notwithstanding. In opposition to Bromley's view, the present book contends that a substantial part of le Carré's achievement lies in his clear-sighted attention to the mutual influence of personal and political material.

For similar reasons, Jerry Palmer's stimulating analysis of the thriller's ideological function proves only partially appropriate to le Carré's fiction. Insistently, for example, le Carré ensures that the justification for 'reprehensible acts' is never assumed; neither are the competence, 'superiority' or 'personal worth' of his agent-heroes offered as naturally endorsed givens.

In these areas, le Carré subverts the ideological assumptions of the genre. On the other hand, of course, the ideological 'fear of conspiracy' that Palmer identifies is undoubtedly 'incarnate' in his work together with further ideological traces and omissions which I shall consider below. It is not the objective of recognizing ulterior and hidden functions that is at fault here but the selectiveness which ignores literature's other functions.

There is probably an unavoidable tendency in genre criticism to neglect differences or departures from the norm but the basic problem with the Palmer–Bromley approach resides not so much there as in a more fundamental misconception about the relationship between (any) literature and ideology. In a useful related discussion, the Marxist critic Cliff Slaughter challenges the idea of literature as *exclusively* acting to reflect and recommend the 'prevailing ideology' of the class whose rule it helps sustain:

> Surely there remains, after all, the question of the objective content within the ideology itself as well as, possibly, within the literary work as against the prevailing ideology. (1980, p. 205)

Slaughter adds that it is 'a caricature of Marxism to reduce literature to just an ideological mechanism' (p. 206) and concludes his argument with an admirable defence of literature's capacity to form valid images of the real:

> Literature and art undoubtedly share with all forms of cognition the characteristic of expressing ideology. The historical study of the ideological influences upon and ideological content of literary works is of course essential to any Marxist analysis. But cognition is not exhausted by ideological content. The social relations engaged in by the men of a particular society . . . are not to be comprehended solely in terms of the fact that they express or confirm that particular social formation. Ideological and 'reproductive' functions are only part of cognition as a whole. They are *relative* to the growth of man's knowledge and control of nature and history. (p. 212)

This is not an argument which necessarily favours realist art – a lyric poem for instance will also produce its particular image of the real world and its processes. That point is important in the present context because in the case of le Carré, the fictional business of spying, secret organizations and their behaviour, provides the form through which an 'objective content' is produced. Real-life spies may well act differently from fictional spies but that is often an interesting yet peripheral concern. Believing that spy-thrillers (le Carré's included) evade reality by presenting actions which rarely correspond 'to the known facts about real-life spy networks and intelligence operations', Bruce Merry (1977, p. 1) betrays a limited and inadequate conception of the relationship between the literary work and the world it encounters. By his statement, Merry (like Palmer and Bromley) neglects completely to acknowledge that thriller writers, alongside artists in general, may:

penetrate, in some way and in some measure, to the source of [the]
ideological structure, and thus be able to expose its contradictions . . .
(Slaughter, p. 201)

Such an 'exposure' indeed begins to occur in the way le Carré tests the
validity of liberalism and the notion of individual self-sufficiency. It occurs
too in his treatment of conflicts between work and home, between the public
and personal spheres, and between the West's self-appointment as the 'Free
World' and its coercive actions. The particular formal methods by which
philosophies and events are made to reveal their contradictions will be
discussed in later chapters, but one needs to consider here the specific
ideological presences in le Carré's fiction in order to distinguish between
what 'mystifies' and what produces 'objective content', between what
incarnates and what undermines the dominant ideology. Le Carré's own
comments on the reception of his novels are very illuminating here. Speaking
in a television interview on the attractions of writing about double-agents
and their intrigues, he said:

> I think that the conspiracy alone is some kind of solace to the reader or to
> the audience: people want to interpret their lives in terms of conspiracy.
> They know that it's around them – they know that they live in an increasingly
> secretive society in many ways where they're cut off from the decisions of
> power – so that a story like *Tinker Tailor*, or for that matter, *Smiley's People*
> does lay out a massive conspiracy for them and lead them to some kind of
> conclusion, and they have that sense of resolution: 'Yes, that is how the
> world is, that is how my firm is – they are all at one another's throats, they're
> all intriguing . . .'   (Bragg 27 March 1983. I.)

These remarks bear directly on Palmer's discussion of the thriller's function
of enacting and fictitiously neutralizing society's 'fear of conspiracy'. It
may be argued that the threat Karla poses, via his 'mole' Haydon,
reproduces the ruling class's self-serving paranoia about the enemy within
being linked clandestinely with the enemy without. The ruling-class's
genuine fears of working-class opposition, of the instability of the prevailing
system, together with its active, hostile destabilizing attempts against 'the
East', are thus masked, and presented for public consumption as *defensive*
acts to preserve the social order from 'foreign' conspiracies. In the course
of the thriller narrative, the supposed threat is displayed as dangerous but
is allayed by the acts of a man who serves the powers-that-be, yet stands
apart from them. The exceptional investigator (like Smiley) single-mindedly
if not single-handedly, takes the necessary action the established Authorities
cannot (by reason of their bureaucratism, their self-interest, their
inefficiency, and their having been temporarily duped by the same
conspiracy). The investigator consolingly discovers an order and safety in
things by defusing the most extreme dangers that face normal society.

However, the scenario is complicated by other factors. In contrast to
Palmer's ideological/generic norm, society is here *not* presented as 'in the
normal run of events, devoid of conflict'. Quite the opposite. Conspiracy,

as le Carré's comments indicate, is given as an inherent part of the social structure. Moreover, it is practised above all by the Authorities themselves, implicitly to the ultimate detriment of society as a whole.

The establishment and the nation

The élite, self-contained groupings which manage, preserve and defend society conspire secretly at the top-most reaches of the social scale. The mass of the population is quite ignorant of their activities (even, it is implied, of their existence) and on the few occasions that 'ordinary' people (actually wives and lovers) are directly affected by them, it is as powerless victims. The secret world is a world apart but it is not united: conflicting personal and policy interests make for a great web of rivalry, pitting at various times Department against Department, Intelligence Service against Ministry, the (British) Circus against their (American) Cousins, Establishment controllers against their petit-bourgeois functionaries, and blatant Cold Warriors against humane liberals. Strict hierarchies lend structure and system to this world but, characteristically, the ultimate sources of power remain undiscovered. Reinforcing this effect, the figures on whom le Carré's narratives concentrate are never themselves in either full or permanent control but are subject to an authority beyond them. Behind Leamas stand the puppet-masters, Control and Mundt; above Leiser and Avery in *The Looking-Glass War* is the Haldane–Leclerc brainstrust, itself the dupe of Smiley and Control, and, so it turns out, the East German Intelligence Service to which with cynical expediency, Control has betrayed the expendable Leiser. In the power games of *A Small Town in Germany* Turner and Harting attempt unsuccessfully to run counter to the British Foreign Service bureaucracy which, to ensure its own preservation, bows to the diplomats in Brussels, the *Abwehr* and, finally, the neo-Nazi Karfeld, who mysteriously has everyone in his power. *The Quest for Karla* novels place George Smiley dominantly in their narratives but, despite his machinations, his capacity to manoeuvre is invariably restricted – *Tinker Tailor Soldier Spy* shows him marginalized as the result of internal power struggles in the Service, while in *The Honourable Schoolboy* and *Smiley's People* he is the temporary caretaker Chief, provisionally interrupting his retirement. Above and beyond him are (first) Alleline and (next) Enderby, themselves subject to the pressure of the Ministry and the Cousins, to say nothing of the power of Karla and his pervasive manipulations.

If le Carré fudges the issue of whether the Intelligence and Espionage Services autonomously formulate policy or if they are merely the executors of policies determined by governmental and managerial forces above them, it is of no great importance. Central to his vision of power, though, is the idea of 'the Establishment'. This term originally entered the public domain in 1955 with Henry Fairlie's *Spectator* article on the defection of Burgess and Maclean (quoted in Hewison, 1981, p. 166) and quickly came to denote the unofficial, conspiratorial power-élite which exercised insidious social influence. It is a notion that has remained with le Carré throughout his career. The Establishment, for him, symbolizes the State not the nation; it pretends to act in the interests of all but is actually accountable to no one below and really serves itself. Ostensibly society's defender, the Establishment in fact defends itself. Undeniably, the image of a self-serving, self-deluding, factional, uncontrollable Authority exposes something of a contradiction in the concept of a free, British (Western) democracy and objectively represents a *partially* valid picture of that democracy's actual structure. But what are its ideological functions? Armed with the author's own description of the 'solace' his stories offer, a Structuralist–Marxist view might well suggest that his novels ideologically promote a knowing, yet cynical quietism, a submission to the status quo. The evidence is already there in the author's statement that his fiction gives the consolation of a confirming knowledge that power-conspiracies exist all around us and proposes *fictional* solutions to a practice that in the real world is perceived as habitual and unresolvable.

Although it would be patently absurd to overemphasize the social significance of this effect (which eventually assumes a readership responding by no more than conditioned reflex to ideological secretions), le Carré's presentation of the exercise of power is particularly noteworthy because, in a significant omission, he gives no indication that the Authorities ever act in defensive reaction to the influence of larger social movements below them. Conspiracy theory excludes the role of class forces. Certainly a sense of class tension is dramatized in the relations between an 'aristocratic' Establishment and its petit-bourgeois functionaries but it exists at the level of snobbery (Hewison, p. 167) and le Carré hardly even gestures towards deeper class conflicts. To be sure, the world le Carré depicts engages interest because it sees itself as a world apart and because it performs its business secretly; and there is no reason why the author should be under any obligation to portray proletarian characters (which he does not), or to describe collective, open, mass activity (which he does only rarely). But as a result, the dominant image is of an élite matrix of power affecting, directly or indirectly, passive, impotent or manipulable social sectors below it. So, even the fascistic mob in *A Small Town in Germany* is seen as the creation and instrument of the demogogue Karfeld: they are his product, he is not theirs. Frenzied and slogan-shouting, the church-wrecking Communist mob which played a small part in the history of Nelson Ko (le Carré, 1977, ch. 11) is described 'without the least hint of rancour' in similar terms–as dehumanized and manipulated, this time by Party 'ideology'. Political mass activity is abnormal, a response to crisis conditions, and whether in the colours of the left or the right (le Carré sees the two 'extremes' as identical), its form is mob rampage. For the first time in *The Little Drummer Girl*, le Carré treats collective action sympathetically but the Palestinian refugee communities depicted there are so placed in the narrative that the real struggle inevitably seems to be played out in the novel's European settings, and again, it is a war principally conducted by the élite – the crack Israeli counter-terrorist unit versus Khalil's highly-organized and highly-successful guerilla group.

Le Carré's vision of power in his fiction may indeed transmit a sense of the impossibility of 'ordinary' people instigating social change but it is perhaps more significant of the way it (ideologically) relegates fundamental class conflicts to concentrate instead on the problem of Authority as, above all, a *national* problem. The crisis expressed, for instance, in the behaviour of the state is, for le Carré, defined as such because that behaviour runs counter to the national purpose, unity and identity which either once was, or now should be, paramount. Many critics and reviewers have noted the tone of nostalgia associated with the character of Smiley and the le Carréan atmosphere of a Britain (even a world) in sad decline. Smiley's age alone contributes to this sense. Though superannuated he is still periodically necessary; brought out of retirement for his archaic soundness, he harks back regretfully to a former time of clear moral values. He is seen as embodying some quiet, almost extinguished spirit of the nation, far removed from vulgar overt professions of patriotism and from crude nationalist political programmes. Of course Smiley is far more complex than this sentimental sketch suggests but his nostalgic strain, acutely and defeatistly critical of the present state of things, indicates that the ideology of the author and the ideology 'incarnate' in his literary works completely coincide in at least one respect.

In his secondary role as political commentator, le Carré champions an ideal nationalism, or perhaps more accurately, 'nationhood', since that term may avoid the flag-waving implications of the former, which are anathema both to the author and to his most famous fictional character. The Introduction le Carré contributed to a book on Philby by the *Sunday Times* 'Insight' team reveals him encountering, not quite head-on, some of the problems involved in his tendency to downplay a language of social class in favour of a language of nationhood. The essay is as harsh an attack on the Establishment as on Philby himself (see Chapter 5 below) and the first-person plural voice le Carré adopts projects significant ambiguities. The author acknowledges his unease over his choice of pronoun, an unease which is actually generated by the desire to assume a national responsibility for the Philby affair at the same time as underlining the difference between those 'privileged Englishmen' of the Establishment and society at large:

> Still, listening to our own judgements we can discern in ourselves the social attitudes and opinions which account as much for Philby's survival as for his own determination to destroy us . . . I am uncomfortably conscious, incidentally, of the 'we': Philby's is one of those cases which force us to define our own place in society. I suppose by 'we' I mean the world to which I myself vaguely belong: middle-class, graduate, intellectual. Philby's world, but indoors. (Introduction to Page et al., 1968, pp. 9–10)
>
> If the secret services were negligent in controlling Philby, so Parliament and we ourselves, society at large, were equally negligent in controlling our own secret services. It was *our* politicians who fronted for them, *our* editors who suppressed for them, *our* dons who informed for them, recruited for them; *our* Prime Ministers who protected them. (Ibid. p. 23)

'We Britons' is what le Carré seems really to mean here, assuming that nationhood is the ultimate donor and guarantor of social identity. The same assumption underlies a piece written twelve years later for the *Observer* on the Prince's Gate siege. Incisively polemical, the article scathingly attacks the gross, patriotic, 'racial?' glorification of the SAS. Le Carré's irony is variously and brilliantly directed against the television channels, Mrs Thatcher, her Army ('shock-troops storming into London's streets'), the police, Mr Whitelaw, Mr Powell, Mr Eldon Griffiths, Government hypocrisy, counter-terrorism itself, and that ignorant, manipulated popular consciousness which was being given 'the first live political siege to be televised on British soil':

> For an audience, take a sensitive, deeply patriotic nation deprived of the fun of war and the status of a Great Power, still bogged down in TV soap opera of how it licked the Germans and tamed the colonial native, and increasingly wedded to such hazardous leisure substitutes as pot-holing, car-racing, hang-gliding . . . (le Carré, 1 June 1980)

But the satirical anger eventually gives way. In the final paragraphs of the piece le Carré's irony all but collapses as the nostalgia for nationhood once more surfaces:

> On the morning following the siege I took an early walk on Hampstead Heath. Sometimes at that time of day, you see a pale blue police car patrolling one of the tarmac paths at a stately five miles an hour. Perhaps it was only my imagination, but on that day the police car seemed to be travelling a great deal faster, and with a lot less concern for the public it was there to protect.
>
> I grabbed my son's dog and tried to wish them good morning because the patriot in me, or the citizen, really wanted to show a human face, and see one in return. They shot past me and all I saw was four hostile eyes looking me up and down. Perhaps they were tired. Perhaps they were hunting for a rapist. But I still wished they'd smiled. Do you know that feeling these days? I seem to get it more and more. (Ibid.)

Fascinated by national 'characteristics' and motivations, le Carré seems inclined to regard nationhood as the natural, normal and authentic source of individual behaviour. Ideally the (British) nation embodies the mostly buried values of humanism, individualism, democracy and decency, which 'good' characters (however few) struggle to defend and maintain, even if that task puts them in opposition to society's purported guardians who have lost sight of their legitimate role. Consequently, betrayal becomes an act against a notion of the entire national organism not just its unhealthy, cynical, compromising leadership and the forces at its command.

Ideology and humanism
This national sense is counterposed, in an unequal antagonism, to 'communism'. In a characteristic opposition, the former denotes a way

of life, the latter a system which masquerades as a way of life. Again, le Carré's complexities should warn against such a simplification: the trials of Leamas in *The Spy Who Came in from the Cold* and Smiley in *Tinker Tailor Soldier Spy* disclose the contradictions in positions which would like to promote themselves as outside 'ideology' (using that term, as le Carré does, in its conventional sense). Leamas and Smiley are forced to recognize their respective 'ideologies', the 'philosophy' they live by. Nevertheless, the way of life versus system opposition persists through le Carré's fiction, thus making for a stimulating (because unresolved) authorial contradiction. The way of life (national, democratic, humanist, individualist, natural) contends — with 'communism' as an unnatural 'ideology' superimposed by idealists, intellectuals and/or power seekers on peoples to whom it is both foreign and frightening. 'Communism' here is actually equivalent to Stalinism. The ex-KGB agent Irina, whose diary entries are reported in *Tinker Tailor Soldier Spy* is led, through her love-affair with Tarr, to reject the 'captivity' imposed upon her by communism and espouse 'Love', 'freedom' and Christianity, thus returning to the natural values of her nation – and dying a martyr's death as a result. In concert, *Smiley's People* nostalgically celebrates the nationalism and religious beliefs of the ageing and long-expatriate white Russian and Estonian communities in Paris and London. It is perhaps not entirely accidental that the publication of that novel in 1980 coincided with the rise of Catholic *Solidarnosc* in Poland and the Red Army's war against the Moslem rebels in Afghanistan. Significantly, the novel also takes to an extreme the mythologizing of the Russian mastermind Karla, whose overriding commitment to communism is seen as an unfathomable fanaticism. But even Karla proves to have a human face in the end; the natural bond (his love for his daughter) is Karla's undoing and, blackmailed, he too defects from the cause. There are 'good' communists in le Carré's fiction but they are either victims or, disillusioned, they desert 'ideology'. Fiedler, the intellectual Stalinist of good heart is murdered by the application of his own 'philosophy' against himself. Nelson Ko eventually wins sympathy by turning aside from the inter-communist rivalries of the Soviet Union and China to return to his brother's arms. Britons who 'go communist' belong to different categories altogether. As a Jew, the young Liz Gold in *The Spy Who Came in from the Cold* is 'understandably' attracted to the communist ideal but she is naive and her naiveté leads her to death; Bill Haydon's communism is given as resistant to full explanation, but as an 'ideology', an abstraction, its status is utterly dubious. An 'authoritarian father' and a 'loveless childhood' (le Carré, 1974, ch. 38) imagines Smiley, may have played their part in Haydon's Marxism.

Gender and personal relationships
Reading for ideology then, the problem of Authority, presented as conspiracy, is pushed forward as part of a process which silences class conflict. A mythology of the past, given for instance in Smiley's evocative nostalgia for nationhood and linked to complementary images of a

transcendent humanism are offered, *finally*, without criticism, as natural – for the reader's 'natural' endorsement. Such a reading is necessarily reductive, taking no account of those sections of le Carré's fiction which illuminate and problematize this same material, not to mention those other (mainly 'psychological') sections which image social behaviour in such a manner as to make the very search for ideology a lame pursuit. If, in the last analysis, a recommendation of nationhood and humanism is clearly discernible, that is not to say that other social practices and assumptions imaged, reflected, secreted, or embodied in le Carré's work must of necessity perform ideological functions.

A nice case in point is provided by le Carré's treatment of the related areas of the family and marriage and the 'personal' or 'intimate' subject-matter they comprise. The question of gender-presentation is obviously central here. Images of the family might well seem particularly prone to ideological saturation, and especially in le Carré's writing where, as I have already implied, family and nationhood seem to enjoy a close relationship. Lost, unhappy, leaving or otherwise distant spouses and lovers, dead or otherwise separated parents and offspring, plus a host of substitutes projected to fill the place of these absent relatives, occupy a large place in the novels. How then does the ideology-conscious reader interpret le Carré's portrayal of marriages and families as parted, broken, estranged or splitting? Do these images *recommend*, through a dewy-eyed nostalgia, the ideal of the harmonious family, a notion ideologically mobilized to maintain the bourgeois order? Or are those same images of separation indicative instead of the generational and male–female disjunctures produced in reality by and in that order? Alternatively, is the concentration on such personal material *in itself* an ideological evacuation of the political (as Bromley thinks)? Or does it implicitly counter-attack the ideological tendency in male popular writing (including the spy-thriller) to avoid 'engaging with the reality of personal and sexual relationships, or, when tackled, denying the mutuality and reciprocity of such relationships' (Worpole, 1983, p. 47)?

Le Carré's project in the area of the personal involves his interest in the psychological manoeuvres of strained domestic relationships (which he presents with great skill) and his fascination with the tension between 'corporate and individual loyalty' (Vaughan, 13 September 1979. I.). His starting-point is quite simple: marital disharmonies are produced and/or exacerbated by the men's exclusive life in Intelligence and Espionage and, as in *The Looking-Glass War* and *The Quest for Karla* trilogy, the fantasies and realities of the secret world help them to retreat from failures in the domestic sphere. For the strong-minded (male) rebels – Leamas, Westerby and Joseph-Gadi – the ultimate rejection of politics in favour of love is an act of courage which, though compromised by circumstance and doomed to defeat, expresses a human value greater than politics can offer. The most professional and powerful men, on the other hand – Control, Smiley, Karla and to an extent Kurtz – are the culpable survivors of either ruined or virtually moribund relationships with their wives. With Avery, Leiser,

Turner and Guillam, Smiley also shares the experience of neither understanding, nor trusting, nor being able to accept the 'otherness' of their partners. Incapable too of expressing an adequate range of feeling, le Carré's male characters make do with guilt, resentment and confusion. Slightly more comfortable in the company of other men they express intimacy in the quasi-familial, quasi-homosexual camaraderie of work. Departing from standard generic practice, le Carré consciously foregrounds 'intimate' male relationships, largely eschews the thriller's eroticism, and either avoids or challenges its characteristic celebration of 'macho' sexuality. In the personal sphere, men are emotionally crippled, and it is to le Carré's considerable credit that he treats with great sensitivity a social phenomenon he seems rather to despise.

As wives and lovers, le Carré's female characters often exhibit a commonsensical and perceptive grasp on the reality around them. Seeing through the fantasies of their men, they 'drive' the latter into deeper self-delusions. For the men, the secret world represents an escape from the tougher pressures of domestic normality and it can be used both as a weapon and an excuse against the women. For the women, the secret world represents an aggravating intrusion into their lives; despite their best endeavours, they are powerless against it. *Smiley's People* dramatizes this feature in the hero's myth-like quest for information. The couples in the novel behave in accordance with a single pattern. One partner (normally female) assumes a protective, insulating role, attempting to restrain the other's (normally a male) anti-domestic impulses. She tries to keep at bay any dangerous or potentially damaging incursion which threatens the stability and normality of their relationship. Repeatedly Smiley has to confront and overcome a barrier put up by a protector before he can reach his target. Stella seeks to keep Willem safe from, in turn, Vladimir, Mikhel and Smiley. When Smiley calls, she begins by claiming that her husband is out 'and, following Smiley's successful persistence, she acts as critical guardian while Willem is questioned. Similarly Elvira guards Mikhel (possibly because she may be the Stalinist agent in the Free Baltic Movement), hovering in the background while Smiley talks to her husband, her expression 'contemptuous'. Toby Esterhase is protected by his secretary-girlfriend who initially denies his availability, and Smiley next faces the more difficult task of by-passing Connie's lover, Hilary, who guards her friend with a jealous commitment. To reach Otto Leipzig, Smiley has to win over his loyal associate Kretzschmar (a spouse-substitute), and when he finds Leipzig dead and requires further information, he is forced to pass the minor obstacle of Frau Kretzschmar. Firmly and politely she informs him that 'Clauschen does no business in the daytime' and that he is the family's 'prisoner till sunset' (ch. 17). Finally, the double blackmailing of Grigoriev, first by Karla and then by Smiley, turns on Grigoriev's relationship with his zealously dominating wife who is unwittingly used by both spy-masters in 'getting to' her unfaithful husband. The wives in *Smiley's People* defend the territory of personal relationships, a territory in which they literally feel 'at home'. This female role is given as normal and natural; it appears, with varying emphases, in all the novels.

The large number and the variety of le Carré's female characters resist instant categorization but there are distinct types of le Carréan women. They are distinguishable in terms of self-knowledge and self-possession where the male characters tend (initially at least) to be differentiated in terms of resourcefulness, competence and purposefulness – externally-directed qualities. The Tribunal President (in *The Spy Who Came in from the Cold*), Sarah Avery, Hazel Bradfield, Connie Sachs, Camilla, Molly Meakin, the 'Colonial Lady' (in *The Honourable Schoolboy*), Madame Ostrakova, Stella, Fatmeh and Smiley's ex-wife Ann figure on an even longer list of 'adult' women who oppose attempts to subordinate them or, by their self-possession, make the very thought of such attempts absurd. 'Adult' here, does not necessarily denote age, but individuality and independence. The latter are expressed in diverse ways – perhaps through defending the family or the marriage, or through an extra-marital relationship, through sexual uninhibitedness, or simply through personal 'presence'. For the men, such women often constitute a threat. Avery, for instance, has no way of dealing squarely with Sarah's no-nonsense realism. Turner is outraged by Hazel Bradfield's adultery because women, his own wife included, are great betrayers. Guillam can 'understand' neither Camilla nor Molly Meakin, who act quite contrary to his expectations. Smiley is even more at sea: for him, Ann is distantly 'other', incomprehensible, strange in all her comings and goings. Perhaps male fears of female self-sufficiency are dramatized here.

Complementing this large group of female characters are 'child' women: Liz Gold, Myra Meadowes, Irina, Phoebe, Lizzie Worthington, Tatiana and Charlie. These women are presented as unknown to themselves but known completely to the reader. They are innocent of the ways of the world, confused, manipulable, vulnerable and, in one way or another, trapped. The extraordinary situations of espionage give the 'child' women opportunities to 'mature' but maturation is costly and uncertain. In such situations their innocence is suddenly charged with a massive self-destructive potential. However, being primarily a masculine world, the world of espionage engages with them indirectly – via male characters. The female sphere is first and foremost personal and so the dangerous innocence of the 'child' women is initially signified by their risky, fragile, compromised love-relationships with men. The adolescent sexuality of Liz, the clandestine affairs of Myra and Irina, Phoebe's 'father-complex', Tatiana's more extreme psycho-sexual disturbance, and the straightforward 'promiscuity' of Lizzie and Charlie, all express innocence in terms of an 'unsatisfactory' sexuality.

The critic Tony Bennett, reading for ideology, has analysed what he describes as 'The sexist code' in Ian Fleming's Bond novels (1982, p. 13). Many of Bennett's observations make for illuminating cross-reference with le Carré's 'child' women and with the 'adult' women who have 'betrayed' their men sexually. The Bond 'girl', argues Bennett, 'constitutes the source of an enigma in being somehow 'out-of-place' sexually' (p. 13). The 'girl', 'orphaned' or 'damaged' by an early sexual experience, is sexually 'deviant', a deviance expressed alternatively by 'challenging aggressiveness', 'frigidity' or 'lesbianism'. Bond's role is to 'reposition' her 'within the structure of sexist ideology', making her properly 'subordinate' to men. Because the girl has been 'insufficiently or faultily positioned sexually', she is also morally and politically displaced:

> Lacking a clear anchorage within the ideological ordering of the relationships between men and women, the Bond girl often functions as a 'drifting subject' within the sphere of ideology in general: unsure of her place sexually, she is also insufficiently attuned to the distinction between right and wrong. (Bennett, p. 13)
>
> The suggestion that the girl is in the service of the villain *because* she is unsure of her position within the system of sexual relations establishes an implicit equation between political deviancy and sexual deviancy that works all the more effectively for being embedded within the plot structure of the traditional fairytale (hero rescues damsel in distress) and its associated system of Manichean opposites.   (p. 15)

The superficial resemblance of Bennett's Bond model to le Carré's novels is immediately apparent. For the 'child' women, a sexually-manifested displacement gives them as 'drifting subjects', unsure or mistaken about what or who is right or wrong. (It is worth recalling though, that moral uncertainty is definitely not an exclusively female issue in le Carré's fiction.) Her sexuality puts the woman in the service of villain-figures. Through her relationship with Leamas, Liz becomes the pawn of Smiley and Mundt. Jenny Pargiter and Hazel Bradfield both betray trust through their attraction to the seeming-villain Harting, who uses them both. Lizzie is the kept woman of the successful crook Drake Ko. Tatiana, so 'faultily positioned sexually' that she is incarcerated in a mental hospital, leads a life totally controlled by Karla. Through her affair with Haydon, Ann Sercombe is also in Karla's service. Believing herself sexually liberated, the radical actress, Charlie, allows herself to be manipulated or mistreated by a succession of lovers of dubious moral status, her choice of whom reflects her own confusions. As with the Bond girls, either the 'absence' or the 'overburdening presence of men' (Bennett, p. 13), often accounts for sexual and moral behaviour. Westerby's free-living, hippy-like companion is known as 'the orphan'; Phoebe 'recruits herself' as a Circus agent on account of love for her dead father. Lizzie, Tatiana and Charlie are all separated from their fathers, and all have intense love-hate feelings towards them. As a rule, such female characters seem in need of 'rescue'.

But le Carré distorts or parodies the knight-damsel scenario in novel after novel, presenting it as male fantasy. Men fail to carry out a therapeutic re-ordering of women; instead, if anything, women tend to rescue them

by the example of their comparatively heightened sensibility. Leamas'
attempt to save Liz ends with both their deaths. When Westerby plays
rescuing knight to Lizzie Worthington's distressed damsel, he is sent up
as a 'Sir Galahad', and in her last appearance in the novel she insists she
has 'kept the faith' with the 'villain' Ko (le Carré, 1977, ch. 21). Tatiana
is last seen in *Smiley's People*, being 'dragged . . . still screaming, back into
the house' (le Carré, 1980, ch. 26), and her impending 'rescue', utterly
downplayed in the narrative, will lead merely to a future of continuing
'treatment' and 'maintenance'. When Joseph-Gadi saves Charlie from the
terrorist Khalil in *The Little Drummer Girl*, the effect on her is deranging.
Rescues are soured by being either unwanted (with Lizzie), or politically
ulterior (with Tatiana) or more emotionally displacing than the 'out-of-
placeness' of entrapment (with Charlie). For the 'adult' women, 'serving'
the 'villain' is itself a rescue from a barely tolerable normality (with Hazel
and Ann), and neither character needs any external male aid in ideologically
relocating her. The endings of le Carré's narratives do not come complete
with ideological closure.

　　Le Carré is not a formula-writer and his work resists the sterilization
of reading exclusively for ideology. It would be simply facile to reduce the
clarity and sophistication of his portrayal of gender transactions to a
mechanism functioning to recommend sexism. All literature will reproduce,
in part, and in one form or another, socially-dominant ideas *and* practices.
An 'ideologically-sound' literature, if such were possible, by denying the
existence of these practices, would simply lie. Therefore, I am not canvassing
the equally untenable position that 'sexist codes' are somehow magically
absent in his texts, nor that they are invariably attacked there. The general
relegation of women to the personal/domestic sphere, the notion of wives
seeking to contain husbands within the boundaries of the home, male fears
of women acting independently (betraying), the sense of non-marital female
sexuality as usefully expressive of immaturity, are all undoubtedly
ideological insofar as they relay 'accepted' ideas and actual practices. But
at the same time (and, it must be added, with a good deal of authorial
consciousness) they implicitly bear witness to the deforming *effects* of the
division of labour by gender in our society, and specifically, to the forms
of women's oppression attendant thereon.

　　The images of women's isolation within the domestic sphere and of their
corresponding 'out-of-placeness' outside of it, of the competing pressures
of work and home, and of men's consequent inability to cope with emotional
matters (except through substitutive relationships), are integral to le Carré's
novels and will be looked at in greater depth subsequently. Perhaps it is
sufficient here to suggest that more fruitful than readings for ideology are
readings which acknowledge the truth embodied in observations such as
the following. The almost off-hand introduction of Jenny Pargiter at work
in *A Small Town in Germany* contains more insight into the reality of female
oppression and here, specifically, its internalization, than any number of
exposés of the thriller's ideology:

Jenny Pargiter was the Information Officer and the only woman present. She read querulously as if she were contradicting a popular view; and she read without hope, secretly knowing that it was the lot of any woman, when imparting news, not to be believed.   (le Carré, 1968, ch. 2)

John le Carré's political fiction

Exploiting to the full an under-used generic resource, le Carré promotes interrogation to a primary position in his stories. Most of his non-domestic dialogues are best described as interrogations because they nearly always involve a dominant voice pressurizing a resistant, defensive voice (although occasionally these roles become reversed in the course of an exchange). Interrogation is sometimes covert and restrained, as when the Circus team interviews Reverend Hibbert in *The Honourable Schoolboy*, sometimes casual, as in Turner's conversations with de Lisle in *A Small Town in Germany*, and sometimes challengingly, insistently overt, as in the encounters between Fiedler and Leamas, Smiley and 'Gerstmann' (Karla) or Kurtz and Charlie. Such formal and informal sessions function to project character and to introduce and deploy 'information' necessary to solving narrative enigmas – the identity of a double-agent, the whereabouts of a defector, the weaknesses of an opponent, for example. But they also allow for intense political dialogue and it is through interrogations that political issues become most exposed and most active in le Carré's fiction.

Some critics and reviewers have noted that alternative trend in thriller-writing which engages with the political world to a degree of greater awareness than is managed in the orthodoxies of a John Buchan or an Ian Fleming. Julian Symons, for instance, distinguishes between the Fleming tradition ('conservative, supporting authority'), and that represented by le Carré:

> The second is radical, critical of authority, claiming that agents perpetuate, and even create, false barriers between 'us' and 'them' . . . The messages of le Carré's novels are that authority is not benevolent, but often destroys those who serve it, that espionage and counter-espionage work is often fumblingly uncertain in its aims and effects, that 'our' men may be personally vicious and 'their' men decent human beings . . .   (Symons 1972, p. 233)

In like vein, Steven Neuse commends the 'exceptional insights', 'meaningful political statements' and the 'critical perspective on political systems' (1982, pp. 293, 295), displayed in the work of le Carré, Deighton and Greene. These writers, Neuse claims, reveal the threat posed and largely effected, not by an 'externalized enemy' but by what he calls 'the bureaucratic state' which stultifies 'individual initiative and motivation', and makes life aimless. In his review of *Smiley's People*, the novelist David Caute is less eager to ignore the 'manichean' anti-communism inherent in the genre and ultimately assented to by le Carré himself, but is still moved to praise le Carré's 'political perception':

> Le Carré is not merely a good writer peddling a shamelessly boyish

mythology; he is equally a most sensitive explorer of the hazy frontier
between politics and crime . . .
     What distinguishes him is the depth and subtlety of his political perception.
However manichean – and to me personally unacceptable – his overall vision
of the Cold War, this is a mind guilty only of dove-tailing brilliant insights
into a final orthodoxy.   (Caute, 8 February 1980)

Caute commends the novel's vision of a little England, 'fuelled by nothing
more vital than adulterated nostalgia', its administration and intelligence
services now run by the inadequate and unimpressive, testimony to the
fact that a devalued 'democracy must find its soldiers where it can'.
     By concentrating on le Carré's 'insights' and 'messages' (undoubtedly
present in his fiction), Symons, Neuse and Caute privilege those
preformulated authorial positions which have implicit in them, at some
level, a remedial programme of action. The underlying assumption here,
quite a natural one, is that political literature is identified as such by virtue
of its tendentious function – its capacity to canvass a preferred politics for
the reader's assent. But le Carré's political novels earn that label by virtue
of much more than their local insights and any articulation therein of an
authorial programme: politics in le Carré's novels are usually the reverse
of propagandist. In spite of the strong opinions on display in his extra-
literary writing (as in the earlier-quoted remarks on Philby and Princes
Gate), le Carré is famed for the political ambivalence of his fiction, an
ambivalence full of contradiction: he told Miriam Gross, 'If I knew exactly
where I stood I wouldn't write' (Gross, 3 February 1980. I.). It is the
absence on the author's part of a clear, coherent political position, complete
with its implied programme, recommendations and solutions, which induces
him to adopt a method of political presentation that dramatizes ambivalence
as problematic. Le Carré's political method acts not to transmit authoritative
opinion but to play out as sharply as possible the conflict between
antagonistic positions. Akin to interrogation, the method tests the self-
consistency of positions and explores the contradictions such testing brings
to light. Akin to debate, it forces opponent ideas against each other, but
unlike debate, it is directed towards no final preference, avoids any
assumption that political viewpoints are equally valid, and is never set at
a level of abstraction. By being sustained through related series of
confrontations which enact specific conflicts, this open-ended method allows
positions to be examined angle by angle in a constantly unsettling process.
The relationship between the work and its readers produced here differs
distinctly both from the general assent required by conventional realism
and from that agreement demanded by fiction more immediately recognized
as political. Where novels as diverse as those of Tressell, Orwell, Malraux,
Greene, Koestler, Upward, Solzhenitsyn (to cite only a few well-known
examples), deliberately prioritize an overall position, most of le Carré's
political novels depart from this convention by refusing to make ultimate
evaluations on their readership's behalf. The political in le Carré's fiction

inheres not in 'message', nor in its political locations, nor even in the presence of political statements, but in the *enactment* of political encounter, an enactment which involves readers as much as characters.

If le Carré's readers choose to resist the temptation of becoming engrossed by the complexities of the thriller-action, they are not accorded the cosy privilege of standing back from his political dialogues. There is no sense at all of occupying some high ground of objective neutrality from which to make dispassionate judgements; the reader is not given the arguments and then asked to retire and consider a verdict like a juror. Instead, active reader-engagement (and discomfiture) are occasioned in the first place by simple strategies. Characters who are subject to political scrutiny are often presented, for example, as the unwilling victims of unfair political assaults they have either not sought or not deserved, they win instant sympathy. Leamas is trapped and brow-beaten by Fiedler, as is Charlie by Kurtz, and, in a bizarre turnabout, as is Smiley – by the silent, self-composed Karla. In each situation the character under pressure is forced to consider his or her stand-point, and the result is subjected to further destabilizing dissection. The dominant character in such encounters (which do not necessarily take place in interrogation rooms) invariably has a more developed, rigorous grasp of politics than the victim, and is usually committed to a stable position. The power this character consequently possesses puts victim and reader in a state of unease which is reinforced by the fact that the substance of the interrogator-figure's politics is generally identified as 'extreme' or distasteful or both by the victim, and, one assumes by le Carré and his audience too. Thus Control, as a Cold Warrior on the offensive, Bradfield as pragmatist and opportunist, Karfeld as Nazi, Fiedler as Stalinist, Karla as Stalinist-'fanatic', Kurtz as Zionist and Khalil as terrorist, play, in their various ways, the part of interrogator. Although their respective positions are also targets for critical analysis, the main focus is reserved for the victim, whose response to the provocation of the other is regarded as of primary importance.

For a writer with ambivalent politics, le Carré is strangely fascinated by people who act politically, and he conveys a great sense of involvement in the process and outcome of political encounter. Himself reluctant to take sides, he ensures that, by their actions, his major characters are already travelling the political road. In this he reverses Graham Greene's paradigm – being less concerned with how the uncommitted are impelled to make a stand than with the soundness of an extant allegiance. The narrative interest here lies initially in a recurring contradiction: though already political by dint of their acts, le Carré's victims resist articulating and analysing their positions; indeed, they often appear unable to do so. Thus, Leamas and Turner consider themselves apolitical in spite of their respective roles as double agent and security investigator, and they avoid political discussion whenever possible. Liz and Charlie, on the other hand, openly advertise their loyalties – the former to the Communist Party and the latter to radical nationalism; but their views, though passionately felt, seem to them to require only minimal exposition, and they both prefer to push aside any material which suggests the fragility of their politics. Avery, Westerby and Smiley (in *The Quest for Karla*) see themselves as naturally espousing common human values which self-evidently need virtually no explanation or justification at all. Forced out of their reluctance by an interrogator's pressure, or by the horror of events, they are made to face the realities of their positions and defend them as best they can. The reader's participation in this business of political reconsideration is invited not just by formal identification with the victim; le Carré addresses his aim towards political positions which are likely to have a considerable resonance for a substantial portion of his readership. Where his heroes and heroines might seem to belong in quite distinctive camps, in fact they do not. Le Carré's principal targets are liberalism and individualism: the home team, as it were, is under fire.

Politics in le Carré's fiction are not confined to what a character thinks or believes in, but are portrayed in the relationship between what a character thinks and what a character does. The ideologies of liberalism and individualism are tested in their practice. Both ideologies pride themselves for opposing dogmatism, both distrust arid, abstract theory, and liberalism in particular, celebrates its impulse to appreciate an issue broadly, to see all sides. Both disparage restrictive, impersonal social institutions which limit human freedom. Liberalism's belief in an essential human decency produces reformist programmes designed to counter the tyrannous autonomy of bureaucracy, and the deforming power of the state. But, asks le Carré, how does the liberal or the individualist react in situations where it becomes necessary to take a side? How feasible is the attempt to remain apart from the cynical manoeuvres of Western Democracy or from Stalinism? How does the liberal reconcile being part of the state apparatus while despising the activities of the state? What results when decent impulses push the liberal into radical causes and organizations which pursue their aims by means which conflict with the liberal's moral assumptions?

Such questions, posed from within liberalism, are therefore formulated as exclusively moral issues. As I suggested earlier, le Carré downgrades or excludes the class and material determinants of political behaviour. But in spite of that, and despite the author's adoption of liberalism's vocabulary – in fact, despite his own preference for a liberal world-view – he nonetheless treats this ideology to a severe dissection which glaringly demonstrates its inadequacies when confronted by the reality of political events and by more hard-headed ideologies. His liberal and individualist victims are never victorious in political encounter and their defeats are always presented as inglorious. Held in the sway of more powerful political forces, liberalism vacillates between stronger alternatives, and invariably ends either in self-destructive defeat, or in siding miserably with what is seen as marginally the lesser evil. Morally attractive and completely untenable, liberalism and individualism are dramatized as contradictory, confused and feeble – 'flabby' is the adjective Smiley chooses to describe his liberal behaviour (le Carré, 1974, ch. 23). Yet at the same time, the more rigorous ideologies and systems opposed to the preferred world-view of le Carré's heroes and heroines are found as unacceptable at the end of the testing process as they were at its beginning.

Through all his thrillers – perhaps 'political novels' is the more appropriate term – from *The Spy Who Came in from the Cold* to *The Little Drummer Girl*, le Carré examines the liberal dilemma in an exhaustive variety of situations without arriving at a satisfactory resolution. The liberal, caught in this dilemma, and now conscious of it, is still left asking, 'Where to now?', and may choose, like le Carré, to remain in that state. Le Carré's political vision does not 'develop' in the course of his writing career because its own basic terms preclude any possibility of development. His novels, therefore, chart a preoccupied repetition, a many-angled attentiveness to an obstinate predicament and, as in the real world, the dilemma remains alive, contradictions and all. Only being fully won over to espousing an alternative position can foreclose the issue, and that necessarily entails the complete rejection of liberalism and individualism.

In a different context, the critic Terry Eagleton defines 'liberal humanism' as 'a suburban moral ideology, limited in practice to largely inter-personal matters' (1983, p. 207). Its 'impotence', he remarks, in the larger political arena

> is a symptom of its essentially contradictory relationship to modern capitalism. For although it forms part of the 'official' ideology of such society . . . the social order within which it exists has in one sense very little time for it at all . . . The truth is that liberal humanism is at once largely ineffectual, and the best ideology of the 'human' that present bourgeois society can muster. (pp. 199–200)

Le Carré vividly portrays that 'contradictory relationship'. The Smiley who is seen in *The Quest for Karla* is one of a succession of characters serving the state machine who simultaneously find themselves in partial opposition to it. He, for instance, quietly objects to the fervent expressions of anti-communism, to the high-minded patriotism and to the limited, opportunist or bureaucratic vision of his colleagues and rivals in the service, favouring a more benign, tolerant acknowledgement of the complexities in things. In their turn, his colleagues consider Smiley's sentiment as sometimes charming but often tiresome, and his idiosyncrasies seem to them out-of-line with their common purpose. Paradoxically though, Smiley still somehow stands for that same purpose, and they know that too. In related instances, Leamas and Turner look contemptuously on all and every pretentious statement of moral justification for their work, preferring to trust only their own commonsense and again, in turn, they are disparaged by their superiors. At times capable of acting as the state's most dedicated and effective warriors, Leamas, Turner, Smiley, Westerby and Joseph-Gadi prove incapable of doing so consistently, nagged as they all are in the end, by liberal doubt and guilt. Utilizing the generic norm, le Carré gives such characters a temporary status in respect of their colleagues. Thus Leamas is re-activated for what the reader presumes is his final mission following ignominious failure as a spy-runner in Germany. Avery is the new-boy of his Department; Turner, Westerby and Joseph-Gadi are all conscripted for one-off missions, as in the trilogy is Smiley, who is semi-retired. Their temporary status of itself suggests partial opposition to the world and world-view of the state's professionals. Smiley's celebrated nostalgia has the same function.

The uneasy coexistence of liberalism's 'humane' language and the prevailing, rightist ideology is mirrored in attempts of Liz and Charlie to reconcile the 'progressive', left-orientated face of liberalism with, respectively, the politics of the Communist Party and the politics of Palestinian nationalism. I shall explore these relationships in detail in later chapters but by way of introduction it is noteworthy that le Carré here deals with how liberalism fares when, admitting its own feebleness, it is taken to its logical extreme and puts itself in the service of a disciplined politics. In these contexts Liz's 'communism' differs categorically from Fiedler's, as Charlie's espousal of radical nationalism differs categorically from the deep-rooted politics of Khalil and Fatmeh. Unable (perhaps justifiably) to make the necessary political leap, Liz and Charlie straddle a self-tormenting middle-ground, not so very different from the middle-ground Smiley occupies.

Le Carré sees a great part of what he would deem the 'moral' interest of his novels as lying in their affective potential. It is a case of inviting the reader to become actively involved in the process of political interrogation, both as experiencing victim and (therefore) as critic and self-critic, deducing the political implications of each argument, position and political event. In his interview on *The South Bank Show*, le Carré said:

> But the ambiguity – what is right to do? – if I were in that position what would I have done? – that I love. (Bragg, 27 March 1983. I.)

Participating in the liberal dilemma, taunted with competing choices the liberal reader asks the same questions, aware of what political practice their 'answers' entail. The aim underwriting le Carré's method of political presentation is not so dissimilar, in the end, to that of the playwright Brecht. It is no accident that Charlie, the little drummer girl of le Carré's most recent novel to date, originates in Brecht's little drummer girl, Kattrin – the dumb, innocent daughter of *Mother Courage and her Children*. Brecht's own remarks on the relationship between this play and its audience have a striking applicability to the relationship between le Carré's novels and their readership. Brecht insisted:

> The chronicle play *Mother Courage and her Children* . . . does not of course represent any kind of attempt to persuade anybody of anything by setting forth bare facts . . . [However] I don't believe that it leaves the audience in a state of objectivity (i.e. balancing the pros and cons). I believe rather – or let's say I hope – that it makes them critical. (Brecht 1964, p. 226)

2 Cold Warriors:
The Spy Who Came in from the Cold

In October 1965, le Carré's third and fourth novels, *The Spy Who Came in from the Cold* and *The Looking-Glass War*, were reviewed in Moscow's *Literaturnaya Gazeta* by a Soviet critic, V. Voinov. The review was fulsome in its praise of le Carré's literary originality and achievement but concluded with a hostile evaluation of the author's political assumptions. Le Carré took considerable offence. He writes that he was profoundly surprised to see his work discussed in the East at all, not least because, following the publication of *The Spy Who Came in from the Cold* 'in many languages and countries', he had awaited reactions from 'the Communist bloc' and receiving none, had himself arranged for copies to be sent to the relevant institutions in the Soviet Union and Eastern Europe. The result of his action was less than promising:

> Rumania, Bulgaria, Czechoslovakia, and Hungary declined the book without comment. Poland took the precaution of protecting even her publishers from its odious qualities: a Polish publishing house twice reported that it had not received my agent's copy, adding in its second letter the injunction: 'We suppose not to risk again with sending it.' One Balkan editor excised the passages he found most obnoxious and returned the remnants. It was a little like recovering one's shirt from a faulty washing machine.   (le Carré, 1966, p. 3)

Le Carré's account of these abortive attempts to elicit public responses to his work in the East is included in his reply to Voinov's unexpected review. He entitled his 'Open Letter', 'To Russia, with Greetings', and it was carried by *Encounter*, a journal as politically partisan as Moscow's *Literary Gazette*. Fulfilling the expectations of its ironical title, the tone of le Carré's open letter is consistently acid; he patronizes Voinov's supposedly self-evident 'bewilderment' and refuses to warm to the review's admiration of his 'realism' and 'cleverness' as compared with the productions of his compatriot, Ian Fleming. Le Carré's principal objection however is to Voinov's designation of him as 'an apologist of the cold war'.

Numerous considerations make it still seem strange that le Carré should have felt so sorely offended by Voinov's accusation, and perhaps even stranger is his evident concern for a positive Soviet reception of his book in the first place. As a genre, the spy-thriller has never been noted as a vehicle for purveying any 'progressive' political content and for all that le Carré's novel eschews the crude and blatant imperialist stereotypes, it is certainly not pro-communist and neither is it neutral. *The Spy Who Came in from the Cold* articulates a similarity between the methods of 'communism' and the West, yet ultimately, and however, uneasily, the balance is tipped in favour of the latter side. This feature of the novel was to become a recurrent theme of le Carré's writing where, over and again, a humanist or humanitarian impulse seems preferred to the political beliefs and postures of both communists and capitalists who are portrayed as virtually identical in their actions. That same humanitarian impulse, however, is shown incapable of sustaining itself independently: it finds itself forced either into an anxious, tortured alliance with the lesser evil (the West) or into its own destruction. In an interview of 1980, le Carré spoke of his own politics in similar terms. Miriam Gross remarked on the 'grey area' his novels inhabit and on the difficulty of locating the author's position. Le Carré replied:

> If I knew exactly where I stood I wouldn't write. I do believe, reluctantly, that we must combat Communism. Very decisively. Of course our own engagement in the cold war is a very well kept British secret, I don't think many British people are aware of the extent to which we are harnessed to the anti-communist effort. (Gross, 3 February 1980. I)

By this time, his character, George Smiley, has appeared in contexts where his earlier restrained ruthlessness is no longer his dominant quality and le Carré admits of the affinity he feels with him:

> His engagement against Communism is really an intellectual one. I think he stands where I stand: he feels that to pit yourself against any 'ism' is to strike a posture which is itself ideological, and therefore offensive in terms of practical decency. In practice, almost any political ideology invites you to set aside your humanitarian instincts . . . He accepts, however reluctantly, that you have to resort to very unpleasant means in order to preserve society, though he sometimes wonders how much you can do in the name of that society and feel sure that it is still worth preserving. (Ibid.)

A comparable dilemma faces Leamas in *The Spy Who Came in from the Cold* (although his consciousness of it is far less developed than Smiley's) and it seems unlikely to have had as much of an appeal to Stalinist reviewers as le Carré had hoped for.

In the light of some of le Carré's subsequent statements on *The Spy Who Came in from the Cold* it is again curious that he should have been so concerned that it was received as a political novel, or at least as a novel dealing in the moral issues implied by specific political positions. In later interviews he has preferred to concentrate on the traditional and general aspects of his novel, and on its construction as a narrative:

> It is a very romantic story: two people fall in love and one has to betray the other and both of them, in a sense, perish in a mental institution; both of them, in the same breath make a statement in favour of humanity. Basically, what was there was a romantic story, and, dare I say it myself, a very well told one . . . (Dean, 5 September 1974. I.)
>   The story of *The Spy* was really a story of loneliness; it was in a cold war context which gave it the edge. (Cameron, 8 September 1974. I.)

It is indeed tempting to downplay the novel's political dimension, to disregard its topicality and view it as romantic in theme, dressed in realist style and structured with clean precision. The serial reversals of the narrative systematically frustrate the reader's expectations, creating and deflating tension with an insistent regularity. Each succeeding stage in the action comprises new information which discredits earlier certainties. The balanced arrangement of trial and imprisonment motifs, the pattern of individual and corporate betrayals, and the symmetry of the attempted frontier crossings which frame the narrative, contribute to the reader's enjoyment of the novel as a well-made fiction. Le Carré's success in crafting his novel so as to balance what Voinov acknowledges as his 'realism' and 'cleverness' is evidenced both by the unobtrusiveness of the narrative's structure and by the author's comments on his choice of material. He prefers, he says, plausibility to authenticity, and his use of the complex potential of the device of the double agent in *The Spy Who Came in from the Cold* represented a toning down of the extraordinariness of double agents in reality. He instances the case of Clemens and Felfe, two senior officials in Gehlen's BND, West Germany's Foreign Intelligence organization:

> Clemens and Felfe . . . were recruited by the Russians, I think, almost on the day they were recruited by the Gehlen organization, and, after ten years service . . . they received, both of them, quite a high decoration from the West Germany Chancellor . . . On the same day, they received quite a high Soviet decoration and they celebrated this double 'honour' with a dinner party at which their wives were present and at which they drank separately to the two governments they had served. (le Carré, 1968. I.)

Such material was unusable; the demands of credibility opposed the formal attractions of incorporating such an albeit authentic event into his narrative. Yet, despite le Carré's literary instincts and interests, his novel's political implications aroused the censure of the Soviet critic and that, in turn, provoked le Carré's astringent reaction. There is no doubt that le Carré intended to elicit responses based on the politics of his novel (at the time of its writing) and that whatever its literary merits and whatever literary choices affected its composition, it was designed to keep the reader's attention on the specific, extra-literary issues it intersected. 1963–66 may have witnessed a slight de-intensification of the Cold War but the Cold War functions not as a fortuitous background but as a principal subject of *The Spy Who Came in from the Cold*.

In *Tinker Tailor Soldier Spy*, the Stalinist double agent, Haydon, claims that the Cold War began in 1917 (ch. 38) and his rival and antagonist, the reluctant cold warrior, Smiley, repeats the same observation as though it were common knowledge in *The Honourable Schoolboy* (ch. 5). Le Carré's first three novels, however, *Call for the Dead*, *A Murder of Quality* and *The Spy Who Came in from the Cold*, published one per year from 1961 to 1963, appeared during a particularly virulent phase of the conflict. It included the West's refusal to withdraw from Berlin, the U-2 spyplane incident, the erection of the Berlin Wall (which le Carré himself witnessed) and the Cuban Missile Crisis. The Moscow–Washington 'hot line' and the Test Ban Treaty that followed soon after doused the flames a little. But in Britian at least, the economic crisis and the record postwar unemployment deriving from it, demanded that society's ideologists keep the Cold War fever running high while diverting popular attention from domestic social problems. The vogue for spy fantasy fitted the bill perfectly. Fleming's novels enjoyed a renewed popularity – a popularity aided, as Christopher Booker has described, by the revelation that President Kennedy was an avid Bond fan (Booker, 1969, p. 179).

The Communist Threat from both within and without was colourfully expressed in the glut of spy trials and scandals which filled feet of newspaper columns during the early sixties and symbolically represented the larger Cold War tensions. March 1961 saw the Old Bailey trial of the five 'Portland spies', including the Russian agent Lonsdale (Molody). George Blake was sentenced to the unprecedented term of forty-two years imprisonment in March 1962 and, later that year, Vassall followed him to gaol. January 1963 brought Kim Philby's disappearance in Beirut and the ensuing Soviet announcement that he had been granted political asylum. Four months later, the British 'businessman' Greville Wynne (actually an MI6 agent) was sentenced in Moscow to eight years, while his contact, the traitor Penkovsky, was sentenced to death. In June, John Profumo resigned his seat in the House of Commons.

It would be foolish to claim that the early spy fiction of le Carré (and Len Deighton, whose first thriller, *The Ipcress File* was published in 1963) could not have contributed in part to the anti-communist hysteria of the period. Le Carré himself acknowledges that to an extent, both his material and his audience were ready-made:

> I believe that the romanticized vision of the spy which was presented by Fleming created a kind of hunger for something more realistic. We'd had the public picture already of the seedy army of spies. We knew about Hiss and Colonel Abel, and the English particularly – we knew them better than we knew our own writers. We could count them off like our best

athletes – Burgess and Maclean, Vassall, Blake and the rest – so that the rather treacly handling of the espionage problem created a counter-market which I was fortunately able to feed.   (le Carré, 1968. I.)

The very existence of a ready market for the sale of a new brand of espionage commodity presupposes that the consumers' responses would be already partially formed but it is a mistake and a simplification to assume, as Booker does, that the popularity of le Carré's novels (and the spy fiction of Deighton and Fleming) was based on what he calls their 'reflection of the *Zeitgeist*':

> They provided, in fact, the perfect vehicle for 'dream-nightmare' stories in which no one's identity was certain, in which self-assertive lone heroes could wander at will, in any disguise, through any social milieu, and in which acts of violence and promiscuity, vaguely condoned by the fact that the heroes were always fighting for 'our side' against 'the enemy', could take place at any time, without any need for elaborate explanation. (Booker, pp. 179–80)

This description of the genre is contradicted at almost every point by *The Spy Who Came in from the Cold*, which consciously and persistently challenges the ideological assumptions Booker identifies. Some part of the novel's enormous popularity (it was reprinted twelve times in six months and after ten years nearly twenty million copies had been sold (Cameron, 8 September 1974)) must have been due to a recognition that it did not simply reproduce the standard generic and political orthodoxies. Nonetheless, not unlike Booker, le Carré's Moscow reviewer thought he had seen through the author's façade of critical objectivity and placed Alec Leamas back where he truly belonged – as the legitimate successor to the pro-Imperialist Bond.
  Le Carré takes it that he is charged on two counts:

1   That I assume the role of impartial observer while my real function is to 'fan the flames of the cold war.'
2   That I elevate the spy to the 'rank of true hero of our age.'   (le Carré, 1966, p. 3)

The second accusation is immediately returned. Le Carré reminds Voinov that the 'supreme decoration of "Hero of the Soviet Union"' was awarded (posthumously) to Richard Sorge in November 1964, and that his controllers, Berzin and Borovich, were also posthumously honoured; that two years later, Colonel Abel was, 'after thirty years' service as a spy, five of which were spent in an American gaol,' made a Member of the Order of Lenin; and that Molody's factoid diaries, relating how Lonsdale, 'super-spy, makes havoc of decadent British society', currently fill the shelves of Moscow's bookshops. The 'Russian Bond', writes le Carré, 'is on his way':

> In the acquisition of intelligence, the weak and even the innocent must suffer; but heroism is the anaesthetic. From the example of Sorge we know definitely what in the past we could only deduce from Lenin: that the Communist Party regards espionage as a fitting profession for a hero. With Sorge, Abel

and Lonsdale as his guides, the young Russian may venture into Soviet Intelligence with as clear a conscience as he would enter the army. (Ibid., p. 5)

Perhaps le Carré protests too much here; the distinction he makes elsewhere in his letter between a morally justifiable counter-intelligence and the immorality of espionage proper seems rather a fine one, especially when considering his own career in the secret world. Le Carré was employed in British Army Intelligence from 1948 to 1950 and by the Foreign Service in Bonn from 1960 to 1964, during which time, according to his long-awaited admission in a recent interview, he was not himself confined to regular diplomatic activity (Bragg, 27 March 1983. I.) In addition, the fact that espionage, like war, in Clausewitz's famous formula, is a continuation of politics by other means seems a central assumption in most of le Carré's fiction. Yet regardless of these possible contradictions, le Carré's main point that spying should not be seen as heroic – is worth dwelling upon because it too is fundamental to his political novels, representing, as it does, his almost obsessive preoccupation with the disparity between means and ends.

Just as in his later condemnatory essay on Kim Philby, whom le Carré describes as having been driven by 'the drug of deceit' (Page et al., 1968, Introduction p. 15), the open letter makes a particularly sharp attack on Richard Sorge as a man who 'devoted all . . . to a life of solitary deceit' (1966, p. 4). Sorge 'implicated others in his work, and led them to their death'. Equally reprehensibly, Sorge was a 'peace-time' recruit and was 'deployed against countries with which the Soviet Union was not at war'. Significantly, le Carré downplays what he rather grudgingly allows as Sorge's 'choice of this most arduous means to defend the working-class movement' (p. 5) and also his 'spectacular achievements' in espionage which 'were not needed in a High Command filled with Stalinist suspicion' – an oblique reference to Stalin's refusal to act upon the information his network had provided on the impending German invasion. Le Carré omits to mention Sorge's grotesque neglect by his Russian superiors following his capture by the Japanese in 1941, and that his reports on Japan's strategic intentions permitted the Red Army to release large units from Far East defence to be thrown into the turning-point battle of Stalingrad. But Sorge is condemned because innocents suffered through his actions and (with perhaps more justification) so too is the bureaucracy which retrospectively and cynically made a martyr of its victim in order to legitimize the 'weapons' of espionage and sanctify its 'mission'.

Le Carré so forcefully rejects the notion that *he* makes spying heroic because it is his main contention, both in the letter and in his novel, that for a 'Communist there is nothing inherently wrong in sacrificing the uncommitted to the course of history' (1966, p. 5), that the collective end justifies any means, but that for the Western democrat such positions are morally untenable. The reviewer Voinov, then, is in contradiction because he ignorantly fails to realize that, for his side, there is 'nothing shabby . . . with the means which Sorge and Lonsdale used', while the West is in contradiction because it conducts itself in the espionage war *indistinguishably* from the East. The rival services use the same methods and 'even the same spies (a point Mr Kruschev made long before I did)' and in *The Spy Who Came in from the Cold*, le Carré sought to draw attention to the implications of this aspect of 'Western hypocrisy':

> . . . I sought to remove espionage from the sterile arguments of the cold war and concentrate the reader's eye on the cost to the West, in moral terms, of fighting the legitimized weapons of Communism. For this reason, my Western agent is at a loss to defend himself in ideological dispute with his Communist interrogator. The Communist *should* be able to reconcile the loss of innocent life with the progress of the proletarian revolution; Western man can't. I tried to tickle the public conscience with the issue of *raison d'état*. (1966, p. 5)

It is clear from the above statement that le Carré wished to shine his spotlight primarily on the Western conscience and his tone of patient explanation here expresses a genuine surprise that a Soviet reader should see anything amiss in his account of the communist ethic. Of course, le Carré is right in assuming that a communist should see means and ends as being interdependent in every society, whatever pretensions it has to complying with an abstract moral code. But the fact that the position canvassed by his 'Communist interrogator', Fiedler, in *The Spy Who Came in from the Cold*, glories so teasingly and ironically in the throwaway cynicism of Stalin's methodology, ensures that it could hardly have failed to provoke Voinov's objection:

> '. . . The Abteilung and organizations like it are the natural extension of the Party's arm. They are in the vanguard of the fight for Peace and Progress. They are to the Party what the Party is to socialism: they *are* the vanguard. Stalin said so' – he smiled drily, 'it is not fashionable to quote Stalin – but he said once "half a million liquidated is a statistic, and one man killed in a traffic accident is a national tragedy". He was laughing, you see, at the bourgeois sensitivities of the mass. He was a great cynic. But what he meant is still true: a movement can hardly stop at the exploitation – or the elimination, Leamas – of a few individuals. It is all one, we have never pretended to be wholly just in the process of rationalizing society. Some Roman said it, didn't he, in the Christian Bible – it is expedient that one man should die for the benefit of many.' (le Carré, 1963, ch. 13)

The stinging and self-composed rhetorical question with which Fiedler concludes his speech turns the reader's attention, however, away from Stalinist amorality and back on to the contradictions in the democratic West's 'evaluation of the individual's place in society' (le Carré, 1966, p. 5), and that is where the novel's focus remains.

Alec Leamas, the anti-hero of le Carré's novel, has a clear generic pedigree; he is a professional agent who behaves with the individualism of an amateur, 'stubborn, wilful, contemptuous of instruction' (ch. 2). He is 'very strong', 'attractive', 'hard to place'; he looks like 'a man who could make trouble' and 'who was not quite a gentleman':

> The air hostess thought he was interesting. She guessed he was North Country, which he might have been, and rich, which he was not. She put his age at fifty, which was about right. She guessed he was single, which was half true.   (Ibid.)

The critic Jerry Palmer describes the typical thriller hero as 'Alone, Sexy, Competitive'. He comments upon his 'dubious status' as deriving from the necessity of his sharing 'the general moral perspective of the community he serves' but being 'forced both to spend most of his time outside it, in an unpleasant world to which he is professionally adapted, and to behave in a way that is only just tolerable to the community' (Palmer, 1978, pp. 24–5). Leamas conforms generally with this stereotype. His sexiness is his least important attribute but it is noted. His intrinsic competitiveness is used by his superior, Control, in building up his persona as the arrogant, self-sufficient spy-runner who cannot believe that an operation could be run on his patch without his knowledge, and it thus provides a crucial element in the mechanism of the plot. He competes successfully with Fiedler, per-suading his antagonist that his cover story is true. The depiction of Leamas as the solitary outsider is emphasized most in the story. He is seen in the opening chapters in the failure of defeat, having lost all of his East German network, and feeling 'written off'. The deception of Fiedler also depends upon the plausibility of his rejection by the 'Circus' and of his subsequent self-indulgent loneliness and resentment which, in Control's scenario, leads him to drink and prison. Leamas is an outsider who must act the outsider.

Leamas's stock individualism makes him, true to genre, a free agent in more senses than one and it is the narrative's ultimate task to expose his freedom as illusory. The terse description which introduces him, given in his 'own' voice, sketches Leamas's ostensible freedom in a succession of negatives:

> Leamas was not a reflective man and not a particularly philosophical one. He knew he was written-off – it was a fact of life which he would henceforth live with, as a man must live with cancer or imprisonment. He knew there was no kind of preparation which could have bridged the gap between then and now. He met failure as one day he would probably meet death, with cynical resentment and the courage of a solitary . . .
>
> Ten years ago he could have taken the other path – there were desk jobs in that anonymous government building in Cambridge Circus which Leamas could have taken and kept till he was God knows how old; but Leamas wasn't made that way. You might as well have asked a jockey to become a totalisator clerk as expect Leamas to abandon operational life for the tendentious theorising and clandestine self-interest of Whitehall.   (ch. 2)

What makes Leamas able to accept the isolation contingent on failure is his 'cynical' self-sufficiency – he feels free from anything which might exert a compromising pressure upon him: philosophy, self-reflection, fear of routine, anonymity, theory, personal loyalty and fear of failure and death.

There is no mention of Leamas having any kind of commitment; he believes only in the means-justifying virtue of pragmatism:

> Intelligence work has one moral law – it is justified by results. Even the sophistry of Whitehall paid court to that law . . .   (Ibid.)

Initially then, Leamas suggests something of the 'hard-boiled' generic hero – tough, masculine, successful, a man apart; in place of glamour and wit, he has the less immediately attractive quality of 'cynical resentment' as his differentiating mark but, at first, he seems to owe as much to Chandler as to Greene. This is by no means the whole story of Leamas; le Carré probes and tests his principal character, dissecting and evaluating the generic features which comprise him and, more important, he marginalizes Leamas's generic 'extraordinariness' to concentrate instead on what makes Leamas socially typical.

If the thriller norm necessitates that its hero be, in Palmer's words, 'of dubious status', 'Alone', 'Sexy', 'Competitive', the more general cultural fashions of the early 1960s made comparable requirements. In fact, many of the adjectives Christopher Booker identifies as keywords of the period – (among others), 'classless', 'straightforward', 'toughly professional', 'sceptical', 'irreverant', 'abrasive' (pp. 23–30), terms used of vogue politicians, entertainers and fictional cult figures alike, seem to apply equally well to the heroes of the standard American detective thriller. Again, all these terms attach to Leamas too, although le Carré uses none of them explicitly. So Leamas is a genre figure and a figure of the moment but he has strong roots also in the two decades which preceded the sixties. He is about fifty-years-old, he served in the war, and intermittently remembers its 'chaos'. Greater emphasis is given to elements of Leamas indicative of the 1950s. Although he is 'hard to place' and only possibly of 'North Country' origin, his apparently 'classless' manner does not obscure his affinity with the real and fictional personae of the writers known collectively as 'The Movement'. The name was coined by Anthony Hartley in a *Spectator* review of 1954 and his famous list of adjectives, defining the school, rivals Booker's in describing Alec Leamas's dominant attitudes:

> The Movement, as well as being anti-phoney, is anti-wet, sceptical, robust, ironic, prepared to be as comfortable as possible in a wicked, commercial world, which doesn't look anyway as if it's going to be changed much by a couple of handfuls of young English writers. (Quoted in Hamilton, 1973, pp. 128–9)

Le Carré implies that Leamas probably comes from the world of provincial grammar schools and that his native intelligence has bought him a free place in an espionage establishment not normally peopled by those of his (presumably) upper working-class or lower middle-class background:

> Leamas, the new men were told, was the old school; blood, guts and cricket and School Cert. French. In Leamas' case this happened to be unfair, since

he was bilingual in German and English and his Dutch was admirable; he
also disliked cricket. But it was true that he had no degree.   (ch. 3)

Leamas shares with the writers of The Movement a more-or-less sup-
pressed anxiety at the individual's incapacity in the face of Authority.
Authority is amorphous – it may be embodied in the Establishment, the
Church, Government, the University, God, politics, social ideals, romantic
love, routine work – anything that might compromise or hinder the
individual in the exercise of his own, experience-based commonsense. The
posture of no-nonsense rebelliousness, of impatience with pretension,
obscures an insular, conservative and petit-bourgeois resignation; the cynical
reliance on the self alone, ostensibly pitted against social limitations, betrays
an equally limited defeatism. Le Carré draws from this stratum for
his portrayal of Leamas and forces him to confront the philosophy he
lives.

Le Carré needs Leamas to straddle the decades – he is the postwar or
Cold War everyman, the 'educated man-in-the-street', so to speak, whom
the thriller format allows to be projected into situations where his attitudes
and assumptions will require more considered definition than normality
asks and where their substance will be proved. A character who religiously
avoids self-reflection and 'philosophy' of any kind is, in the course of the
novel, obliged to discover where he actually stands, what his politics and
morals really are, and whether or not they are justifiable. Accordingly,
The Spy Who Came in from the Cold proceeds via a sequence of confrontations
in which its petit-bourgeois hero is induced to confront the competing claims
of the English political Establishment (in the figure of Control), Stalinism
(in Fiedler) and Left-Liberalism (in Liz), in order that each of these, and
Leamas himself, may be judged. The narrative's attentiveness to keeping
the reader's sympathies with Leamas, in refusing to admit that there
is anything but endorsement of him by the author in each of the
confrontations, constitutes one of the novel's many ironies.

Control is set up as a good candidate for ridicule and his grating
cultivatedness makes for an easy satirical target:

> He was shorter than Leamas remembered him; otherwise just the same.
> The same affected detachment, the same donnish conceits; the same horror
> of draughts; courteous according to a formula miles removed from Leamas'
> experience. The same milk-and-water smile, the same elaborate diffidence,
> the same apologetic adherence to a code of behaviour which he pretended
> to find ridiculous. The same banality.   (ch. 2)

Somewhat surprisingly following this, Control proves very much to have
the upper hand in their discussion. His opinions of Leamas remain
unexplicated but, with what seems a malicious subtlety, he keeps his
subordinate completely outclassed, allowing Leamas no opportunity to
patronize him openly. Control's approach combines an oblique and
mannered vagueness with a disarming, offensive use of direct questions:

'How did you feel? When Riemeck was shot, I mean? You saw it didn't you?'

Leamas shrugged. 'I was bloody annoyed,' he said. Control put his head on one side and half closed his eyes. 'Surely you felt more than that? Surely you were upset? . . .'   (Ibid.)

Leamas flounders, unable to make Control reach his point. Forced into irritation and confusion, he expresses his inability to 'talk like this' and Control proceeds only when Leamas is trapped in his final defence of silence:

'I want you to stay out in the cold a little longer.' Leamas said nothing, so Control went on: 'The ethic of our work, as I understand it, is based on a single assumption. That is, we are never going to be aggressors. Do you think that's fair?'

Leamas nodded. Anything to avoid talking.

'Thus we do disagreeable things, but we are *defensive*. That, I think, is still fair. We do disagreeable things so that ordinary people here and elsewhere can sleep safely in their beds at night. Is that too romantic? Of course, we occasionally do very wicked things'; he grinned like a schoolboy. 'And in weighing up the moralities, we rather go in for dishonest comparisons; after all you can't compare the ideals of one side with the methods of the other, can you, now?'

Leamas was lost. He'd heard the man talked a lot of drivel before getting the knife in, but he'd never heard anything like this before.

'I mean you've got to compare method with method, and ideal with ideal. I would say that since the war, our methods – ours and those of the opposition – have become much the same. I mean you can't be less ruthless than the opposition simply because your government's *policy* is benevolent, can you now?' He laughed quietly to himself: 'That would *never* do,' he said.

'For God's sake,' thought Leamas, 'it's like working for a bloody clergyman. What *is* he up to?'

'That is why,' Control continued, 'I think we ought to try and get rid of Mundt . . .'   (Ibid.)

Control has many voices at his disposal and they are all the voices of the English Establishment. His deployment of the pronoun is masterly: he varies his choice of 'person' in a virtuoso performance which demonstrates a complete ease with the entire linguistic register of his class. He ensures, for instance, that what comprises 'we' and 'our' remains both elusive and exclusive and contrasts it with his formulaic and self-deprecating 'I' which pretends that he is merely on the fringes of, or subordinate to, that apparently shared ethic. 'I' also performs the role of independent adjudication ('That, I think, is still fair') in such a way as to preclude the possibility of any come-back, any criticism. And Control's use of 'you' throughout, the deliberate slippage into colloquialism, is a magnificently condescending appeal to the popular, governing rhetorical questions which insidiously keep the addressee in helpless silence ('you can't compare . . . can you now?', 'you can't be less ruthless . . . can you now?'). When 'we' reappears at the end of Control's display its content has been completely obscured and the reader is left, like Leamas, wondering whether 'we' signifies the powers-that-be, or just Control and Leamas, or if it is simply a euphemism, meaning not 'us' at all but 'you' – Leamas – on his own.

Control's manner is ingeniously effective but that is not to say that his argument is obscured by it; there is a sophisticated logic there too:

1 We are not aggressors.
2 We are defensive.
3 We do 'disagreeable things' for agreeable reasons.
4 Like should not be compared with unlike; it is dishonest to compare our ideals with their methods.
5 Our methods and theirs have become identical.
6 Therefore we have to act as ruthlessly as if we were the aggressors.

The full irony of Control's argument only emerges at the end of the novel when it proves to have been the justification not for getting rid of Mundt at all but for eradicating his rival, Fiedler, while destroying Liz and writing-off Leamas en route. Leamas, it turns out, has been induced to volunteer for his own fall. Yet le Carré leaves the overall status of Control's position ambiguous. The reader is invited to entertain the thought that his alleged ideal – doing 'disagreeable things so that ordinary people . . . can sleep safely' – has its own validity, regardless of the speaker's deviousness and superciliousness. Certainly, the reader does not share Leamas's view that Control is talking 'drivel'. But the disparity in terms of social class between Control and Leamas, between the Establishment and 'ordinary people' which underwrites the scene nicely complicates the simple moral dilemma which is dramatized here. Le Carré wishes to find an acceptable morality to validate a corrupt practice carried out by a corrupt and élitist class which claims to act in the interests of society as a whole. Le Carré finds himself torn between disgust at this class's hypocrisy and his 'reluctant' belief that 'Communism' must be fought 'decisively'.

In his Introduction to *Philby*, le Carré takes the British Intelligence Services and the Establishment as one and the same, and he describes them as an autonomous 'withdrawn', 'initiated élite', quite divorced from those they supposedly serve:

> . . . SIS would not merely *defend* the traditional decencies of our society; it would embody them. Within its own walls, its clubs and country houses, in whispered luncheons with its secular contacts, it would enshrine the mystical entity of a vanishing England. Here at least, whatever went on in the big world outside, England's flower would be cherished. '*The Empire may be crumbling; but within our secret élite, the clean-limbed tradition of English power would survive. We believe in nothing but ourselves.*' . . . An inescapable concomitant of this mental condition was the identification of the fortunes of the Service with the fortunes of the nation. They themselves replaced the ideologies they dismissed. *Their* image, *their* repute, were the nation's prestige; *their* infallibility the nation's bond; their survival evidence of the inarticulate supremacy of the English gentleman.   (Page et al., 1968, pp. 17–18)

The figure of Control implies this self-advancing tradition but, unlike the gentlemen le Carré is referring to above, Control is not 'inarticulate' when it comes to advocating an 'ideology' – his single professed belief of acting in the name of 'ordinary people' is breathtakingly crude and remains completely unexplored, yet it is an articulated position. Leamas, on the other hand is silent. He says virtually nothing in his interview with Control, not simply because Control's rhetoric discourages replies, nor because he despises his boss, and evidently not because he has any feelings of social inferiority, but because, at a deeper level, he has nothing to say. Control states a credo: Leamas, it seems, has none.

In a quite different context, the subject of Leamas 'philosophy' is quickly reopened. After a cosy supper in her flat one evening, Liz asks:

> 'Alec, what do you believe in? Don't laugh – tell me.' She waited and at last he said:
> 'I believe an eleven bus will take me to Hammersmith. I don't believe it's driven by Father Christmas.'
> She seemed to consider this and at last she asked again: 'But what do you believe in?'
> Leamas shrugged.   (ch. 4)

Liz persists, ignoring his dismissals and in this exchange too, there is considerable silence. Eventually he submits and supplies a barely patient answer:

> 'Sorry, Liz, you've got it wrong. I don't like Americans and public schools. I don't like military parades and people who play soldiers.' Without smiling he added, 'And I don't like conversations about Life.'
> 'But, Alec, you might as well say – '
> 'I should have added,' Leamas interrupted, 'that I don't like people who tell me what I ought to think.'   (Ibid.)

His characteristic negatives do reveal an easily recognizable attitude – world-weary, chauvinist, 'knowing', anti-pretentious, anti-privilege, chip-on-the-shoulder – and his assertive tone betrays pride in his opinionatedness although it also implies that his opinions, gained from experience, need no voicing. Liz is unimpressed:

> 'That's because you don't *want* to think, you don't dare! There's some poison in your mind, some hate. You're a fanatic, Alec, I know you are, but I don't know what about. You're a fanatic who doesn't want to convert people, and that's a dangerous thing. You're like a man who's . . . sworn vengeance or something.'   (Ibid.)

Vengeance is not Leamas driving force. Le Carré gives him ample opportunity to express himself in terms of revenge – the agents he ran have all been betrayed and killed – but it is made perfectly clear that Leamas is no avenging angel. When he agrees to 'get rid of Mundt' he tells Control that he's 'game' but Control reminds him that he doesn't '*have* to say it':

' . . . I mean in our world we pass so quickly out of the register of hate or love – like certain sounds a dog can't hear. All that's left in the end is a kind of nausea . . . Forgive me, but isn't that rather what you felt when Karl Riemeck was shot?' (ch. 2)

And if, as Leamas thinks, both sides are the same, the moral justification for revenge is compromised almost to the point of extinction from the outset. Leamas' fanaticism is an extreme bloody-mindedness which won't and can't 'convert people' because it is unaware of its own source. Leamas realizes this partly and it is a sore point; as soon as he can he returns Liz's question – what does she believe in? 'History,' she replies, bravely. After a moment's shock, Leamas draws the right conclusion and laughs:

'Oh, Liz . . . oh *no*. You're not a bloody Communist?'
She nodded, blushing like a small girl at his laughter, angry and relieved that he didn't care. (ch. 4)

A more demanding test of belief comes with a Party Member of more advanced political consciousness than Liz, (because *her* philosophy is also interrogated and also found wanting in the course of the novel). Masquerading as a potential defector, Leamas consolidates his contact with the opposition and is moved 'East'. His last debriefing session with Fiedler takes place in woodland seclusion. The brilliant, young East German counter-intelligence man questions him in a long, finely observed exchange:

He asked about the pay, the leave, the morale, the canteen; he asked about their love-life, their gossip, their philosophy. Most of all he asked about their philosophy.
   To Leamas that was the most difficult question of all.
   'What do you mean, a philosophy?' he replied; 'we're not Marxists, we're nothing. Just people.'
   'Are you Christians, then?'
   'Not many, I shouldn't think. I don't know many.'
   'What makes them do it, then?' Fiedler persisted; 'they must have a philosophy.'
   'Why must they? Perhaps they don't know; don't even care. Not everyone has a philosophy,' Leamas answered, a little helplessly.
   'Then tell me what is your philosophy?'
   'Oh for Christ's sake,' Leamas snapped, and they walked on in silence for a while. But Fiedler was not to be put off.
   'If they do not know what they want, how can they be so certain they are right?'
   'Who the hell said they were?' Leamas replied irritably. (ch. 13)

On one level, Leamas' replies are those of the trained agent, the responses of a professional trained to resist interrogation and in this dialogue Leamas is seeking to convince Fiedler that his defection is genuine, that it has been occasioned not by any 'ideological' reversal but on account of his mistreatment by his ungrateful former employers. But he is given no chance to pursue his prepared script. Not expecting, and not really understanding Fiedler's line of enquiry, Leamas endeavours to deflect the curious questions about 'philosophy' and cover things over with an impatient, negative uncooperativeness, which in other circumstances comes naturally to him. Yet le Carré ensures through Fiedler's cool, probing insistence and from the hitherto unseen extent of Leamas' irritation that the reader perceives Fiedler revealing something of the man behind the spy.

The dialogue now devotes considerable time to Fiedler's amused and approving description of Stalin's 'philosophy' (quoted above) but, although it stands well in its own right and as a recapitulation of the novel's ends-and-means theme, the focus of the scene is kept securely on Leamas. Fiedler's Stalin speech serves mainly to taunt his victim's superficiality and expose his theory-despising short-range 'commonsense' as naive. Leamas is embarrassed and begins to feel foolish. Once more he finds himself trapped and once more he surrenders, supplying an answer (of sorts) which might stop his interrogator's intrusive pressure:

> 'Then what do you think? What is your philosophy?'
>   'I just think the whole lot of you are bastards,' said Leamas savagely.
>   Fiedler nodded, 'That is a viewpoint I understand. It is primitive, negative and very stupid – but it is a viewpoint, it exists. But what about the rest of the Circus?'
>   'I don't know. How should I know?'
>   'Have you never discussed philosophy with them?'
>   'No. We're not Germans.' He hesitated, then added vaguely: 'I suppose they don't like Communism.'
>   'And that justifies, for instance, the taking of human life? That justifies the bomb in the crowded restaurant; that justifies your write-off rate of agents – all that?'
>   Leamas shrugged. 'I suppose so.'   (Ibid.)

Fiedler is not to know that Leamas' feeble and bad-tempered statement of a position ('I just think the whole lot of you are bastards') is as much directed against Control as against him but that is by the way; the outburst delights him even though he controls his triumph with customary restraint. As the interrogator correctly surmised, there *was* a rationale underlying Leamas' off-handedness all along – 'primitive, negative and very stupid' but 'a viewpoint' nevertheless. The assumption that people do not act in accordance with ideas but for private and obvious reasons – if they have any at all – is exposed in this dialogue as embodying, despite its denials, a 'philosophy' as strong, at root, as Christianity or Stalinism. As part of his attempted resistance to Fiedler's questions Leamas allows himself to acknowledge that Fiedler has a point here and there but the interrogator's observations hurt and, realizing the poverty of his own responses, Leamas is forced to snap back either with a self-deprecating and escapist irony or with an equally powerless infantile venom. In making Leamas 'at a loss to defend himself in ideological dispute' with a Stalinist, le Carré both dramatizes and criticizes that insular, English, petit-bourgeois 'viewpoint' which pretends to take the world as meaningless and retains an obstinate, arrogant, and, as here, rather pathetic faith in cynical individualism. When Leamas hesitantly and vaguely offers the opinion that the Circus personnel 'don't like Communism' his tentative statement disturbs him (and any reader who has identified with his attitude during the exchange) because, as a collective position, it evaporates the fantasy of complete individual self-reliance and because, at a more general level, it reveals that Leamas (and those he symbolizes) exist in a culpable ignorance of the ideological foundations of their actions.

Leamas moves through the novel in possession of an unresolved contradiction. At one and the same time he believes that both sides are identical and that, therefore, there is nothing outside himself worthy of belief, and seems also grudgingly to accept Control's view that there is something worth defending in Britain and the West. Le Carré keeps the contradiction sharp. In Leamas' final conversation with Fiedler he admits that London would kill 'an innocent man':

> 'It depends . . . it depends on the need . . .' 'Ah,' said Fiedler contentedly, 'it depends on the need. Like Stalin, in fact. The traffic accident and the statistics. That is a great relief.' (ch. 18)

Fiedler is subsequently killed by the application of Stalin's philosophy by the British and, in the terms of the novel, he is just such an 'innocent' – an honest victim, like Liz, and, like her, a Jew. As the action approaches its climax – the lovers' deaths on the Berlin Wall – Leamas is yet again required to rehearse a credo. Now arguing against Liz's outraged disgust at the way they and Fiedler have been abused by London, he takes the offensive and in so doing echoes Control:

> ' . . . What do you think spies are: priests, saints and martyrs? . . . Do you think they sit like monks in London balancing the rights and wrongs? I'd have killed Mundt if I could, I hate his guts; but not now. It so happens that they need him. They need him so that the great moronic mass that you admire can sleep soundly in their beds at night. They need him for the safety of ordinary, crummy people like you and me.' (ch. 25)

Liz returns to her familiar tack – 'You're trying to persuade yourself' – and Leamas immediately and unconsciously switches back towards his other position:

> 'Christ Almighty! . . . I don't believe in anything, don't you see – not even destruction or anarchy. I'm sick, sick of killing but I don't see what else they can do . . .' (Ibid.)

'It makes you the same,' she says, and he replies, 'But it's the world . . . everywhere's the same'. Broken, Liz resigns herself to his argument.

Le Carré is ambivalent in his attitude towards Leamas: he is critical of the inadequacy of his 'philosophical' confusion and of his resentment in facing the fact that he *does* support one side and *does* have a 'viewpoint', yet sympathetic both to that same confusion and to Leamas' 'decent instincts' (1966, p. 5) which raise him (along with Fiedler and Liz) above the ruthless cold warriors whom le Carré sees as fighting on both sides of the Wall. Le Carré projects a comparable ambivalence in his treatment of Liz. She belongs (roughly) to the same social class as Leamas – 'lower-middle' – and, like him, she is a character caught in contradiction. She is in her early-twenties, innocent, impressionable and honest about herself. She is a member of the British Communist Party but is of a quite different order to the novel's other 'Communists': 'Ashe, the mercenary, Kiever the fellow-traveller, . . . Peters, for whom the end and the means were identical' (ch. 8), Fiedler, the intellectual and ideologue, Karden and the Tribunal President, hard as nails. For Liz, membership of the Party derives from and answers emotional needs, and her beliefs (in peace and social good) are sincerely felt but not rationally analysed. Le Carré concentrates on her youth and innocence, portraying them as at once dangerously naive and as objects of paternalistic celebration. The reader is asked to bemoan her simple-minded idealism, admire her tenacity and her moral sense, and take pleasure in her charm.

The novel's female characters are divided into two categories: the tough, powerful and self-sufficient (Elvira, the unnamed President of the Tribunal and the Prison Commissar), and, set against them, the child-like. Control's wife and Miss Crail, the head librarian, are mother-dependent, while 'debutante secretaries' people the Circus and Control's coffee is brought to him by 'Such a *silly* girl' (ch. 2). When Leamas is taken to meet Kiever in a tawdry club, the two men watch an embarrassingly sad stripper, oppressed and bruised, who watches them 'with the precocious interest of a child in adult company' (ch. 7). This woman-as-child motif is explored most fully with Liz who is frequently referred to, both by narrator and characters, in such terms. Liz herself becomes acutely conscious of how close she still is to her childhood experience and identity; alone in her cell, following the Tribunal, she recalls the horror of her infant recognition that 'with every step she made, thousands of minute creatures were destroyed beneath her foot' (ch. 24). Her membership of the Party allows her to explore tentatively her developing, adolescent sexual awareness. She is shown as both fascinated and disgusted by the imagined or real sexual advances made towards her by acquaintances in the Party. The implication is that her maturity has been somehow retarded. With Leamas, she permits herself romantic feelings which mainly seem to express her desire to be protected:

> He never spoke to her much and once, when she asked him if he loved her, he said he didn't believe in fairy tales. She would lie on the bed, her head against his chest, and sometimes he would put his thick fingers in her hair, holding it quite tight, and Liz laughed and said it hurt. (ch. 5)

In counterpoint to the 'adult' Leamas, whose autonomy the novel questions, the 'child' Liz is projected into situations in which her innocence may be given its full destructive rein – in her love-commitment to Leamas and in her experience as a Party member.

Liz's uncomfortable alliance with the Party, and the contradictions she lives as a member, are related with a complete absence of explicit narrative condescension. The Party's secrecy 'didn't appeal' to her much but 'she supposed it was necessary, and Heaven knows, there were plenty who got a kick out of it' (ch. 15). The form of address – 'Comrade' – 'she'd never quite got used to'. The letter from the Centre inviting her on an educational exchange to the GDR puzzles and surprises her but she accepts it, over-riding her doubts, as good coin. Le Carré reproduces the letter in full and authentically captures the 'house style' of Communist Party communications: Liz's response unconsciously relays his mild satire. The letter is unusually '*long*', 'so efficient, so well typed it might not have been done at Centre at all' but it has that 'awkward, semi-bureaucratic, semi-Messianic style she had grown accustomed to without ever liking'. Receiving it brings home to her all her half-expressed anxieties about membership and so takes her away from too detailed an enquiry about its source and the motivation behind it:

> It was stupid to say she had a good record of stimulating mass action at street level. She hadn't. As a matter of fact she hated that side of party work – the loudspeakers at the factory gates, selling the *Daily Worker* at the street corner, going from door to door at the local elections. Peace Work she didn't mind so much, it meant something to her, it made sense.   (Ibid.)

Engaging, incidental (and for the most part accurate) details representing one of the more moribund branches of the British Communist Party pepper this chapter: the unsold papers and lies about sales, the voting for a secretary who would 'do the work and not try and make them go canvassing at weekends', the desire for 'a decent little club, nice and revolutionary'. The rationalizations Liz produces to deal with the Party's self-deception are the products not only of her naiveté but, more generally, of a liberal consciousness compelled to political commitment but caught in disagreement with both the programme and practices of the very organization which allows her to express her commitment:

> It was such a little world, and she wished they could be more honest. But she lied to herself about it all, too. Perhaps they all did. Or perhaps the others understood more *why* you had to lie so much.   (Ibid.)

Liz covers her confusion in fantasy, sustaining herself with a sentimental 'warmth' towards the essential decency of the membership and 'gratitude' to the authority of the Centre, 'such a wonderful thing':

> – stern, benevolent, impersonal, perpetual. They were good, good people. People who fought for Peace.   (Ibid.)

Trusting that the Centre is different, other Branches must be different,

East Germany must be different, she accepts the invitation. The Branch meeting in Leipzig opens her eyes. Expecting an 'exhilarating experience', an instructive and exemplary discussion on peaceful coexistence, she is bitterly disappointed. Seven people attend:

> It was like the meetings in Bayswater, it was like mid-week evensong when she used to go to church . . .
> But seven people were nothing: they were worse than nothing, because they were evidence of the inertia of the uncapturable mass. They broke your heart. (ch. 19)

Le Carré forgoes a description of the meeting's political content, concentrating instead on the sense of irritation and hurry, and on Liz's attempt to cope with her shattered illusion. Perhaps Alec was right:

> you believed in things because you needed to; what you believed had no value of its own . . . No, Alec was wrong: truth existed outside people, it was demonstrated in history, individuals must bow to it, be crushed by it if necessary. (Ibid.)

Liz vacillates between the two alternatives; the narrative emphasis inclines the reader to prefer her pessimism to her unconvincing retreat into generality, but the subjectivity and self-pity which underwrite the former make that 'viewpoint' inadequate too. Where Leamas, who 'knows', purportedly believes in nothing, Liz, who 'believes', seems to know nothing. The point is hammered home in the chapter called 'The President' where the character of the title, terrifyingly and benevolently maternal, advises Liz on how to behave in giving her evidence. Liz has entered the courtroom 'like a half-woken child' and is addressed with the patient clarity of a firm parent, the President playing mother to Prosecutor Karden's father. Liz adapts accordingly, responding with submissive nods and fearful whispers, remembering that she is an adult in an afterthought which fools no one:

> 'And have you been told never, never to ask questions of another Comrade on the organization and dispostion of the Party?'
> Liz nodded again. 'Yes,' she said, 'of course.' (ch. 22)

She is told, 'It is better for you, far better, that you should know nothing', and this is insistently repeated. On her crucial admission that Leamas never mentioned he had any 'friend', the ensuing silence is 'terrible' to her:

> because like a blind child among the seeing, she was cut off from all those around her; they could measure her answers against some secret standard, and she could not know from the dreadful silence what they had found. (Ibid.)

And in his attempt to rescue her in the following chapter, Leamas confesses Control's plot, adding, 'She knows nothing. Nothing at all. . . . She knows nothing, I tell you' (ch. 23). By this time, as far as the reader is concerned, Liz's lack of knowledge is in no way confined to her ignorance of the intrigue but has assumed a far larger dimension. At the end of her witness, Karden passes judgement:

> ' . . . I am sorry that a girl whose perception is clouded by sentiment and whose alertness is blunted by money, should be considered by our British comrades a suitable person for Party office.'
>
> Looking first at Leamas and then at Fiedler he added brutally: 'She is a fool . . . (ch. 22)

Just as Leamas' alleged lack of belief is exposed (together with its contradictions) as false, so too is the quality of Liz's belief. Karden's judgement on her is that of a Stalinist, the product of a particularly distasteful consciousness, but the reader is given, at this point, no option but to accept it.

In formal terms, le Carré's novel is deftly resolved, satisfying the desire for closure with its symmetries. The death of Riemeck, betrayed by a trusted companion, began the narrative; it ends with two deaths also consequent on (both intentional and inadvertent) betrayals. The Berlin Wall frontier with Smiley on one side and Mundt on the other suggests, for the last time, the identity of the East and the West. The novel's final images of Leamas 'astride the wall', Smiley calling to him to jump back to the Western side, Liz, 'lying still' on the Eastern side, show the innocent, ordinary hero trapped between morally unacceptable and merely seeming alternatives. Leamas' final act is portrayed as a decent and baffled disengagement from the Cold War – suicide in a tiny no-man's land which suddenly becomes a floodlit 'arena'. Both hero and heroine have been led to understand the mechanism of the entire intrigue but, in a precise paradox, they die in confusion, Leamas, 'blinded', 'Shielding his eyes', 'glaring round him like a blinded bull' just as Liz has been left blind. The overall status of hero and heroine, however, remains as ambiguous as it has been for the duration of the narrative and, with regard to its debates on 'philosophy', the reader leaves the novel without the clear answers it has so systematically canvassed for throughout.

Certainly, le Carré wants to keep the moral issues open and certainly wishes them transplanted alive from his fictional world to the world of the reader. In his 'Open Letter', le Carré spells out the question that captures his main interest:

> . . . how long can we defend ourselves . . . by methods of this kind, and still remain the kind of society that is worth defending? (1966, p. 5)

The Spy Who Came in from the Cold does indeed ask this question and, moreover, it induces the reader to challenge its premise, the assumption contained in 'still remain'. Yet, what the novel has presented as untenable in Liz's 'innocent' liberalism and Leamas' myopic cynicism and self-reliance, seems finally to earn a larger measure of authorial endorsement than the bulk of the narrative might have led the reader to expect. With its final concentration on the innocent victims of the Cold War, the novel compromises its criticism of them: the culpably confused, self-deceiving, poor little anti-heroic dupes become, through their deaths, *preferable* to the overt cold warriors who force them into destruction. Through their deaths, Leamas and Liz (and to an extent, Fiedler) attain a kind of heroism. Voinov's objection to le Carré's professed political impartiality and his downplaying of the novel's astringent attacks on the British Establishment has more to commend it than le Carré himself cares to admit even though the Russian critic, collapsing Leamas into Control, distorts his evidence:

> 'From time to time, we take very unpleasant steps,' say the characters in le Carré, 'but such is life, what is one to do? You see, our methods, ours and those of our antagonists, are completely identical.' So a lie about the East about-turns into an argument for the war-cries of the Imperialist Intelligence Service . . .
>
> Le Carré's moralistic conception is extremely primitive; the Western Intelligence Service is conscripted 'To protect the people's peace', but modest rank-and-file spies at the front lines of the Cold War (cleansed by the author of any cheap gilt and tinsel) are the authentic heroes of our century. It is not surprising that le Carré's books are so well inserted into the propaganda fanning the flag of the 'Cold War' . . .
>
> Le Carré is already beating Fleming. He is more ingenious, deeper, more 'human'. As a replacement for the fearless good-looker, with muscles but no brain, the ordinary 'Little man' has arrived, with his doubts, weaknesses [and] vulnerability. In place of frontal 'agitation', the moral-psychological novel has arrived, with its claims to realism. (Voinov, 16 October 1965)

Here, Voinov identifies something of the ideology underlying le Carré's stated purposes in writing *The Spy Who Came in from the Cold*. The ending of the novel, so satisfying in formal terms, blunts the impact of those moral questions the author wishes his readers to consider when, the final page turned, they have set the book aside. The unfortunate deaths of Leamas and Liz assume a romantic grandeur and, almost in spite of the narrative's intentions, a reappraisal of the two characters is required. Their bafflement becomes preferable to the clarity of their manipulators, their ordinariness more sympathetic than the cold élitism of their masters, where formerly their insistence on acting ordinarily in extraordinary situations won large measures of authorial rebuke. Leamas' previously untenable individualism now becomes invested with a new approved life, expressing itself through love. He dies 'for' Liz, turning his back on the political world and in his so doing the novel also vacates the moral-political site it has previously occupied. With its generic conclusion, the novel leaves behind its anxiety over the doing of 'disagreeable things' for agreeable reasons, the 'squalid' business of spying, and avoid the fact that Leamas dies with his duty done in protecting the peace of 'the great moronic mass'. Leamas is 'saved' by love, but in any other than personal terms, it hardly matters.

3   Little Games:
The Looking-Glass War

'The game justifies their very existence. They're all fantasists talking endlessly about team spirit, which I take to be a euphemism for homosexuality and reiterating the myths they create around themselves as monotonously as banging a ball against a wall.'   (le Carré on *The Looking-Glass War*. Oakes, 11 September 1977. I.)

Because there is so little opportunity for intimacy in daily life, and because some forms of intimacy (especially if intense) are psychologically impossible for most people, the bulk of the time in serious social life is taken up with playing games. Hence games are both necessary and desirable, and the only problem at issue is whether the games played by an individual offer the best yield for him.   (Berne, 1967, pp. 54–5)

Although some of its action is again set in a Cold War German borderland and although it replays its predecessor's theme of the discrepancy between the means and aims of espionage, le Carré's next novel, *The Looking-Glass War*, in fact takes a quite new perspective on the Intelligence world. From its title, the reader might initially expect to find in its pages some further treatment of the mirrored identification of East and West, a notion that lay at the heart of *The Spy Who Came in from the Cold*, but such an expectation remains unfulfilled. For the most part, the characters of the new novel are not forced to confront their present activity and justify it – they are not led into attempts to articulate a coherent and consistent philosophy which might stand up to the scrutiny of interrogation – these characters bury their heads in dreams and myths of the past and participate in games designed pathetically to revive it. In *The Looking-Glass War* le Carré turns his attention to the fantasies of nostalgia.

The Department depicted here is a run-down Military Intelligence section of the War Office staffed by a handful of remnant veterans from World War Two. Dreams of security, ostensibly military and actually personal, inform the action. From a smug, knowing distance, one of the Department's sister services, the surrogate SIS of Control and Smiley, watches quietly as it carries out a series of lethal blunders. The Department seeks to perpetuate the spirit of some long-departed camaraderie and it acts, in whatever it does, with a grotesque, archaic amateurism. *The Looking-Glass War* divides into three sections, 'Taylor's Run', 'Avery's Run', and 'Leiser's Run' and each describes an incompetently planned and incompetently executed mission ending in failure. Each mission has its own distinctive tone and quality, which is signalled initially by the wry quotation heading each section. The first is from Kipling's *Kim* (*A fool lies here who tried to hustle the East*), the second from John Buchan's *Mr Standfast* ('*There are some things that no one has a right to ask of any white man*'), and the last from a poem by Rupert Brooke (*To turn as swimmers into cleanness leaping/Glad from a world gone old and cold and weary*). 'Taylor's Run' has an atmosphere of confusion and anxiety concluding in violent and mysterious death. 'Avery's Run' is satirical, ending with the deflation of farce; 'Leiser's Run' approaches the tone of tragedy but lacks that genre's glamour. Yet these differentiated missions, all separate species of the thriller, do not, in themselves, constitute the novel's primary interest.

Heading the Contents page, and thus the whole novel, is another literary quotation, this one from *Alice Through the Looking-Glass*:

> *I wouldn't mind being a Pawn,*
> *if only I might join* – Alice

There is no strict counterpart to Alice in le Carré's novel, although some of its female characters share some resemblance with her, and there is only a faint echo in Lewis Carroll's Red and White Queens of le Carré's Cold War context of Communist–Capitalist conflict. Nonetheless, the Alice allusion serves to state a major theme. Here it is in full:

> 'I declare it's marked out like a large chess-board!' Alice said at last. 'There ought to be some men moving about somewhere – and so there are!' she added in a tone of delight, and her heart began to beat quick with excitement as she went on. 'It's a great huge game of chess that's being played – all over the world – if this *is* the world at all, you know. Oh, what fun it is! How I wish I was one of them! I wouldn't mind being a Pawn, if only I might join – though of course, I should *like* to be a Queen, best.'   (Carroll, 1970, pp. 207–8)

Le Carré's novel has its own Looking-Glass House and Looking-Glass World and its 'great huge game' takes up Alice's chess-board fantasy and also the 'Great Game' of espionage both from *Kim* and from the real-life Soviet spy, Leopold Trepper, whose 'Red Orchestra' of wireless-operator agents played 'The Great Game' with the Gestapo during World War Two. The irony is clear. Le Carré's absurdly small-scale British fiasco has nothing great about it at all. It is a little game – chess at novice level, the pieces Pawns who think they're Knights, the players bureaucrats who think they're Kings and Queens. The chess-game though, signifies more than espionage – it is a 'relationships' game too, played by husbands and wives, a game in which men strive to be winners but actually lose hands down and seek, in consolation, to cement ties with other men and memories of other men. Fantasy is everywhere in *The Looking-Glass War*, which is not itself a fantasy but a realist novel about fantasy.

The collective or interpersonal fantasies here find expression in the more or less sophisticated playing of games. These non-recreational games function to provide useful pay-offs of various kinds. Played at work (in the Department or its 'safe-house' in Oxford), they are team games, played by only one team, with the achievement of group security as their aim. Played at home, in domestic or otherwise normal situations, they are games of power and self-protection with the aim of keeping wives and home-truths at bay. Mostly, the two playing areas are kept separate but sometimes they collide head-on, and sometimes they intersect each other. The ostensible content of the domestic games concerns the possession of secret knowledge. Despite the assumption of secrecy in the Department's work, the wives and girlfriends of its employees (Joanie Taylor, Sarah Avery, Woodford's wife, and Leiser's companion, Betty) are all, to varying extents, aware of what their men do, and have been told details of their operations. The women use what knowledge they have to challenge their men's motives, pretensions and inadequacies, while the men give and withhold information for their own private, ulterior purposes, using it as currency in transactions of control. In two subsequent novels, *The Honourable Schoolboy* and *The Little Drummer Girl*, le Carré refers to the 'Transactional Analysis' of Eric Berne's *Games People Play* (first published in 1964 – the year before *The Looking-Glass War*) and Thomas Harris's *I'm OK – You're OK*. Berne's vocabulary seems essential in describing the games le Carré dramatizes.

Berne's two defining characteristics of games – their 'ulterior quality' and their progression towards a 'payoff' (1967, p. 44) are present in all of John Avery's conversations with his wife. Their dialogues are represented with a minimum of narrative commentary or explanation and what few narrative remarks there are indirectly voice one or other character's unspoken thoughts. That is to say, the 'ulterior quality' is largely implicit and it is the reader's task to recognize and decode it. The Averys are introduced in Part II of the novel conducting a strained middle-of-the-night exchange:

> Avery put down the telephone, woke Sarah and said, 'Taylor's dead.' He shouldn't have told her, of course.
>   'Who's Taylor?'
> A bore, he thought; he only remembered him vaguely. A dreary English bore, straight off Brighton pier.
>   'A man in the courier section,' he said. 'He was with them in the war. He was rather good.'
>   'That's what you always say. They're all good . . .'
>   'He wants me to go to the office. He wants me. You don't expect me to turn over and go back to sleep, do you?'

'I was only asking,' Sarah said. 'You're always so considerate to Leclerc.'

'Taylor was an old hand. Leclerc's very worried.' He could still hear the triumph in Leclerc's voice: "Come at once, get a taxi; we'll go through the files again."

'Does this often happen? Do people often die?' . . .

'You're not to tell anyone,' said Avery. It was a way of keeping her from him. 'You're not even to say I've gone out in the middle of the night. Taylor was travelling under another name.' He added, 'Some one will have to tell his wife.' He was looking for his glasses.   (le Carré, 1965, ch. 2)

Every statement and every action has an ulterior function. Le Carré forgoes the narrator's privilege to explain fully – these meticulously recorded transactions are left to speak for themselves, and they do. Throughout, the reader's task is purely interpretative: to 'read through' the ostensible content of their relationship and register its authentic substance. The narrative allows that Avery's injunction 'was a way of keeping her from him' but lets the reader believe he is thinking this and offers no further comment as to why he acts to distance her. Similarly, the knowledge that both partners behave like children ('marriage had made her childish' and 'The motion of the taxi comforted him, as rocking consoles a child') is only minimally explanatory and the reader is left alone to identify each specific infantile response in the game's manoeuvres: the manipulations of giving and withholding, the gratuitous punishment by inducing jealousy, the deliberate 'put-downs' through ignoring and mishearing, and the self-sustaining and self-torturing guilt.

Avery's strategy in the marital game is to put into play information which his partner is forbidden to use. In so doing he is disobeying Departmental rules, but he is following established precedent all the same. Unknown to Avery, the unfortunate Taylor had committed the same offence: 'He'd told her, of course, he wasn't supposed to, but Leclerc didn't know Joanie . . .' (ch. 1). Pretending to intimacy by pretending to be candid Avery in fact rejects and excludes Sarah, seeking to imply his own indispensability in the exclusive Departmental group. He lies blatantly, almost obliviously, in suggesting Taylor's legend-like worth: the 'dreary English bore' becomes, for Sarah's consumption, proficient, experienced and impressive.

The game doesn't all go Avery's way. When his complacency leaves him momentarily exposed Sarah seizes her opportunities: 'That's what you always say. They're all good.' But she neglects to follow up an advantage, preferring to take it only so far and then defuse the challenge: 'I was only asking'. Anyway, Avery has no difficulty in dealing with her sarcasm. When she has expressed the jealousy he wanted her to feel he simply rides right over it:

'You're always so considerate to Leclerc.'

'Taylor was an old hand. Leclerc's worried'.

That this is another lie bothers him not at all. His last comment is game point – 'Someone will have to tell his wife' – a line of wilfully brutal insensitivity. She responds with an angrily resigned commonsense; 'For God's sake stop talking like a cowboy', but too late, for the game has already been won. Victories such as this, however, are at best provisional and Avery's ingenious improvizations cannot be sustained. He claims that a car is waiting for him at a 'secure' distance but loses all composure when he finds that he has to borrow money from her. The secret work fantasy now backfires completely as, watched by a neighbour ('as she watched everybody night and day') and by Sarah ('he knew she was crying because he hadn't kissed her'), he walks first up the street only to turn around and proceed in the opposite direction: 'He took half an hour to find a taxi to Blackfriars Road'.

The Avery-Sarah relationship surfaces intermittently during the novel in a counterplot which obstructs the thriller-reader's desire to become 'lost' in the atmosphere and mechanics of the espionage action proper. While much of their subsequent dialogue is given over to one of the novel's political themes, 'Loyalty without faith' (ch. 5), and to the ramifications of that predicament in a marriage which quite autonomously manifests loyalty without faith, le Carré is offering the Averys as a more general social example. Those pressures that the myth of the Department is allowed to exert upon their marriage stand, in extreme form, for other more typical and normal challenges to domestic security. Invariably, the political and moral issues in Avery's work (isues of which he is acutely conscious) are immediately superseded whenever the chance arises of his playing the relationship game. With a mixture of bravado, disgust at the senselessness of Taylor's death, and an uncomfortable feeling of being irreversibly cut-off from Sarah, Avery makes a sudden decision to resign. But Sarah telephones with news that pushes him straight back into the game. She has been visited by detectives and has 'told them about Taylor'. The former tone of sarcastic control is eschewed; now the game is played with hysterical emotionalism:

> 'What did you tell them? For Christ's sake, Sarah, what else did you say to them?'
> 'Don't swear at me! I should be swearing at you and your beastly Department! I said you were doing something secret; you'd had to go abroad for the Department – John, I don't even know its *name*! – that you'd been rung in the night and you'd gone away. I said it was about a courier called Taylor.'
> 'You're mad,' Avery shouted, 'you're absolutely mad. I told you never to say!'
> 'But, John, they were *policemen*! There can't be any harm in telling them.' She was crying, he could hear the tears in her voice. 'John, *please* come back. I'm so frightened. You've got to get out of this, go back to publishing; I don't care what you do but . . .'
> 'I can't. It's terribly big. More important than you can possibly

understand. I'm sorry, Sarah. I just can't leave the office.' He added savagely, a useful lie, 'You may have wrecked the whole thing.'

There was a very long silence.

'Sarah, I'll have to sort this out. I'll ring you later.'   (ch. 9)

Whatever impulses he had to resign fall into insignificance beside the attractions of playing for the kill, the pay-off in this game scenario. Sarah's transgression has been so gross that Avery is permitted a much wider range of manoeuvres than he has previously had at his disposal. Although Sarah is distraught, all of her remarks are coherent and justified but her guilt at having betrayed him is so strong that he is able to capitalize on it at will and completely ignore the content of her sane objections. Certainly he feels a real sense of panic but this is secondary and he turns his child-like tantrum to his own advantage: 'I told you never to say!'. He loads all the responsibility on to her shoulders with malicious intent, 'You may have wrecked the whole thing', and this 'savagely . . . useful lie' is a masterly move in the face of which she has no alternative but to capitulate, again giving game-point to Avery. His outrageous use of officialese, purportedly adult, actually infant, keeps her out in the cold, but his rejection of her is admirably ambiguous; the promise to ring later offers the faint hope of future forgiveness and leaves him the field open for further play.

Their last dialogue in the novel is like *déjà vu*; the game they begin seems tired: 'It was like children: parallel playing' (ch. 15). After some standard exchanges Sarah suddenly stops playing 'as if the speeches were over and this were the choice' (Ibid.). A significantly transformed recapitulation of Liz's question to Leamas in *The Spy Who Came in from the Cold* follows:

'John, I want to know, I've got to know, now, before you go. It's an awful, unEnglish question . . .

You've been telling me you've found a vocation. Well, who calls you, that's what I mean: what *sort* of vocation? That's the question you never answer: that's why you hide from me. Are you a martyr, John? Should I admire you for what you're doing? Are you making sacrifices?'

Flatly, avoiding her, Avery replied, 'It's nothing like that. I'm doing a job. I'm a technician; part of the machine . . .'   (ch. 15)

Where Leamas 'belongs' to his Department, Avery is stuck at the stage of persuading himself that he *should* belong. And where recognition of the disjuncture between personal and political commitment is forced on Leamas by circumstance, Avery's dilemma is more complex because he has chosen to keep the two separate in order to play them off against each other and to keep his options open. Like Leamas, Avery evades. The question of his commitment to his marriage is at stake. He retreats into fantasies of the past ('the house in Chandos Road, remember?') and the future ('if we lived in the country, bought a house') and tries for a tone of intimacy, even agreeing to spend Christmas at her mother's:

'That'll be fine. Look . . . about the office. They owe me something now, after all I've done. They accept me on equal terms. As a colleague. I'm one of them.'

'Then you're not responsible, are you? Just one of the team. So there's no sacrifice.' They were back at the beginning. Avery, not realizing this, continued softly. 'I can tell Leclerc, can't I? I can tell him you'll come to dinner?'

'For pity's sake, John,' she snapped, 'don't try to run me like one of your wretched agents.'   (Ibid.)

These are Sarah's last words in the novel. Le Carré leaves Avery a victim of his own games and Sarah the clear-sighted moral winner whose victory is meaningless, in real terms. The fate of their relationship stays open and undecided. In counterpoint, the narrative sketches comparable domestic games in which male fantasies of worth are challenged by women.

As did Sarah initially, both Leiser's Betty and Woodford's Babs suspect that their men are chasing other women, unable to believe that their partners could be at all valued in the work which takes them away from home. As did Taylor's wife, both women drink, to pass the time and as an accompaniment to their distress and frustration. Like Avery with Sarah, Leiser and Woodford attempt to impress their women with the mystique of work. Woodford is typically indiscreet about what he does, revealing information in the set moves of his ulterior relationship game. Leiser has been out of the espionage business for years and feels more at home not divulging professional secrets. The information he employs in his play is all false – he tells Betty he has been approached by a man 'from one of the big companies' – but it serves the same purpose. Their games-playing is even less successful than Avery's. Less proficient players, they have partners who participate less readily than Sarah, being more estranged from their men than she is. Both men have recourse, crudely, to attempts to buy off their partners, whom they both fear. Woodford takes Babs out for lunch at a large, London department store while Leiser, to Betty's suspicious amazement, suggests a romantic restaurant dinner, with dancing. None of it succeeds. Demoralization is the domestic norm, the acknowledgement of incompatibility and failure. The novel's alternative domestic action maintains a critical female perspective on the professional world of its men.

In all the marital scenes of *The Looking-Glass War*, dialogue predominates; there are only the barest traces of a narrator's presence. The act of decoding the ulterior is left to the reader with his or her own knowledge of similar situations gained in the real world. These scenes work in the classic way through the delight of recognition. The narrative voice remains as quiet and neutral as possible – as if to explain any more than is minimally necessary were an intrusion on the unintimate intimacies of personal relationships: almost as if it would be a kind of voyeuristic bad form to analyse, in the way that I have done, the private games couples play. The illusion of the narrator's respectful care works well. The reader is induced gently to patronize the characters and is permitted to do that privately, as if unconsciously. The manner, and thus the response, changes when the narrative's attention is turned towards the fantasies of nostalgia, the 'sweet anachronism' of the Department.

Play in the normal, domestic world of marriages is mirrored on the other side of the looking-glass by play in the almost exclusively male world of bureaucracy and espionage which the Department embodies. Le Carré makes it clear that *The Looking-Glass War*, like its predecessor, is about the Cold War, and elements of the new novel's plot have obviously been borrowed from a contemporary historical and political reality. For instance, the reader is asked to accept as more or less factual, the spying overflight of the scheduled civilian airliner whose pilot has been contracted to veer, as if accidentally, off-course in order to photograph sensitive military installations in East Germany. Such an incident is designed to be read as the kind of thing that probably did, and probably does, go on. An article on the Korean airliner KAL 007 in an American newspaper of 1983, dealing with a more recent Cold War overflight, quotes an ex-NSA official allowing distractedly that the United States 'might at one time have used commercial aircraft for spying, "perhaps in the Berlin corridor"' (*Philadelphia Inquirer* 4 September 1983), and thus furnishes exactly the kind of tentatively plausible rumour which le Carré drew on nearly twenty years earlier. The routine 'weather flight' of U-2 pilot Gary Powers in 1959 is, of course, a specific source; Leclerc even makes a joke about that incident while conducting his briefing meeting in an early chapter of the novel. The East German counter-espionage team we see towards the end, and the Cold War atmosphere of silence, fear, closed areas and Russian troop movements in the novel's finale, are also presented as alluding to political reality. So too is the rivalry between different sections of the British Intelligence Service, and the background of the Western Alliance, for the stability of which the loyal agent Leiser is sacrificed. But all such business is supportively peripheral to the novel's main interest. With *The Looking-Glass War*, le Carré tried 'to touch new ground':

> The ideological deadlock which provided the background to *The Spy Who Came in from the Cold* is replaced by the psychological deadlock of men whose emotional experiences are drawn from an old war. The piping has stopped but they still dance. In the opening chapters of the book we therefore follow two searches: one for the dead and one for the living. Sometimes the searchers are conscious of anachronism as drug addicts are conscious of drugs. This does not save them from addiction. I tried to touch new ground when I discussed the phenomenon of committed men who are committed to nothing but one another and the dreams they collectively evoke. At heart, I said, professional combatants of the Cold War have no ideological involvement. Half the time they are fighting the enemy, a good deal of the time they are fighting rival departments. The source of their energy lies not in the war of ideas but in their own desolate mentalities; they are the tragic ghosts, the unfallen dead of the last war. (le Carré, 1966, p. 5)

The unfallen dead haunt the Department's building, which is a protected space wherein the collective dreams can be freely produced:

> It was like a house eternally for sale. No one knew why the Ministry put a wall round it; perhaps to protect it from the gaze of the people, like the wall round a cemetery; or the people from the gaze of the dead. Certainly not for the garden's sake, because nothing grew in it but grass which had worn away in patches . . . The building had that unmistakable air of dilapidation which characterizes government hirings all over the world. For those who worked in it, its mystery was like the mystery of motherhood, its survival like the mystery of England. It shrouded and contained them and, with sweet anachronism, gave them the illusion of nourishment. (ch. 27)

Le Carré's narrator steps forward in passages such as this, unashamedly creating and milking the symbol for all that it is worth, but doing so with the ease of enjoyment, without moralizing. Inside is Leclerc's office, hung with signed photographs of the 'boys who had fought in the war . . . There were no surnames, but sobriquets from children's magazines: Jacko, Shorty, Pip and Lucky Joe'. For the Department's members names have a peculiar importance; the concern with naming and forms of address seems obsessional. In a fantasy world where identities can be reformed and be more fluid than in the normal world 'of the people', naming serves a larger purpose than that of mere recognition. The nicknames of past agents mythologize their owners and lend a religious aura to the present. Even if the boys from the past are now gone, their names can survive to endorse the current activities of the Department. Taylor's cover name is Malherbe and it has been chosen mysteriously by Leclerc. Taylor is unsure both how to spell and pronounce it. 'Malherbe' becomes an embarrassment for Avery too, when he is sent to collect Taylor's body because the dead man's effects are all in his real name. Leclerc, it transpires, borrowed the name 'Malherbe' from a young flier he was close to during the war and his gesture of homage in resurrecting it proves sentimental and foolish. This is not to say that only Leclerc is caught in bondage to the past – Taylor himself is fascinated and stimulated by the mystique of designation, which has, for the reader, a strong flavour of quaint archaism. He dreams of 'making a stir' in the coyly named Alias Club on his return from Finland and is momentarily unbalanced by hearing his contact's name spoken aloud at the airport desk:

> In the outfit, they simply never did it. They favoured circumlocution, cover names, anything but the original: Archie boy, our flying friend, our friend up north, the chappie who takes the snapshots; they would even use the tortuous collection of letters by which he was known on paper; but never in any circumstances the name. (ch. 1)

Here, pseudonyms and circumlocutions do not stop at their function as security devices but help perpetuate Departmental ideology. Leiser's code-name, 'Mayfly', also chosen by Leclerc, has a romantic ring about it too, although the ironical implication of short-livedness is lost on all who use it – and who forget to be consistent in using it rather than the agent's real name. Inexplicably, Leiser objects paranoiacally to his cover-name, Freiser, and investigation into this produces no explanation; a second choice, Hartbeck, has no superstitious associations for Leiser and he seems happy to accept it.

The play with names reaches beyond questions of group conspiracy and individuals' sense of identity into areas of Departmental hierarchy and man-to-man intimacy. In accordance with a tradition of professionalism, the names of wives and children are never mentioned:

> They never talked about Sarah. It was as if they shared a single relationship to Avery's wife, like children who are able to share a toy they no longer care for. Leclerc said, 'Well, she's got that son of yours to keep her company.'
> 'Yes, rather.'
> Leclerc was proud of knowing it was a son and not a daughter. (ch. 2)

The decorum of which this is part incorporates further subtleties. Reproducing public school and military models, the use of either forename or surname acts either to distance or unite, depending on context. And the names are qualified with other verbal formulae which enhance the sense of group-unity. All of them resonate vaguely and jarringly with echoes of an outmoded discourse:

> He noticed that they ascribed – it was a plot in which all but Haldane compounded – legendary qualities to one another. Leclerc, for instance, would seldom introduce Avery to a member of his parent Ministry without some catchword. 'Avery is the brightest of our new stars' – or, to more senior men, 'John is my memory. You must ask John.' (ch. 6)

But when, later in the novel, men need to talk to men as equals, as more than comrades, their forenames are heard voiced with a self-conscious and consoling familiarity:

> 'You there, John?'
> After a moment he heard him sit up. 'Nice time, Fred?'
> 'You bet.'
> 'Woman all right?'
> 'Just the job. See you tomorrow, John.'
> 'See you in the morning. Night, Fred. Fred . . .'
> 'Yes, John?'
> 'Jack and I had a bit of a session. You should have been there.'
> 'That's right, John.' (ch. 13)

All the examples I have given above instance the kinds of inauthentic behaviour which constitute most of the novel's fabric; all are variants of a single, utterly serious game: maintaining each individual's sense of worth and stability and sustaining him in that illusion, through acting out fantasies of purposeful behaviour. Any cynicism in the games-play is barely conscious because the members of the Department, lacking intimacy in their domestic lives, require a substitute, corporate fantasy they can submit to. Haldane is the only conscious cynic – he is the one exception, but that does not mean that he is exempt from play. The more formal the site for the game, the more closely it resembles ritual, the harder the players play. The institutional life includes a variety of automatic, gestural, substitute behaviour as le Carré fixes the reader's gaze, mainly through powerful implication, on the ulterior interactions of bureaucratic functioning. In the Departmental meeting which briefs the team on Operation Mayfly, the reader's attention is kept on what is actually going on between the participants in terms of jockeying for position and attention, a series of complex transactions beyond the technical, ritual, official procedures which are undertaken. The briefing is like the prelude to combat mission from World War Two. For Leclerc, who is at the helm, the session provides him with the opportunity to display his grasp of every relevant detail. Self-confidently, and with some degree of success, he indicates his familiarity with military geography, with photography and with large-scale weaponry; he puts on show his cognizance of the interpretative problems offered by the limited information they had at their disposal, admits the initial sense of puzzlement he experienced but gives no acknowledgement of any lack of control or weakness in the face of these difficulties, presenting them, rather, as the welcomed challenges which test a good professional. Not to be seen as a mere tactician, he refers, as though drawing on a different and deeper fund of knowledge, to the political and diplomatic aspects of it all. Leclerc's ulterior, and partly conscious motive in the game as it functions for him is to confirm his leadership role, affirm the Departmental hierarchy, remind the assembly that he is in touch with higher centres of power and, at the same time, suggest that there is a personal bond, based on tradition and a sense of unstated purpose which welds the company together.

The others respond according to rank and personality. Standford, McCulloch and Avery, the functionaries, choose to signify their awareness of their parts as subordinates in this play. While they offer the odd helpful comment and laugh loyally and supportively in the right places, Woodford and Haldane, their superiors, feel obliged to compete with Leclerc by diverting attention to themselves. Third in rank, Woodford is concerned simply to remind everyone of his presence and he accomplishes this small task by supplying the occasional good-natured and irrelevant remark or gesture, which Leclerc tolerates because Woodford, despite his stupidity, does do his bit to foster the myth of the Department's club-like traditionalism, and thus endorses Leclerc:

'The first indicator came exactly a month ago when we received a report from our representative in Hamburg, Jimmy Gorton.'
Woodford smiled: Good God, was old Jimmy still going?
'An East German refugee crossed the border near Lubeck . . . Since the

Foreign Office will not even give us the facilities of its bag service it is unlikely' – a thin smile – 'that they will assist us by buying military information.' A nice murmur greeted this joke. However, by a stroke of luck Gorton got to hear of the man and went to Flensburg to see him.'

Woodford would not let this pass. Flensburg? Was not that the place where they had located German submarines in 'forty-one?'

Leclerc nodded at Woodford indulgently, as if he too had been amused by the recollection. (ch. 4)

Haldane, on the other hand, is more dangerous an opponent, and is harder to deal with. Leclerc's rival, he alternately sulks in silence or challenges his superior's self-important enthusiasm with commonsensical but niggling objections which Leclerc inexpertly fends off. The functionaries cover their embarrassment as best they can:

'This is Jimmy's report', he said. 'It's a first-class bit of work by any standard.' The cigarette looked very long between his fingers. 'The defector's name,' he added inconsequentially, 'was Fritsche.'

'Defector?' Haldane put in quickly. 'The man's a low-grade refugee, a railwayman. We don't usually talk about men like that *defecting*.'

Leclerc replied defensively, 'The man's not only a railwayman. He's a bit of a mechanic and a bit of a photographer.'

McCulloch opened the file and began methodically turning over the serials. Sandford watched him through his gold-rimmed spectacles. (ch. 4)

Every detail is precisely drawn; the narrative stays consistently alert to the Department's tense transactions. For the characters, planning and executive ability are self-justifying. Hints of incapacity in these areas are treated with injections of nostalgia and communal endeavour which provide a comforting anodyne. Internal rivalry is registered and then carefully moved aside so as to preserve the hygienic façade. The gross errors in each of the Department's three missions, errors of preparation, casting and overall conception, which contribute to the failures of the three agents, are similarly treated in the effort to sustain the illusion of competence.

At many points in the novel the reader wonders whether he or she is reading about a specifically Cold War phenomenon or about kinds of activity encountered in any professional or social environment where corporate behaviour is engaged in. Le Carré seems to want *The Looking-Glass War* to show the sharp edge of a commonplace wedge. Steven Neuse has pursued the question of the common applicability of le Carré's work in the context of administrative systems in general. His article, 'Bureaucratic Malaise in the Modern Spy Novel', contends that public administrators have much to recognize in the 'bureaupathological behaviour' reflected in the thriller genre:

Essentially, we see here a non-academic variant of the argument that modern political systems are increasingly plagued by the loss of ideology or purpose, '*a development from politics to administration, from principles to technique*'. (Neuse, 1982, p. 301)

What are the ramifications of this tendency? Neuse supplies the answer: 'The loss of purpose or vision is followed by the triumph of technique' (p. 302). *The Looking-Glass War* provides ample evidence, for the psychological effect of acting without a substantial or satisfactory philosophy leads to a situation in which technique, inadequate and antiquated as it may be, becomes fetishized, an end in itself. Le Carré's novel enacts the fetishization of technique; in its third and longest section, technique is paramount. The reactivated agent, Leiser, is retrained in the practical business of spying and le Carré reproduces the process methodically: 'small arms training, unarmed combat, mental exercises, tradecraft' (ch. 12) and, above all, practice in Morse Code on the vintage radio set – a gift from Control's Department. Curiously, for a standard thriller, at the very place where the action should be gathering momentum, le Carré slows it right down. Some of the reviews which appeared at the time of the novel's publication took issue, to greater or lesser degrees, with this feature: *The Times* (24 June 1965) spoke of 'too much description and not enough action' while the *New Statesman* (25 June 1965) found the story-line 'curiously inert'. In his (later) study of the genre Brucc Merry agreed, seeing the problem as residing in the novel's structure:

> This is an expanding, rather than diminishing, funnel, as in *The Day of the Jackal* . . . But there is another structural canon which Forsyth follows instinctively, and which *Looking-Glass War* disregards: digression from the story-line should be placed at a further, rather than lesser, distance from the climax. (1977, pp. 51–2)

Such comments mistake le Carré's design; moving away from those generic norms by which the thriller characteristically accelerates to culminate in focused climax, he prefers to retard the pace of the bulk of the last part of the novel, leaving the climax as a brief crescendo at the very end. For its third part, *The Looking-Glass War* proceeds expansively into an area where the minutiae of technique have obliterated almost completely considerations of its underlying principles. Whether the reader finds this either suspenseful or frustrating in terms of plot resolution is not really pertinent; as usual, le Carré's interest and emphasis is elsewhere than in plotting. As the fetishization of technique is to seduce all the main characters in its fantasy to some extent (and kill Leiser as a result), details of technique must become so central in the narrative that the reader too is tempted to subscribe to its attractions, to become also a victim of the illusion.

The Circus, in the person of Smiley, watches from a distance as the game unfolds and eventually intervenes to write off both agent and operation in order to pacify the American Service. Smiley's role throughout the novel is to warn Avery, who liaises between the Departments, of the dangers inherent in trusting to technique. Smiley's periodic appearances in the action take on a choric form:

> [Smiley to Avery] – 'When you have that film, put it in your pocket,' he suggested, 'and carry the briefcase in your hand. If you are followed,

they tend to watch the briefcase. It's natural really . . . But don't *worry*. It's such a mistake, I always feel, to put one's trust in technique.' (ch. 5)

[Smiley to Leclerc] – 'I just thought I'd make the point. It's so easy to get hypnotized by *technique*. I didn't mean to imply . . . How is Haldane, by the way?' (ch. 11)

[Haldane to Smiley] – 'You too: I find you contemptible. You shoot us, then preach to the dying. Go away. We're technicians, not poets. Go away!'

Smiley said, 'Yes. You're a very good technician, Adrian. There's no pain in you anymore. You've made technique a way of life . . . like a whore . . . technique replacing love.' (ch. 22)

Devoid of authentic content, technique becomes pure game; its supposed purpose and payoff apparently lie somewhere beyond the individual players but its genuine function is to maintain each individual in the dream of security. The game has been played time and again, and le Carré emphasizes its repetitive quality. Invariably, each match sees pawns taken, pawns who are themselves playing games. Significantly, Leiser's heroic and technically accomplished mission in the last war ended, even then, in the failure of capture, a fact the Department seeks to block out of consciousness. When the game is played in the real world of the here and now, and lost, the remaining players suffer momentary shock but fortunately morale can be recovered, for most of them, by withdrawal to the baseline or home, represented by the Department's buildings away from the front line.

Certainly, the characters themselves are not completely duped by their own fantasies – that would make them too easy a satirical target. They are shown both unconsciously and consciously constructing fantasies so as to justify their lives. It is the conscious part of this process that gives rise to what is described in the novel as 'the second vow'. The first vow, evidently, consists in the recruit's declaration of loyalty and secrecy, something akin to signing the Offical Secrets Act. But the second vow is different: a kind of secondary and advanced recruitment oath undertaken by each individual alone. It is much more than a supplementary act of faith because in it the member: 'experiences self-knowledge but does not withdraw' (le Carré, quoted in Hicks, 24 July 1965). It becomes necessary when the individual commits himself wholly to the organization in the face of, and because of, the reservations about it he has come to feel.

Avery is shown experiencing an almost debilitating phase of doubt about the Departmental 'dream factory' and its criminal divorce from the 'real people . . . out there'. His doubt borders on despair and he considers resignation. Leclerc's response is priest-like; he rebukes the younger man gently and tells him about the often tenuous basis on which covert operations had been conducted during the war:

'Often we had scruples like you. We had to overcome them. We used to call that the second vow.' He leant against the desk, informally. 'The second vow,' he repeated.

'Now, John, if you want to wait until the bombs are falling, till people are dying in the street . . .' He was suddenly serious, as if revealing his faith. 'It's a great deal harder, I know, in peacetime. It requires courage. Courage of a different kind.'

Avery nodded. 'I'm sorry,' he said.

Haldane was watching him with distaste.   (ch. 9)

Haldane has moved way beyond the second vow, espousing a technique reinforced with cynicism, but for Avery and Leiser, the vow is yet to be taken. Le Carré comments, 'In Haldane, the most corrupt, this is hardly an issue. In Avery it is more of one; in Leiser it is acute' (quoted in Hicks, 24 July 1965). The second vow has, of course, a particular applicability to le Carré's position in the Cold War mentality and it is also nicely pertinent to a discussion of the group psychology of bureaucracies, or even to the membership of any organization requiring commitment but, in the context of *The Looking-Glass War* as a whole, it seems to have most relevance to the exploration of the nature and quality of personal relationships among groups of men who take a second vow to one another. The male intimacies of the second half of the novel are, without doubt, substitutes for the absence of intimacy in domestic and sexual contexts and in the slightly unsatisfactory and worrying parts of the formal, executive side of their profession. Moreover, it is true that the close male relationships also resemble games-play in that their real content remains private, hidden under fantasies of comradeship, professional support and a shared sense of mission but, notwithstanding, these relationships are regarded by the novel as comparatively authentic.

In treating the subject of male intimacy, le Carré investigates a field uncommon to recent fiction. What is unusual is that the substance of the male relationships comprises that which is normally the material of either female, or male-female interactions. Le Carré writes about the standard male needs of comradeship and group solidarity merely as the superficial and transferred expressions not only of the ideologically adrift but also of men seeking the deeper intimacies of contact that are, in slightly different form, normally reserved for their individual personal transactions with women. Homosexuality is not really the issue; if these relationships have psycho-sexual origins, that possibility is left unvoiced. What le Carré actually depicts is the phenomenon of male friendship. The conventional professions of male intimacy are included in the novel but these are exposed either as fraudulent power-games, or as masking more genuine, difficult, barely acknowledgeable feelings.

Le Carré deals with this subject with insight and care. Avery's relationship with Leclerc and the Avery–Leiser–Johnson triangle offer the cases in point. Avery is put into a filial role by his superiors who take advantage of their surrogate son. According to le Carré, Avery:

reflects the moral search of the weak and unhappy recruit who banishes doubt with action. He is young; it is his youth and attraction which the others deploy to revive themselves and ensnare their victim [Leiser].   (Quoted in Hicks, 24 July 1965)

But Avery responds to them, and in particular, to Leclerc, not only as a son but as a parent:

> There were times when Avery felt for Leclerc a deep, protective love. Leclerc had that indefinable quality of arousing guilt, as if his companion but poorly replaced a departed friend. Somebody had been there and gone; perhaps a whole world, a generation; somebody had made him and disowned him, so that while at one moment Avery could hate him for his transparent manipulation, detest his prinking gestures as a child detests the affectations of a parent, at the next he ran to protect him, responsible and deeply caring. Beyond all the vicissitudes of their relationship, he was somehow grateful that Leclerc had engendered him; and thus they created that strong love which only exists between the weak . . .   (ch. 3)

His real, unacknowledged, role as protector and support sustains Avery; it affirms his place and importance in the team as a whole. Both as child and parent he becomes a brother in the exclusive fraternity of the Department:

> . . . he felt his heart thrilling with love. Woodford with his pipe and his plain way became part of that secret élite to which Avery now belonged. Haldane, Haldane above all, with his crosswords and eccentricities, fitted into place as the uncompromising intellectual, irritable and aloof. He was sorry he had been rude to Haldane. He saw Dennison and McCulloch as the matchless technicians, quiet men, not articulate at meetings, but tireless and, in the end, right. He thanked Leclerc, thanked him warmly for the privilege of knowing these men . . .   (ch. 6)

Remembering a little later that, 'A man must steel himself against sentiment', he cannot afford to take his own advice and the sentimental haze of quasi-religious devotion stays with him even after his period of doubt, bolstered by his timely introduction to the 'second vow'. It is true that his doubt is never effectively banished (it eventually wins out and breaks him) but Avery tries to compensate by giving himself wholeheartedly to Leiser as mainstay and friend.

Leiser's need for Avery is matched by Avery's need for Leiser. In one shy moment, where Leiser has 'slipped his arm through Avery's' as they walk, he feels the touch of Leiser's hand 'dry and warm'; in another, when the agent is sweating over his difficulty in completing a written memory test, Avery 'silently changed his paper for Leiser's. Haldane, turning round, might not have seen' (ch. 12). Such child-like complicity and equality guarantees the relationship as real, as does its slightly wilful defiance of the parent-figure, Haldane, who is disgusted by their extra-professional bond:

> Once or twice Avery suspected that Haldane resented this intimacy with

Leiser. At other times it seemed that Haldane was deploying emotions in
Avery over which he himself no longer disposed.   (ch. 12)

Avery asks Haldane if he intends to visit friends during some free time
while they are in Oxford and earns a snide rebuke for his trouble:

> 'Besides' – a dour smile – 'we are not all so prolific in our friendships.'
>   'You told me to stay with him!' Avery said hotly.
>   'Precisely; and you have. It would be churlish of me to complain. You
> do it admirably.'
>   'Do what?'
>   'Obey instructions.'   (ch. 12)

But when Haldane is out of the way, friendship between Leiser and Avery
begins to flower, eschewing its childish stage and entering an adolescent
dimension; the conversation is about sex. Leiser talks either 'about his
women or the war', but mostly about the former which subject he relates
in great detail assuming, to Avery's mild irritation and embarrassment,
that he too leads 'an intense and varied love life'. Le Carré's perceptive
narrative voice explains:

> It was not vanity which made him thus but friendship. These betrayals and
> confessions, whether truth or fantasy, were the simple coinage of their
> intimacy. He never mentioned Betty.   (ch. 12)

Johnson, the radio instructor, constantly invokes a discourse of sexual
innuendo with regard to Leiser and this has a slightly competitive edge
as Johnson subscribes vicariously to the myth of Leiser's sexual prowess,
but it too functions as the offered currency of warmth. Leiser sustains the
myth in deference to his two friends. On his day off, he goes to a blue
movie, refuses a pimp, dials Betty but receives no answer and buys her
a present with his subsistence money: 'He waited till evening in order not
to disappoint Avery, then caught the last train home to Oxford'   (ch. 13).
   In the build-up to the novel's climactic ending, Leiser is at last seen acting
out the sexual fantasy about himself. In the temporary haven of Anna's
flat, a world with its 'own names' and 'own rules', he finds the perfect
audience for, and counterpart to, this fantasy identity which comes to have
a sustenance in itself. It offers more satisfaction than friendship because
it obliterates the need to bargain:

> She followed him, clasped him round the chest, pressing herself against his
> back. He turned and seized her, wild, held her without skill, forced her across
> the room. She fought him with the rage of a daughter, calling some name,
> hating someone, cursing him, taking him, the world burning and only they
> alive; they were weeping, laughing together, falling, clumsy lovers, clumsily
> triumphant, recognizing nothing but each himself, each for that moment
> completing lives half-lived, and for that moment the whole damned dark
> forgotten.   (ch. 21)

When the Vopos come in the final chapter he and his other fantasy (Leiser as spy) are one also:

> As they came in he was standing away from her, the knife at her throat, his thumb uppermost, the blade parallel to the ground. His back was very straight and his small face was turned to her, empty, held by some private discipline, a man once more intent on appearances, conscious of tradition.   (ch. 23)

The Looking-Glass War contains many ironies in its unseen repetitions of behaviour and in its twists of plot, which make characters think they are going in one direction, when really they are heading in another; but irony is not the defining quality of the novel. What distinguishes *The Looking-Glass War* is the fact that almost its entire action is not ironical but ulterior. That is to say, the fantasies and games that the reader recognizes are not presented in order to undercut or moralize on the characters (as standard irony does) but to indicate a mode of acting in the world whereby the genuine motivations for behaviour remain unacknowledged because the cost of facing them is impossible to pay. To reproduce this phenomenon, le Carré seduces the unwary reader into thinking that this 'thriller' can be taken at face value, the value its characters try to take it at, when, in fact, its real action is almost invariably coded in the subtexts of each of its personal transactions. Irony implies an alternative to the mode of behaviour it points to, le Carré's ulterior does not. The fantasies and games are integral to the way of living given in the novel; although the little games are played in earnest, there is no way of playing games for real.

4 A Sense of History: A Small Town in Germany

'. . . Most of all, it was a sense of something left undone.' Turner said this
as if it were a problem which applied to his own case, and to which he had
no solution. 'A sense of history if you like.' He hesitated, 'Of time. The
paradoxes caught up with him and he had to do something about it . . .'   (le
Carré, 1968, ch. 16)

To the extent that they accord with narrative structures familiar in the
thriller and in detective fiction, le Carré's stories in general move towards
the disclosure of enigmas of motivation and fact: a hunter hunts his prey
and finds him, an agent undertakes his mission and completes it. In this
fulfilment of the task an unexpected or repressed truth is uncovered.
Normally in le Carré, the disclosure of the enigma is gradual and
evolutionary, and normally it is achieved through an intensive retrospection.
The secrets in his narratives were there to be discovered all along if only
the right people had asked the right questions and had looked in the right
places. Often, the object of the enquiry knows and embodies the enigma
and often the investigator's superiors or other figures of authority and power
are also in the know but the investigator himself, by the definition of his
role, never is. It is not that new actions occur which help the final completion
of the evolving picture, for the actions comprising the enigma are almost
invariably historic and lie inertly awaiting revelation. When the past is
subjected to an inquiry of sufficient critical rigour, when trial overcomes
error, the dark secrets emerge into the light.

The Spy Who Came in from the Cold is slightly abnormal in this respect,
and more like the standard thriller in that its plot looks forward more than
it looks back. Yet that novel too has its retrospective dimension in Leamas'
desire to discover the cause of the destruction of his network of agents and
in the revelatory deduction, at the end, concerning exactly what Mundt
has been all along; these features conform to a favourite pattern whereby
the past, decoded, explains the present. Leamas' unwillingness, however,

66

to analyse his reactions to the past, together with his unregarding, unwitting acceptance and defence of the lies Control has fed him, keep the retrospective impulse largely under-employed. Full comprehension, for both character and reader, does not arrive gradually; when, finally, revelation comes, it comes as an explosive shock – it is 'blinding'.

In *The Looking-Glass War*, looking back is a semi-conscious means of coping with the present and avoiding its implications. The past is remembered as a myth of tradition and is available for re-enactment in waking dreams. History is regarded with obsessional nostalgia in a haze of protective fantasy. The eventual truth awaiting disclosure is one that the reader, Smiley, and, to an extent, Avery, intuit from the first – that Leiser's mission must fail. The secret in *The Looking-Glass War* is, in one sense, open; it merely requires proof. In both novels, the uncovering of the enigma functions as literary device because thrillers, indeed narratives in general, love disclosure, but it also claims to attest to real truths in the non-fictional world: the near-as-damn-it identity of the Cold War opponents in *The Spy Who Came in from the Cold*; the effects of tactical and personal evasiveness, part of the same Cold War context, in *The Looking-Glass War*; in both, the Establishment's wish, at all costs, to sustain only itself.

With *A Small Town in Germany*, le Carré again focuses on the past, but this time not as a vague atmosphere but as a specific, causal series of recoverable events. To make sense of the present and its ramifications in the future you must first lay bare the past. Two characters in the novel – the hunted, missing, apparent defector Leo Harting, and his hunter, the brusque Foreign Office trouble-shooter, Alan Turner – are the archaeologists of knowledge. Their antagonists, the members of the British diplomatic community in Bonn (The West-German Establishment) personified in police-chief Siebkron, and Harting's target, the 'ex'-Nazi leader of the nationalist Movement, all conspire for their various reasons to leave the past buried. The pasts under investigation are diverse; they include the recent past of Harting's disappearance, his career, his personal and political history, Karfeld's recent and wartime activities, Turner's own personal and professional life, the political history of the new, postwar West-German state and that of the decline of Britain's imperialist power during the same period. The secret histories here are set against those histories already in the public domain; the uncovering of the former are to elucidate the latter.

A novel with such a marked historical interest offers great opportunities for its treatment of time and le Carré accepts the challenge, manipulating the temporal aspects with considerable sophistication. *A Small Town in Germany* was published in 1968 and it draws heavily on contemporary events but it is set in a near future, some time in the early nineteen-seventies. Its temporal scale stretches from the tail end of World War Two through to the developing future political crisis projected as the fruition of mid-sixties' *détente*. Comparisons between Germany's war generation and its successor attract le Carré especially and so the Cold War interim, for this and other thematic reasons, is largely left unexplored. The novel concentrates on a point at the end of the scale, telling of the rapid rise to prominence of the Movement and its charismatic figurehead, and of the last few months, weeks, days and hours in the career of Harting, a German Jewish Second Secretary on the British Embassy staff who has vanished together with forty-odd diplomatic files. Turner's investigation of the missing man brings into play a provisional enigma in Harting's past – he had been involved, so it turns out, in a strange and ferocious bar-brawl in Hamburg five years beforehand, a notable and uncharacteristic event in a life of diplomatic service that began, after an obscure previous career, in the period of postwar German reconstruction.

The action we witness, the 'real time' of the novel, covers a very brief time-span – just one week. The contrast between a single week and a quarter-century makes for a continually unsettling double focus in which time is both minutely charted and also generalized in an atmospheric haze. Both Prologue and Epilogue contribute to this sense as the novel begins on the night of Harting's last embassy appearance that Friday morning and ends with Karfeld's rally the Friday following, but the time of both these framing chapters is kept unspecific. It is not until the Epilogue, for example, that the reader can deduce exactly when the Prologue's action took place, and the Epilogue itself, with the claustrophobia of its crowds, police, music, darkness, floodlights and torches, has the quality more of nightmare than mere night-time. Time is of the essence throughout. Public knowledge of Harting's defection threatens to jeopardize crucial negotiations currently in progress in Brussels as Britain makes its last pleading effort to enter the E.E.C. It could also swell the rising tide of anti-British and anti-American German nationalism, especially dangerous at the moment, so it seems, as Karfeld's Movement is seeking accommodation with the Soviet Union. If Harting is a Russian spy that danger is multiplied.

Turner charts time methodically, keeping it in the reader's consciousness. The technique of the novel is largely interrogative – twelve of the nineteen chapters are almost exclusively devoted to dialogue through which the diverse histories are related. As the action makes its slow, day-by-day progression, and Harting appears less and less a spy and more the privately motivated anti-Nazi avenger he really is, other temporal factors emerge. The Statute of Limitations, it turns out, is now in force, preventing any further trials of war criminals making, as Bradfield approvingly observes, 'a law of forgetting' (ch. 17); more than twenty years have passed since the war and Karfeld is thus guaranteed immunity from prosecution in spite of what Harting has found in proof against him. The assassination attempt he is to make at the Friday rally is deduced only hours before it takes place and the novel's climax is built around its prevention.

The standard thriller pattern of finding the quarry and averting the disaster, its standard dynamic of resolving tension in climax and of disclosing the enigma, are counterposed to the novel's more powerfully static structure of interrogation. In plot terms this is frequently digressive and episodic but, in fact, it carries the novel's main substance. The second structure is no functional complement to the first but is a challenge to it. Turner, who is to turn Harting's stolen key and thus unlock the plot-enigma, also, significantly, turns away, until the end, from the vast amounts of what he regards as irrelevant and uninteresting political and historical opinion yielded in the course of his interrogations. Only gradually does he come to understand that Harting's motives have their source in and among the attitudes displayed by the embassy diplomats. It is not only in interview, though, that the novel's pervasive historical and political matter is laid out, and it is only a part of le Carré's design that the prolific allusions to the real world relate, retrospectively, to an understanding of Harting.

For all that it is set in a near future, *A Small Town in Germany* recalls quite strikingly real events from the contemporary (mid-sixties) West German situation. It would be naive to read this fiction as barely-disguised and unmediated history but equally it would be wrong-headed to assume that its reference points, its regard to the social real, were simple conveniences of the fiction. Certainly, the reality the novel reflects is partial and selective; there is no attempt to present an all-things-considered historical overview – not only would that be impossible, it is not the novelist's project. Nonetheless *A Small Town in Germany* is extremely alert to social reality; the quality of its reflection of events is akin to an intelligent and vivid political journalism while its reproduction of political opinions resembles the commentary in serious periodicals and the conversations of their readership. It is no accident that newspaper reports and reporters figure prominently, nor that the kind of incident and situation alluded to are like those that made headline news world-wide at about the time the novel was written.

The novel's selection of historical information, and the relative narrative weight each piece is given are geared in part to the requirements of literary interest – the events of the action, after all, must be engaging. This same selectivity perhaps also signifies something of the author's own ideology; what he includes and what he omits both stand out. Thus, le Carré foregrounds his concern with national characteristics and national identities and improvizes around the idea of a society that is 'classless', yet pays scant attention to the economic and industrial issues relevant to the real situation he is alluding to. So, the Common Market problem is viewed – as it then appeared to many contemporary commentators and as it partially was – as resulting from mainly nationalist tensions. Similarly, the rise of the Movement is seen as the reaction of the young post-Hitler generation, in Praschko's words, 'blaming their parents for *losing* the damn war, not for starting it' (ch. 17). Merely glancing regard is accorded West Germany's economic and labour predicament which, by late 1966, was in a state of crisis. When Cork, the cypher-clerk, muses on his investment opportunities facts such as the deterioration in profitability, unemployment, strikes and the immigration of foreign workers, if they are alluded to at all, are done so at a level of very deep implication. Maybe, on the other hand, no more is needed than the brief, distracted formulation we are given:

> If the Krupp labour front was going on like this, he might take a little look
> at Swedish steel, just an in-and-outer for the baby's bank account . . .
> (ch. 1)

Much more idiosyncratically, le Carré presumes an alliance between left-wing youth and the right-wing Movement. Mid-sixties student and youth 'extremism', whether of the left or right, appear to le Carré in this novel as two sides of the same coin: the student leader, Halbach, is singled out as the Movement's rising star. A thematic justification for this would reside in the fact that all the power centres in the novel are looking to what they can get from Karfeld's popularity and, anyway, the novel's fictitious future must allow its author some leeway of prediction. Possibly le Carré is merely following those commentators who invariably identify the extreme left with the extreme right but here he does depart somewhat from both fact and plausibility.

    Such excursions from the real are few. Le Carré draws heavily, and with considerable accuracy, on contemporary history, and particularly with regard to what is commonly thought of as the political sphere proper – the world of Parties, Government and Diplomacy. Thus Karfeld's Movement suggests von Thadden's NPD – a party formed in 1965 which scored electoral successes the following year in the state elections in Hesse and Bavaria; a party whose membership reached thirty thousand, a third of whom were under thirty years old; a party whose rallies, heavily protected by both police and squads of its own stewards, elicited comparisons with the SA. Everything seemed to point to the beginnings of a new mass movement of the radical right; the NPD's programme of nationalism, anti-Americanism, its anti-immigrant stance and its revanchist ambition for the reconquest of East Germany held it in the limelight for over two years and it seemed, at the time, that it would continue its rapid growth. The Movement/NPD is not alone in contributing to the atmosphere of threat surrounding the diplomatic community in the novel; police-chief Siebkron is Karfeld's twin in enjoying a comparatively unchecked and uncheckable malign potency. His undisclosed and disturbing political machinations together with the claustrophobic protection his men afford the embassy staff, severely limiting their movements, make reference to the policies and practices of West Germany's massively centralized Grand Coalition government, the right-wing alliance of Christian Democrats and Social Democrats. In 1967, its proposed Emergency Laws seemed to sum up a sinister tendency in the government apparatus itself which looked to be moving towards a totalitarian militarization and political coordination of public life. The Grand Coalition described itself as transitional and a mood of transition informs le Carré's novel – Karfeld's overtures towards Moscow are a transferred expression of Foreign Minister Brandt's tentative moves in the same direction and Karfeld's legally forgotten Nazi past is suggestive, in extreme form, of a new situation in which accounts with history could now be deemed settled: the Coalition's Chancellor, Kiesinger, for instance, had been a member of the Nazi Party from 1933 to 1945. What le Carré is doing is singling out an implicit potential in the real and projecting it into a hypothetically predicted future in order to ask a series of 'what if . . .?' questions, constructing, at the same time, a feeling of incipient turmoil in which history is seen in the process of repeating itself. That, at any rate, is Harting's view:

> 'He could get very worked up about that. It could happen again, he said, and the West would just stand by . . .' (ch. 5)

> 'He saw it all happening again; he told people that: history repeating itself.'
> 'Was it really Marx who said that: "History repeats itself, but the first time it's tragedy, and the second time it's comedy?" It seems *far* too witty for a German. Though I will admit: Karfeld does make Communism awfully inviting.' (ch. 7)

> 'That's why he took the Green File! To show them: *Children look*, he wants to say, *history really is repeating itself, and it isn't comedy at all!*' (ch. 17)

References to Chamberlain and appeasement recur; the novel's Epilogue carries allusions to tragedy. History tells where politics will lead.

Of course, it is true that the terms politics and history are abstractions of what in reality is a single process but where Harting, and later Turner, seek to prove the point, the diplomats and politicians insist on obscuring it. In *A Small Town in Germany*, politics and history become antagonists. The Embassy personnel and Bonn's foreign journalist community partake of a life of high political consciousness. In this, they both diverge radically from the espionage departments of le Carré's two previous novels where the business of politics is taken as happening above, beyond, or otherwise elsewhere than in the active world of controllers, agents and double agents. Here though, the natural subject-matter of conversation comprises not only the immediately pressing topics of the Common Market – the farmers' demonstrations, youth unrest, the nationalist revival and moves towards West German–Soviet *détente* – but also the larger issues related to these which are the substance of the experience of political people – the decline of Britain as an imperialist power, its shrinking Commonwealth, military cutbacks, monarchy, democracy, neutralism and the role of the USA. Sundry references to Vietnam, De Gaulle, the Rhodesian embargo, Aden, the Congo, Grosvenor Square, the Berlin airlift, the Cultural Revolution and the like abound; these are not included just as the incidental paraphernalia required by any realist novel dealing with modern politics but serve the more important intrinsic function of character construction and le Carré's extra-literary desire to engage in political diagnosis and speculation.

The interest of journalists and diplomats in politics seems more than professional. Although Pargiter's quotations from the comment columns of the German press at the daily Chancery meeting (shown at the beginning of the novel) are received with less than enthusiasm, the diplomats theorize in their own time, and at length on matters of politics. But for all that, the diplomats blinker themselves against a view of both the future and the past. For them, politics are facts and moods not process. When de Lisle is first introduced in the novel he remarks:

> 'You chaps don't know a thing, do you? Federal Foreign Minister's just left for Moscow. Top level talks on Soviet–German trade treaty. They're joining Comecon and signing the Warsaw pact. All to please Karfeld and bugger up Brussels. Britain out, Russia in. Non-aggressive Rapallo. What do you think of that?'
> 'We think you're a bloody liar,' said de Lisle.
> 'Well, it's nice to be fancied,' Allerton replied, with a deliberate homosexual lisp. 'But don't tell me it won't happen, lover boy, because one day it will . . . That's what you stupid flunkies don't understand! Karfeld's the only one in Germany who's telling the truth: the Cold War's over for everyone except the fucking diplomats!' (ch. 7)

Equally significant is the (at first) curious absence, on the part of the diplomats, of allusions to the Nazi past, which is a massive unspoken subject in their normal discourse. De Lisle's languid reply to Turner's question about Karfeld's record is stylishly deflective:

> '. . . There are the usual boring rumours that he was Himmler's aunt or something of the sort. No one pays them much heed; it's a sign of arriving in Bonn these days, when the East Germans dig up an improbable allegation against you.' (ch. 7)

And Bradfield is stubbornly resistant to Harting's quest, stonewalling wherever an opportunity alerts Turner's inquiries in that direction.

Where the British wish to bury any traces of Karfeld's past, Harting's self-imposed and covert task is to dig them up and so cure what seems a generalized and legal amnesia. It is a nice touch that Harting is never seen at work on his historical project; the history of his researches has itself to be reconstructed through Turner's investigation of the man and the material he worked on. Turner encounters a continual refusal to reveal information about Harting. At one level, this stems from personal loyalty, jealousy or guilt, depending on the individual concerned; at a higher level, it is the result of a political conspiracy that reaches beyond the Embassy confines; at yet another, it arises from an almost pathological desire not to face truths. The sense of politics that the diplomats display, acute in some respects though it is, acts as a smokescreen, where what is of moral moment in history is expediently forgotten. Retracing Harting's footsteps, Turner brings it back into memory.

It would be perfectly understandable if le Carré, who looks for the morality in political behaviour, had informed the narrative of *A Small Town in Germany* with a rhetoric to ally the reader unequivocally with the Harting–Turner endeavour. It would also be uncharacteristic of him. No moralizer, le Carré delineates all the contradictions he can to produce a story whose reader is invited to take a side, but is simultaneously prevented from doing so. This technique is reminiscent of *The Spy Who Came in from the Cold* where the reader's confusion in the face of the moral and social contradictions represented there is reproduced here. Although all the moral arguments are on the Harting–Turner side, the positions of both characters are shown compromised by their contexts. The 'real world' offers an unresolved challenge to their idealism, a real world of expediency embodied in the novel by the élite power groupings – the Embassy, the Police, the Movement – even though *their* positions are all based on lies and illusions. Le Carré keeps the contradictions raw and unsynthesized.

De Lisle and Bradfield are the spokesmen of the Establishment; de Lisle is facetious, knowing, urbane and gay – and Bradfield is his antithesis, conservative, reserved, pompous, masculine, formal. But both men speak variants of the same language. For de Lisle, all the old definitions have broken down yet only he, he implies, has realized it, and definition continues apace around him, absurdly and erroneously. He mentions to an unconcerned Turner that the Embassy has brought in tins of blood plasma, 'just in case':

> 'Apparently none of us belongs to groups any more: *uniblood*. I suppose it makes for equality.' (ch. 7)

This symbol attracts him so much that he applies it politically:

> 'Artificial definitions. Yes. They absolutely bedevil us here. Always the same: in a grey world we reach frantically for absolutes. Anti-French, pro-French, Communist, anti-Communist. Sheer nonsense, but we do it again and again. That's why we're so wrong about Karfeld. So dreadfully wrong. We argue about *definitions* when we should be arguing about *facts*. Bonn will go to the gallows arguing about the width of the rope that hangs us. *I* don't know how you define Karfeld; who does? The German Poujade? The middle-class revolution? If that's what he is then we *are* ruined, I agree, because in Germany they're *all* middle class. Like America: reluctantly equal. They don't want to be equal, who does? They just are. Uniblood.' (Ibid.)

Continually asked by London to define the social base of the Movement, he replies:

> 'The man in the street . . . the disenchanted . . . the orphans of a dead democracy, the casualties of a coalition government . . . How do you *define* a mood?' (Ibid.)

What is the status of de Lisle's remarks? The narrative events punctuating his speech merely complicate the problem of its interpretation by extending quite separate strands of the action. Turner 'appears not to have heard . . . his pale eyes had returned to the Petersberg', he was 'still lost in thought'; when he speaks it is in an irritated and vain attempt to bring the focus to bear on Harting. His disinclination to attend to de Lisle tells more about him than about the validity of de Lisle's set-piece. Similarly, de Lisle's intermittent flirtation with a waiter brings a parallel light to bear on the diplomat but in no way undercuts his vocalized meditation. Even his apologetic retractions ('I'm sorry. This is my hobby-horse. *Do* tell me to shut up . . . What a bore I've been') fail completely to guide the reader in making full sense of his comments. Of course, de Lisle is clear – there is nothing incoherent about him at all – but does his argument instruct the reader to accept as objectively valid its claims for the redundancy of definition and the dissolution of social class? The 'grey world' epigram has an appeal in its acknowledgement of complexity but at the same time it could connote avoidance and subjectivism, perhaps even the tired expression of an out-moded class trying to come to terms with its impotence. The reader's response is to wait and see, but help never arrives and exactly the same problem recurs when, for instance, the same speaker reaches the subject of democracy:

> 'Both we and the Germans have been through democracy and no one's given us credit for it. Like shaving. No one *thanks* you for shaving, no one *thanks* you for democracy. Now we've come out the other side. Democracy was only possible under a class system, that's why: it was an indulgence granted by the privileged. We haven't time for it any more: a flash of light between feudalism and automation, and now it's gone. What's left? The voters are cut off from parliament, parliament is cut off from the Government and the Government is cut off from everyone. Government by silence, that's the slogan. Government by alienation. I don't need to tell *you* about that; it's a British product.'
> He paused . . . but Turner was still lost in thought.   (Ibid.)

In respect of the novel's ostensibly major narrative strand (finding Harting), de Lisle's episodic observations function to make the reader wait. The latter is placed, as it were, somewhere between the speaker and the intended auditor, who, in this case, is still not listening. What is signified here is bewilderingly plural and a reader spurred on to regain the Harting plot may well be inclined to skim the passage. On the other hand, remaining loyal to the text means facing these interpretative choices:
1   that de Lisle is expressing an authorially endorsed empirical truth concerning the history of democracy ('only possible under a class system . . . an indulgence granted by the privileged');
2   that these opinions describe accurately the recent political development of Britain and West Germany ('Both we and the Germans have been through democracy . . . We haven't time for it any more . . . Government by silence . . . Government by alienation');
3   that regardless of the referential truth of his statements, de Lisle has a capacity for insight; this being signified by his rational tone and his lucidity;
4   that de Lisle is cynical, self-indulgent and narcissistic, therefore to be treated with scepticism ('no one's given us credit for it. Like shaving. No one *thanks* you for shaving . . . I don't need to tell *you* about that');

5   that de Lisle is making snide criticism of Turner's distasteful profession
and is distancing himself from it ('Government by alienation. I don't need
to tell *you* about that; it's a British product').

Most, but not all, of these alternatives are mutually compatible and most,
but not all, seem to give credence to the speaker, making Turner's uninterest
and his attempts to redirect the conversation seem crude and inappropriate.
The dialogue moves towards a hiatus involving a change of scene as
de Lisle draws his conclusions, bringing us back to the more negotiable
le Carréan terrain of justification in political actions:

> '*I* don't know what I'm defending. Or what I'm representing; who does?
> "A gentleman who lies for the good of his country," they told us with a
> wink in London. "Willingly," I say. "But first tell me what truth I must
> conceal." They haven't the least idea . . . Perhaps we need a Karfeld? A
> new Oswald Mosley? I'm afraid we would barely notice him. The opposite
> of love isn't hate; it's apathy. Apathy is our daily bread here. Hysterical
> apathy. Have some more Moselle.'   (Ibid.)

Turner continues to ignore him; at this point in the novel, just over a third
of the way through, he has not yet needed to challenge the attitude de Lisle
represents. Apathetic himself in this context he has not yet learned that
Harting – the dedicated researcher and would-be avenger – finds his
motivation in a militant opposition to apathy.

When, at the novel's denouement, Turner confronts Bradfield with the
truth about Harting their ensuing row is at last one between two equally
engaged combatants. Like de Lisle, Bradfield represents a stage beyond
Control's Machiavellian loyalty, Leamas' confusion and *The Looking-Glass
War*'s self-deluders; he knows he is defending nothing of substance:

> 'What am I to do about Harting? Tell me what else I can do but disown
> him? You know us here now. Crises are academic. Scandals are not. Haven't
> you realized that only appearances matter?' . . .
>
> 'What else is there when the underneath is rotten? Break the surface and
> we sink. That's what Harting has done. I am a hypocrite,' he continued
> simply. 'I'm a great believer in hypocrisy. It's the nearest we ever get to
> virtue. It's a statement of what we ought to be . . .
>
> 'And unlike yourself,' he added, 'I did not contract to serve a powerful
> nation, least of all a virtuous one. All power corrupts. The loss of power
> corrupts even more . . .
>
> 'We've learnt that even *nothing* is a pretty tender flower. You speak as
> if there were those who contribute and those who do not. As if we were all
> working for the day when the world could pack and cultivate its allotment.
> There *is* no product. There is no final day. This *is* the life we work for . . .
>
> 'We are all looking for the wider freedom, every one of us. It doesn't
> exist. As long as we accept that we can dream at will . . . Harting has broken
> the law of moderation.'   (ch. 17)

Turner takes none of this on board – he insists that Bradfield is leaving
Harting out in the cold because his wife, Hazel, has had an affair with

him. But Turner's outraged moralism makes no impression at all on his opponent – Bradfield's defences are impregnable and make quotation from Turner's attack unnecessary here. Bradfield's discourse of abstraction, his justification of hypocrisy and moderation, rapidly disarm the reader who submits long before Turner. Bradfield's triumphant tone is engineered in a brilliant rhetorical play of pronouns: his first-person singular questions, which initially suggest that his hands are tied ('Tell me what else I can do') are reinforced by a succession of personal statements ('I am a hypocrite . . . I'm a great believer . . . I did not contract to serve') which become subsumed in the alliance of first-person plural expressions, each signifying an authoritative, collective and realistic received wisdom ('It's the nearest we ever get to virtue . . . We've learnt that . . . We are all looking . . . As long as we accept that . . .'). Turner is cast as very much a second-person singular in Bradfield's gloating dismissal of him ('unlike yourself . . . You speak as if . . . as if . . .'); only Turner's stubbornness keeps him still standing in this exchange.

With Harting, Turner has been left upholding a notion of a British morality which *should* reside in its natural home, the Establishment, but which the Establishment ridicules for its 'simplicity':

> 'He isn't a Communist. He isn't a traitor. He thinks Karfeld's a threat. To us. He's very simple. You can tell from the files – '
>   'I know his kind of simplicity.'
>   'He's our responsibility, after all. It was us who put it into his mind back in those days: the notion of absolute justice . . .'
>   '. . . I know very well how they thought. I was here myself. I saw what he saw; enough. He should have grown out of it; the rest of us did.'   (ch. 16)

The two positions presented in this quotation and in the two dialogues I have discussed above are exclusive of one another and, as I have suggested, the reader is invited to choose between them; yet at the same time, choice is almost impossible. The reader is led to the brink of partisanship but is firmly held there, in contradiction. The very concept of taking sides *vis-à-vis* a novel's characters and attitudes is unusual; the appreciation of ambiguity and complexity is generally regarded as the limit of a reader's task in traditional literary criticism. But political fiction, such as le Carré's, which enjoys a close and specific reference to the real world (mediated though that must be) has the capacity to overturn the traditional, protective, confined role that readers accord themselves. The political novel may give its readers tasks which do not stop short at receptiveness but require them to negotiate its ideas in terms of preferences made partly on the basis of experience gained outside of fiction. There is, of course, a question of emphasis here, since literary works of whatever kind reflect the social, and since no reader comes ideologically blank to any piece of writing. But political literature (and in particular le Carré's) strives to make that socially referential emphasis powerful enough to push its readership into either the affirmation or the rejection of its contents. Le Carré's political fiction is especially stimulating because the quality of its images of the real continually expose social contradictions, which remain unresolved – as open questions for the reader – in spite of the articulate, formal resolutions demanded, and given by, the logic of his narratives. Which positions are correct, then – those of Turner and Harting or those of de Lisle, Bradfield, Siebkron and Karfeld? And over and above that question, how is 'correctness' determined in the first place?

There should be no contest in making the first of these choices. Turner and Harting should win hands down. They have the moral absolutes on their side where their opponents are all betrayers. The ending of the novel, which comprises a multiple sell-out on the part of the Establishment characters, should decide the issue unequivocally but it doesn't. The past Karfeld boasts about (his war service at the Russian front) is a fabrication, a cover for the atrocities he actually committed. Bradfield, Siebkron and Praschko (the ex-communist and ex-friend of Harting, who is now a Free Democrat MP), have all been, as Turner puts it, 'trying to make [their] number with tomorrow's lucky winner' (ch. 17) – all of them have made secret deals with Karfeld. Turner's disgust at Bradfield and Praschko is open and unrestrained but the reader may not easily take his side. The mechanism of this hindrance is found in Turner's characterization which constructs him as emotionally unstable and incapable of defending his position intellectually against his many antagonists. Here he is in confrontation with Praschko, Bradfield at his side:

> 'You betrayed him,' Turner said. 'You put Siebkron on to him. You sold him down the river. He told you the lot and you warned Siebkron because you're climbing on the bandwagon too.'
>
> 'Be quiet,' said Bradfield. 'Be quiet.'
>
> 'You rotten bastard,' Turner hissed. 'You'll kill him. He told you he'd found the proof; he told you what it was and he asked you to help him, and you put Siebkron on to him for his trouble. You were his friend and you did that.' (ch. 17)

Praschko first tries to make excuses for himself but quickly turns that into counter-accusation:

> '. . . What do you think the world is? A damn playground for a lot of crazy moralists? Sure I told Siebkron. You're a clever boy. But you got to learn to forget as well. Christ if the British can't who can?' (ch. 17)

Turner's outrage has a tone of incredulity and impotence in the face of the facts; his aggression accords with his characterization as a blunt but effective individualist, yet in this context it makes him seem little more than petulant. Bradfield's injunction to silence is headmasterly and distastefully pathetic but it also gives a strong sense that Turner is simply naive. Praschko's rebuke has the same effect and his final barbed jibe allows Turner no reply; this section of the chapter ends with the remark still ringing.

A reviewer in *The Listener* (31 October 1968) thought 'the lovable Turner', unlike Harting, 'a little hard to take' and it is true that there is a quality of incompleteness and confusion about him. Sensitive and caring, brusque and brutal, determined, careless, logical, emotional and resentful, he gives the impression of a character who lacks a central core of personality. Le Carré needs a character who can probe, cajole and embarrass in the process of revealing his quarry and therefore requires that a wide range of strategies and responses be at his disposal, but as a result Turner lacks the solidity, and perhaps the credibility, of the other characters. Moreover, as one of the novel's two 'heroes' (the other is Harting) and as one of the two decent, honest liberals in it, he is potentially likely to capture the reader's unthinking approval. Le Carré guards against that potential by destabilizing Turner's character, guarding against the reader's inclination to feel comfortable with him, and to place full, approving trust in him. Harting, on the other hand, is strangely more substantial, even though he only appears directly in the novel's framing chapters. But his enigmatic disappearance, present whereabouts, history, motives and intentions, all of which Turner must deduce, mean that for almost the entire action he is also unable to offer much in challenging the attitudes of the novel's philosophers and dissemblers.

Like his precursor Leamas, Turner seeks to avoid all collective ties and loyalties but ends up in attempts to defend them. Harting, in turn, is reminiscent of Leiser – the expatriate Polish Jew of *The Looking-Glass War* who desperately desires admission into Englishness. The resemblances between Turner and Harting however are stronger still and they are frequently identified with each other. Both men are outsiders and social irritants, and in the Embassy world they seem displaced: *déclassés* and *dénationalisés*. Their origins are obscure and abnormal. Turner's London colleagues knew:

> he was a late entrant, never a good sign, and a former fellow of St Anthony's College, Oxford, which takes all kinds of people.   (ch. 3)

Harting's file reveals his German Jewish refugee background and that he was brought up by his communist uncle in Hampstead. Bradfield explains that he 'wasn't quite dinner-party material' (ch. 4), and that goes for Turner too. Both characters are 'temporaries', and therefore discardable. Both are engaged in a manhunt, which becomes a private obsession. Both characters fail in their respective missions at the point where each is in sight of success. Harting's assassination attempt brings about his own death, while Turner catches a glimpse of his quarry just a moment before Harting is killed. As underdogs and victims, they project a pathos that invites the reader's sympathy, but through his political method, le Carré prevents full and final identification with them.

In the Epilogue, immediately prior to Harting's operatic death, Turner experiences a confused revelation; he finds himself speaking to himself in Harting's voice, a voice he still does not quite 'own':

We've got to kill him, Praschko, Alan Turner told himself in his confusion, *or
we shall be wearing the labels again . . .*
   'Kill who?' he said to de Lisle. 'What are they doing?'   (Epilogue)

This is the chapter of the rally – it includes, in slow, tense detail, the chaotic
threat of the crowd, the sinister police activity, the expectation of Harting
making his move and its probable thwarting; most of all, it is Karfeld's
chapter, whose speech is faithfully reported as if it were being replayed
in Turner's mind, with the minimum of explanatory comment. All the
differences between the previously oppositional Embassy characters have
now been rendered irrelevant – Karfeld's speech supersedes them. The scene
is about understanding amidst confusion. But the nature of its revelation
is withheld:

   Afterwards, Turner could not say how much he had understood, nor how
   he had understood so much.   (Epilogue)

On the basis of the narrative so far, retrospection should make things clear
but here the reverse applies: 'Afterwards . . . he could *not* say . . .'. The
device is ingenious. It signifies that Turner's new-found awareness is
particular, and it prepares for his final empathy with Harting. More
important, the device excludes the novel's readers from knowing what
Turner now knows. Evidently the revelation has little to do with the
knowledge that Karfeld is dangerous and evil – that has been known all
along. But understanding the content of Karfeld's speech is crucial for
readers of the novel and they are left alone with the privilege and necessity
of judging it in all its specifics. Le Carré could easily have made Karfeld
maniacal or ridiculous in order to aid his readers in this task. He doesn't:

   How then, if Germany was so rich, if she possessed the largest standing
   army in Europe, and could dominate the so-called Common Market, how
   was it possible for her to be sold in public places like a whore? . . .
      In seeking, then, a rational explanation for this curious – and, for Germans
   at least, highly relevant – historical fact, objectivity was essential. In the first
   place – the first shot upward again – we had twelve years of Nazism and
   thirty-five years of anti-Nazism. Karfeld did not understand what was so
   very wrong about Nazism that it should be punished eternally with the whole
   world's hostility. The Nazis had persecuted the Jews: and that was wrong.
   He wished to go on record as saying it was wrong. Just as he condemned
   Oliver Cromwell for his treatment of the Irish, the United States for their
   treatment of the blacks and for their campaigns of genocide against the Red
   Indians and the yellow peril of South-East Asia; just as he condemned the
   Church for its persecution of heretics, and the British for the bombing of
   Dresden, so he condemned Hitler for what he had done to the Jews; and
   for importing that British invention, so successful in the Boer War: the
   concentration camp.   (Epilogue)

Karfeld's own irony momentarily eclipses the underlying narrative irony.
His evidence is based on truths readers are asked to assent to – and that

puts them in an extremely invidious position. Karfeld's appeal to rationality and objectivity, together with his condemnation ('on record') of Nazi persectuion, has a seductive effect, and, however disturbing for them, readers must find themselves understanding something of the mass psychology of fascism. Here le Carré invites his readers to stand among Karfeld's audience. It is this, rather than the torchlight and the sense of impending tragedy, which makes the scene nightmarish. Karfeld's real subtext, ironically presented as its opposite, is a programme of nationalist terror – history tells that and history is repeating itself – but his justification is founded on facts of history and history, in this novel, stands for truth. For the reader, the revelation is one of bewildering contradiction. Does rejecting Karfeld in disgust mean rejecting the charges of genocide levelled against the Western Democracies? And if those charges are accepted as valid, why is Karfeld so wrong? The narrative supplies no answers, preferring not to let its readers off the hook of contradiction.

It would be a distortion to view *A Small Town in Germany* as exclusively devoted to the predicament of the new West Germany. Karfeld may dominate the novel's climax but le Carré aims to keep his discussion directed towards Bonn's British populace – the fear of a revived fascist menace forces the diplomatic community, welded together through its sense of threat, to articulate its ideology. The (British) reader's feeling of contradiction must not be experienced as distant, 'out there', but must come home as pertinent to the contemporary British situation. In the broadcast interview given at the time of the publication of *A Small Town in Germany*, le Carré explained the project underlying his depiction of Britons in a German setting:

> the English and the Germans have something in common and that is a great obsession with the problem of an élite. The Germans, as an emerging country, are looking for a national identity (the West Germans), they're looking for a posture . . . a dignity. An Englishman in Germany at the moment may not be very clever about Germany but experiencing the German scene he can become a great deal more clever about his own country and this is what draws me constantly to describe Englishmen in a German context, which I've done three times now, in the last three books . . . the English scene illustrated in the German context.   (le Carré, 1968. I.)

Relocating their national identity is the task of the British élite in le Carré's novel. The Establishment characters, the representatives of the ruling class, are seen attempting to come to terms with (le Carré's words again), 'fading power' and 'the British adjustment' to it. In spite of the incipient emergency and in spite of the self-evident decline of British influence, the diplomats struggle to carry on as if Bonn were England and the Empire still existed. De Lisle's blithe admission that 'We're trained to regard Karfeld as an irritant, not an epidemic' (ch. 4) is symptomatic of an overall attitude that wants to regard the British presence in West Germany, and the British 'way-of-life' itself, as permanent and secure. The attitude is self-conscious however; it knows itself to be false.

The life of the diplomatic community replicates life back home; 'the Embassy has built itself a modest piece of suburban Surrey' with 'comfortable stockbrokers' houses' and Church on Sundays:

> Bradfield, though theoretically a Roman Catholic, regarded it as his iron duty to attend the Embassy Chapel; it was a matter on which he declined to consult either his Church or his conscience. (ch. 2)

Saturday has seen a children's sports day complete with prize-giving as Britain plays host to diplomatic families from the Commonwealth countries. It is so English it even rains:

> Inside the marquee, the surviving children, mostly coloured, had rallied to the mast. The small flags of the Commonwealth, creased by storage and diminished by secession, swung happily in disarray. (Ibid.)

English chauvinism and condescension are mildly present everywhere. But although the old roles are still being played, in deference to the facts of the past and the necessary fictions of the present, the imperial ideology has actually and quietly been replaced. The Harting crisis reveals how. The community closes ranks and keeps tight-lipped – wherever Turner looks he encounters a brick wall of unhelpfulness. The group loyalty, however, is no longer loyalty to the nation or to the social class or to the profession: it is loyalty simply to itself. For those on the lower rungs of the Chancery hierarchy, Cork, Gaunt, Pargiter and Meadowes, the sustaining ideology is one of either keeping out of things or of remaining true to a colleague or friend (in this case, Harting) whatever he might have done. For those higher up, the personal motive does not apply; de Lisle's ideology comprises a series of negations – convictions, motives and definitions are all dangerous and false. Apathy is the only legitimate alternative. His boss Bradfield has a credo complementary to this, in which 'only appearances matter'; he believes (as his wife, Hazel, formulates it on his behalf) that 'Some things aren't true till they're said' (ch. 14). Hazel herself seems to share something of all three attitudes. For all these characters, history is either wilfully evaded or revised or denied; for some of them, that goes for their own personal histories too. When Bradfield loses his temper and seems about to break down in the confrontation with Turner referred to above, he acknowledges defiantly that political and personal preservation depends on a controlled refusal to allow threatening realities to touch him:

> '. . . Harting has broken the law of moderation.'
>   'We're *not* automatons! We're born free, I believe that! We can't control the processes of our own minds!'
>   'Good Lord, whoever told you that?' He faced Turner now and the small tears showed. 'I have controlled the processes of my own mind for eighteen years of marriage and twenty years of diplomacy. I have spent half of my life learning not to look, and the other half learning not to feel. Do you think I cannot also learn to forget? . . . (ch. 17)

Bradfield's defence has at least as much dignity as pathos and Turner is made to seem morally right but callow. With this exchange le Carré both evokes disgust with and asks distanced sympathy for the remnants of Britain's traditional administrative élite.

Hazel's affair with Harting, which Bradfield refuses to see, is just part of a context of sexual indiscretions and incompatibilities occupying the Embassy world. Myra Meadowes nearly caused a breach of security, and nearly succeeded in killing herself over it, on account of an affair in Warsaw. Jenny Pargiter gives Harting her keys in an act of love which will ruin her career. Gaunt protects his wife from Harting's sexual influence which, on her own, she feels unable to resist. Crabbe's marriage is one that has had to come to terms with his impotence, while Cork discovers, to his amazement, that the long-awaited birth of his child reveals an enormous gap between himself and Jenny:

> '. . . She wouldn't let them send for me while I was on shift.' His pink eyes were wide with fear. 'She didn't even need me. She didn't even want me there.' (ch. 16)

As the man from Security, Turner investigates the transgressions and in so doing punishes Myra, Jenny and Hazel for his own wife's adultery and for his own sexual inabilities:

> . . . Alan darling, you're supposed to take me, not fight me. It's rhythm, it's like dancing, can't you understand? And Tony's such a *beautiful* dancer, Alan darling, and I shall be a little late tonight . . .   (ch. 9)

The strain in all the relationships parallels the political strain, pointing, in the personal domain, to a generalized British (male) incapacity. Where the Embassy men cope and control by forgetting, Turner is obsessed by disgust for past betrayals, losses and failures, just as Harting is. Neither of them forgets or ignores; Turner is as much a 'memory man' (ch. 6) as Harting and his jealousy corresponds with Harting's obsessional guilt.

Harting has had himself put in charge of the Embassy's Personalities Survey and his official task is the Destruction of old files. In his secret 'glory-hole' in the heart or womb of the Embassy building, he works not on the destruction of the past but on its reconstruction. Like Turner, he is searching not only for his quarry, but for 'the childhood he never had' (ch. 7) and he hopes to discover it there. The glory-hole is a cellar reminiscent of the cellar in which he interrogated Karfeld with Praschko just after the war, and of the Hapstorf cellar, with its 'torn' brick walls where Karfeld committed his crime. Here, he enters into the horror of his compulsion, ignoring Praschko's advice:

> '. . . I said to him: Listen it's not your *fault*. It's not your *fault* you survived! . . . (ch. 17)

Harting takes the guilt of surviving upon himself, neither forgetting nor forgiving. Turner follows him into the underground corridors, 'his sense of time and place . . . almost lost' (ch. 15). Turner's journey giddies, confuses, blinds and disgusts him as he passes through door after door into the glory-hole, eventually finding the light switch:

> domed like a woman's breast, and when he pressed it down it thumped like a punch against his own body . . .   (ch. 15)

At last safely inside he begins to relive Harting's search:

> alone like Harting . . . living like Harting on borrowed time; hunting, like Harting, for a missing truth.   (Ibid.)

His reappearance, bringing the truth of the past back to the present, is a kind of rebirth. The sexual connotations here are not gratuitous. They function to indicate a mutual exchange between personal and political preoccupations and obsessions. In *Tinker Tailor Soldier Spy*, the next of le Carré's novels to consider the interplay of personal and political motives, sexuality again figures prominently, but now as a component part of a more complex network of multiple betrayal.

5   Absent Friends:
Tinker Tailor Soldier Spy

Like a great novel, and an unfinished one at that, the story of Kim Philby lives on in us . . .   (le Carré, Introduction to Page et al., 1968, p. 9)

It is difficult not to adopt a tone of journalistic hysteria when writing of the spy 'scandals' and 'revelations' of the past thirty years which have provided so much sensational newspaper copy. Headlines such as, 'TRAITOR! Mole flees: How many more spies are there? . . . MAURICE and BASIL The scandal' from the *Daily Express* (16 November 1979), although by now familiar through repetition, invariably retain their gleeful and horrified impact. The Blunt revelation – that word must be used – which occasioned these headlines and a dozen similar, was prompted by the publication of Andrew Boyle's *The Climate of Treason*, an *exposé* relying for its evidence on 'confidential sources', mainly of CIA extraction. Margaret Thatcher's statement to the House of Commons naming Blunt as 'the fourth man' came ten days after the appearance of Boyle's book and thus suddenly ended one chapter of anxious and seductive speculation as another, again fed by semi-official leaks, was just beginning. The identity of 'the fifth man' now became a minor national obsession.

The Blunt affair had followed immediately the conclusion of a serialized television adaptation of le Carré's 1974 novel, *Tinker Tailor Soldier Spy* and the unmasking of the fictional mole Gerald was still very much in the public mind. However 'scandalous' and 'sensational' the discovery of Blunt, or Prime, or Bettaney, or their precursors, Burgess and Maclean, Blake and Vassall, it had always been Kim Philby who stood out, depending upon one's point of view, as either the most shocking or impressive Soviet agent in the British Intelligence Services. Although le Carré's mole Bill Haydon is in many ways a composite creation, above all he is Philby's fictional counterpart.

In 1968, six years prior to the publication of *Tinker Tailor Soldier Spy*, le Carré contributed his introductory essay to *Philby: the Spy who Betrayed a Generation*, a book written by three *Sunday Times* reporters, Page, Leitch and Knightley. As an essayist, le Carré is uncompromisingly unambiguous in giving his opinions. He is both fascinated and repulsed by Philby, powerfully unsympathetic towards him. At the same time, he finds only slightly less reprehensible the 'citadel' of the Establishment which the 'avenger stole upon' and 'destroyed . . . from within' (p. 9). Philby is seen as the sick expression of a sick Establishment, which is itself the expression of a sick Britain. He writes:

> . . . in times of dismay and national corruption [the Secret Service] sinks swiftly into intrigue, slovenly security and inter-departmental rivalry. I believe that SIS in its worst years, far from being a putrescent arm upon a healthy body, was infected by a general sickness which grew out of the sloth and disorientation of after-war. It is arguable that Kim Philby, spiteful, vain and murderous as he was, was the spy and catalyst whom the Establishment deserved. Philby is a creature of the postwar depression, of the swift snuffing out of the Socialist flame, of the thousand-year sleep of Eden and Macmillan. (pp. 22–3)

The high rhetorical tone is meant, I suppose, to suggest the massive dimensions of Philby's treachery and the society which helped produce it and cover it up. Trading on the spy's literary namesake, Kipling's Kim, le Carré (like the authors of the main text) makes full use of the fortuitous coincidence whereby the century's first fictional secret agent invites comparison with the real-life Kim. Nonetheless, the comparison seems to irritate or even anger him:

> He would root out the old fort with . . . the amoral loyalty of Kipling's chosen boy . . . (p. 9)

> Like Kipling's boy, one feels, he was already waiting for the call: '*It was intrigue, of course – he knew that much, he had known all evil since he could speak – but what he loved was the game for its own sake – the stealthy prowl through the dark gullies and lanes . . .* ' (pp. 12–13)

> On either side of the Iron Curtain they will lift their glasses to Kim, the Felix Krull of the intelligence war. '*He crossed his hands on his lap and smiled, as a man may who has won salvation for himself and his beloved.* ' Thus ended Kipling's boy.
> I have no such affection for Philby and no admiration. (p. 23)

Like Kim, Philby is caught in the autonomous logic of deceit, but where for Kipling's character deceit constitutes a kind of freedom, for Philby it is a dependency, a kind of sordid addiction.

The question of motivation for le Carré and his characters is always complex and ultimately indefinable. Smiley ends his part in *Tinker Tailor Soldier Spy* 'distrustful as ever of the standard shapes of human motive' (ch. 38), and that sentiment is very much le Carré's own. Philby is seen therefore, not as having freely chosen his loyalties on the basis of an adul rationality but as the unfortunate product of diverse determinations. His unknown Soviet recruiter 'recognized, courted and consciously seduced [the] children of Cambridge' (p. 10) and Philby was already ripe for manipulation; as the son of a 'slightly beserk English gentleman', 'an empire man . . . a collector of intelligence in the best Kipling tradition; an Arabist, a Lawrence mystic, a solitary adventurer capable of violence and rapacity' (p. 12), he 'could hardly fail to inherit many of his characteristics'. Le Carré paints Philby as a disturbed and naive child whose incarceration within the secret world prevented him from growing up:

> I do not much believe in the political motive of Kim Philby; but I am sure that the British secret service kept it alive as no other environment could have done. The British intelligence world described [in this book] is apolitical. Once entered, it provides no further opportunity for spiritual development . . . he took into the soundless shrine of the secret world the half-formed jargon of his intellectual betters, the brutal memories of his father, Vienna and Spain; and from there on, simply ceased to develop. He was left with a handful of clichés whose application had ceased in 1931 . . . the early life of Kim Philby is doubly important: all Kim's life was early. (pp. 11–12)

Since deceit, so le Carré claims, was Philby's nature, it invaded his personal life too; he used women, for instance, 'as he used society':

> he performed, danced, phantasized with them, begged their approbation, used them as a response for his histrionic talents, as a consolation for a manhood haunted by his father's ghost . . . But whatever they were, they were second to that one elected mother who held his heart: Russia.
>
> As the authors repeatedly demonstrate, Philby was not a political animal. We do not find him plunged into an agony of doubt during the Stalin purges, the Doctors' plot, the Hungarian revolution . . . Mother Russia was the boy's absolute. (p. 14)

Reading the foregoing quotations one may well have the feeling that le Carré's sermonizing approach succeeds more in offering its subject in symbolic than in historical terms. The traces of wounded fury in this psychopathological explanation are perhaps designed to provide the kind of condemnation the Establishment had an interest in not expressing.

Philby himself had read the original *Sunday Times* articles when they appeared in 1967 and in the following year his autobiography, *My Silent War* was published. Introduced, this time sympathetically, by Graham Greene, Philby's memoirs included a dignified statement 'in the form of gross over-simplification', so he says, on exactly those political motives le Carré disbelieves:

> It seemed to me, when it became clear that much was going badly wrong in the Soviet Union, that I had three possible courses of action. First, I could give up politics altogether. This I knew to be quite impossible. It is true that I have tastes and enthusiasms outside politics; but it is politics alone

that give them meaning and coherence. Second, I could continue political activity on a totally different basis. But where was I to go? The politics of the Baldwin–Chamberlain era struck me then, as they strike me now, as much more than the politics of folly. The folly was evil. I saw the road leading me into the political position of the querulous outcast, of the Koestler–Crankshaw–Muggeridge variety, railing at the movement that had let *me* down, at the god that had failed *me*. This seemed a ghastly fate, however lucrative it might have been.

The third course of action open to me was to stick it out, in the confident faith that the principles of the Revolution would outlive the aberration of individuals, however enormous. It was the third course I chose, guided partly by reason, partly by instinct. Graham Greene, in a book appropriately called *The Confidential Agent*, imagines a scene in which the heroine asks the hero if his leaders are any better than the others. 'No. Of course not', he replied. 'But I still prefer the people they lead – even if they lead them all wrong.' 'The poor, right or wrong,' she scoffed. 'It's no worse – is it? – than my country, right or wrong. You choose your side once and for all – of course, it may be the wrong side. Only history can tell that.'   (Philby, 1968, p. 16)

The motive Philby gives for continuing to remain loyal to a social class and a kind of state other than those he was ostensibly serving, in spite of the criminal horrors being perpetrated in the name of his chosen workers' regime, is not idiosyncratic, nor is it unique. In his autobiography, for instance, the communist spy Leopold Trepper gives a not dissimilar reason for his continuing struggle to defend the Soviet Union, despite the knowledge of Stalin's betrayals, through the Great Game his Red Orchestra of agents played (many to the death) against fascism:

Between the hammer of Hitler and the anvil of Stalin, the path was a narrow one for those of us who still believed in the revolution. Over and above our confusion and our anguish was the necessity of defending the Soviet Union, even though it had ceased to be the homeland of the socialism we had hoped for. This obvious fact forced my decision . . . [By] fighting far from Moscow, in the forefront of the anti-Nazi struggle, I could continue to be what I had always been: a militant revolutionary.   (Trepper, 1977, p. 88)

Both Trepper and Philby speak of the anguish involved in their commitment and their initial decisions to fight for the cause were, both claim, not taken lightly. And as far as Philby's recruitment is concerned, it now seems unnecessary to explain it in terms of a conjunction of sick psychology and devious manipulation. Le Carré is of course not alone in making ingenious and patronizing speculations on the power of some sinister Russian mastermind brilliantly manoeuvring Britain's honourable schoolboys of the thirties into the evil fold of communism. Certainly Philby's recruiter and controller could well have exerted a charismatic influence but it is likely that the Cambridge radicals turned to what they saw as the revolutionary left for more obvious political reasons. In Philby's words:

. . . the real turning-point in my thinking came with the demoralization and rout of the Labour party in 1931. It seemed incredible that the party should be so helpless against the reserve strength which reaction could mobilize in time of crisis. More important still, the fact that a supposedly sophisticated electorate had been stampeded by the cynical propaganda of the day threw serious doubt on the validity of the assumptions underlying parliamentary democracy as a whole . . . It cannot be so very surprising that I adopted a Communist viewpoint in the thirties; so many of my contemporaries made the same choice. (Philby, pp. 15–16)

New York Times columnist Claud Cockburn points out that 'there was no need of' any 'mastermind':

The circumstances at that time were quite enough to do the trick. The gilded popinjays were living on a small lush oasis in the middle of an economic desert and all but the oafs among them knew it. (12 November 1979)

The three authors of *Philby* do not underestimate the leftist climate of the times (how could they?) and even le Carré is forced, reluctantly to acknowledge it:

In our very notion of the 'Thirties Spies' there is an implicit confession of weakness. 'The Thirties', we say, 'The Thirties' were the last lot to care . . . (Page et al., p. 10)

If Kim Philby is the source and evocation of Bill Haydon in *Tinker Tailor Soldier Spy*, Haydon is not Philby's duplicate. Although not a version of the autobiographical Philby nor of the Philby offered in le Carré's essay, Haydon is delicately suggestive of both, and overshadowed by neither. With Haydon, le Carré eschews completely his moral venom for the real-life spy and gives instead a character whose motives and determinations alike, though ultimately intangible, are worthy of balanced appreciation. The last chapter of the novel is mainly devoted to two low-key interrogation sessions, really no more than conversations, which Smiley conducts with the man he has intuitively suspected all along and now encounters as if for the first time in what may be his true colours. The chapter concerns itself with attempted explanations of Haydon offered by the mole himself and weighed up with a subtle, tentative, qualifying reserve by his victor. For Smiley, summing it all up, Haydon eventually remains an unsolved puzzle to be regarded from a quizzical distance and then set aside:

Smiley . . . settled instead for a picture of one of those Russian dolls that open up, revealing one person inside the other, and another inside him. Of all men living, only Karla had seen the last little doll inside Bill Haydon. (le Carré, 1974, ch. 38)

And Haydon himself has suggested a complementary analogy:

He was touched to hear that Ionesco had recently promised us a play in which the hero kept silent and everyone round him spoke incessantly. (Ibid.)

Le Carré is clearly attracted here by the notion of an absent centre – even perhaps one absent centre superimposed on another, as Karla, the Soviet spymaster, is also a central but unknown substance. Haydon is ultimately definable as the cause of a series of acts: the betrayal of friend and lover (he sets up Prideaux for capture and possibly death), the betrayal of friend and colleague (he has an affair with Ann, Smiley's wife so as to cloud Smiley's perception), the betrayal of his institution, country and class. These actions are all revealed in full but the nature of their cause is indeterminate. Le Carré, however, is pulled in a contrary direction by the character of Haydon. Had he gone straight for the Russian doll metaphor in the concluding chapter he would have laid himself open to the charge of evasion: the seductive appeal of the absent centre might well leave the reader feeling cheated. Haydon could have been left as little more than a sophisticated device or mechanism; he is not. Almost as unsatisfying, the contradictions and ellipses in Haydon's statements, which cast doubt on his explanations, could have reproduced quite uncritically that aspect of liberal ideology which takes refuge from definition in the cosiness of multiple, self-cancelling ambiguities; this also is not the case. Last, it would have been possible for le Carré simply to sidestep the issue of Haydon's substance by writing exclusively of Smiley's emotional response to his betrayer. In fact, Smiley's Russian doll conclusion is a shrugged admission of surrender following an authentic attempt to grapple with Haydon's motives in serious political terms.

From Philby, Haydon inherits the personal qualities of amiability and sexual charm, intelligence and professional competence. Haydon's affair with Ann is probably designed to suggest some comparison with Philby's affair with Maclean's wife following his defection. The successful isolation and forcing out of Control is reminiscent of Philby's skilfully engineered removal of the director of the SIS counter-intelligence department in 1945. Politically, however, and despite their shared espousal of Marxism and Russia, the real-life and the fictional spy differ significantly: le Carré suggests for Haydon possible motives evocative in a curiously unintended prediction more of Michael Bettaney than Philby. Early on in the novel the testimony of Karla's agent Irina describes some 'typical' varieties of recruitment:

> Most of the English moles were recruited by Karla before the war and came from the higher bourgeoisie, even aristocrats and nobles were disgusted with their origins, and became secretly fanatic, much more fanatic than their working-class English comrades who are slothful. Several were applying to join the Party when Karla stopped them in time and directed them to special work. Some fought in Spain . . . Others were recruited in the war during the alliance of expediency . . . Others afterwards, disappointed that the war did not bring Socialism to the West . . . (ch. 8)

Where Philby certainly falls into one of Irina's categories, Haydon seems not to. In his second and final interview with Smiley he lets slip a remark about his 'lifelong relationship with Karla' but refuses to discuss it: 'The assertions of yesterday appeared suddenly nonsensical, but Haydon would not elaborate'. Perhaps then Haydon *was* a typical thirties spy after all, and this comment puts into cloudy question the veracity of Haydon's entire explanation but 'the assertions of yesterday' are sufficiently supported in the bulk of the novel to give them some credence in their own right.

Haydon claims that he was not recruited in the thirties and that while at university 'he was genuinely of the right'. His 'apologia', only partially recalled by Smiley, rests on three assumptions or observations which drew him to Karla: that Britain no longer has any 'relevance or moral viability in world affairs'; that the American masses suffer so 'institutionalized' an 'economic repression' that revolution is impossible for them; and that although the Cold War has been fought since it began in 1917, 'the bitterest struggles lie ahead of us, as America's deathbed paranoia drives her to greater excesses abroad' (ch. 38). Any reader wishing to dismiss these assertions out of hand is immediately checked by Smiley's response:

> With much of it, Smiley might in other circumstances have agreed: it was the tone, rather than the music, which alienated him.   (Ibid.)

Haydon's despair in the capacity of the working-class for revolution is not at all out of step with the political line of the national Communist parties ever since Lenin's death and it also has something in common with the political diagnoses of the New Left popular in the sixties. His anti-American posture, too, has leftist equivalents: 'He hated America very deeply, he said, and Smiley supposed he did'. He had at last realized Britain's 'trivial' role in the world and:

> after prolonged reflection he had finally to admit that if either monolith had to win the day, he would prefer it to be the East.
>   'It's an aesthetic judgment as much as anything,' he explained, looking up. 'Partly a moral one, of course.'
>   'Of course,' said Smiley politely.   (Ibid.)

Haydon's contempt for Americans and his hurt Little England patriotism make for a strange comparision with the thirties spies. Although Smiley is 'conscious all the while that even the little Haydon was telling him was selected with meticulous care from a greater, and perhaps somewhat different truth', Haydon's curious vestigial nationalism is often referred to in connection with him throughout the novel. In his second interview he recounts his gradual metamorphosis into a spy:

> From about 1950 onwards, if he was to be believed, Haydon had made Karla occasional selected gifts of intelligence. These early efforts were confined to what he hoped would discreetly advance the Russian cause over the American; he was 'scrupulous not to give them anything harmful to ourselves' as he put it . . . The Suez adventure in fifty-six finally persuaded him of the inanity of the British situation . . . The sight of the Americans sabotaging the British action in Egypt was paradoxically an additional incentive.   (Ibid.)

Earlier in the novel Smiley remembers him 'fuming about Pentagon arrogance', claiming that 'the time had come to do a deal with the bloody Russians instead (ch. 16) and, even more significantly, there is Smiley's sense that Haydon himself had been betrayed:

> Connie's lament rang in his ears: 'Poor loves. Trained to Empire, trained to rule the waves . . . You're the last, George, you and Bill.' He saw with painful clarity an ambitious man, born to the big canvass, brought up to rule, divide and conquer, whose visions and vanities all were fixed, like Percy's upon the world's game; for whom the reality was a poor island with scarcely a voice that would carry across the water.   (ch. 36)

This explanation has the added credence of following instantly upon Haydon's unmasking.

It may well be that le Carré finds it difficult to account for an ideological espousal of the Soviet Union for a Briton in the postwar period and so invents negative impulses for Haydon which incline him at least initially to make a choice against rather than for. Hence Haydon's extreme resentment against the United States and his reaction against Britain's spiritual bankruptcy and ineffectiveness. If this is le Carré's intention, it is not unusual, as a recent *Times* editorial on Michael Bettaney and Geoffrey Prime well illustrates:

> Bafflement arises from the continuing ideological pull of the Soviet Union. It is just possible to believe that Stalin's Englishmen in the 1930s had no real knowledge of the Soviet tyranny. But, in an age when the details of the Gulag are well-known . . . how it is possible for an intelligent civil servant to treat Moscow as the repository of his idealism beggars belief . . . Mrs Thatcher was utterly wrong in the Commons in May 1982 to have assumed such spiritual blight had afflicted only a single generation of tainted, upper-class Englishmen.   (17 April 1984)

The case of Bettaney, the would-be MI5 spy, retrospectively gives more plausibility to what seems to be one of Haydon's driving-forces. In his public statement following sentence, Bettaney claimed not to be acting against Britain so much as against her government's 'slavish adherence' to an American administration; like Haydon, Bettaney also had a youthful interest in right-wing politics. And just as the newspapers could not resist discovering the root-cause of Bettaney in a supposedly disturbed upbringing and psychology (as le Carré does with Philby), Haydon too fails to escape those suggestions. As Smiley puzzles over the 'contradictions' in Haydon's account, he remembers:

> the ghost of Bill's authoritarian father – Ann had called him simply the Monster – and he imagined Bill's Marxism making up for his inadequacy as an artist, and for his loveless childhood. Later of course it hardly mattered if the doctrine wore thin.   (ch. 38)

Le Carré himself provides an instructive coda to the discussion of patriotism and anti-American chauvinism which runs, to a greater or lesser extent

through most of his political fiction. In a BBC Radio interview he explained
it at first in terms of literary convenience:

> If you're using British society as the microcosm for your Cold War story
> you have somehow to place the Americans in the scheme of things, and one
> of the most convenient ways of dealing with that problem is to make them
> unpopular and therefore take them out of the picture. And I'm afraid I've
> been guilty of that tactic . . .   (Vaughan, 13 September 1979. I.)

Convincing though this reason is, the theme of chauvinism goes deeper;
though dialectically changing into its opposite in Haydon's Marxism, it
normally constitutes part of le Carré's recurrent debate over 'philisophy'.
Le Carré's Britons, drawn from the petit bourgeoisie upwards, all need
to negotiate the disorientation caused by what can be summed up as the
loss of empire, which situation throws all aspects of social living into doubt
and contradiction. For most of his major characters the sense of
disorientation expresses itself in a foregrounding of the problem of belief;
for others, residual commitments from the past re-emerge in extreme form,
often unthinkingly, as a shield against admitting the implications of present
realities. It is in the latter category that the chauvinism naturally falls:

> I think there is, also – in all my later books anyway – a strong line of
> simplistic, wishful, chauvinist thinking in one or another character, people
> who, for very honourable reasons, often for reasons of their own natural
> intellectual limitations, are loyal, decent, unashamedly patriotic blokes, like
> Jerry Westerby in *The Honourable Schoolboy* or Jim Prideaux in *Tinker Tailor
> Soldier Spy*. People who have almost deliberately foreshortened their critical
> faculties in order to believe their country right or wrong, and those chaps,
> ironically, always get the worst drubbing in the story, because you simply
> cannot cease to criticize, however noble one's reasons.   (Ibid.)

The political ideas of *Tinker Tailor Soldier Spy* are discussed within a pattern
of intersecting political stances emphasized to different degrees in different
characters: patriotism (Prideaux, Haydon?), anti-Americanism (Prideaux, Control, Haydon), pro-Americanism (Alleline), anti-communism
(Prideaux, Alleline, Bland), communism (Karla, Polyakov, Haydon?),
cynicism (Lacon, the Minister, Alleline, Bland, Esterhase), and doubting
liberalism (Smiley). Although Smiley is the reader's guide through the
discussion, it transpires that Haydon is at its centre. Le Carré achieves
in Haydon the paradox of a character who is in political terms sufficiently
definable to play his role as a mouthpiece for extra-literary political positions
and who is also sufficiently indefinable to play his role as enigma, even
after his 'discovery'. The twin parts of the paradox meet in the question
of Haydon's truthfulness about his motives and beliefs, their quality and
their origins. Like Philby's, his story is 'an unfinished one' too.

As in *The Spy Who Came in from the Cold*, it is communism (again, for
le Carré, viewed as identical to Stalinism) which serves as the firm, if
inflexible, political position against which the novel's alternative ideologies

are articulated. For Prideaux, communism is a clearly comprehended evil; it has no capacity to induce in him any self-reflection. East and West both offer nothing of value in comparison with 'the privilege of being born an Englishman':

> 'Best place in the whole damn world!' he bellowed once. 'Know why? Know why, toad?'
> Spikely did not, so Jim seized a crayon and drew a globe. To the west, America, he said, full of greedy fools fouling up their inheritance. To the East, China–Russia, he drew no distinction; boiler suits, prison camps and a damn long march to nowhere. In the middle . . .   (ch. 1)

The simplicity invited by talking to schoolboys suits Prideaux well and his cartoon naiveté is touching; his unquestioning faith in England, principled, reactionary and absurd, is unassailable. His response to Haydon's betrayal has none of Smiley's ambivalence – he takes his vengeance and returns, after a brief period of recovery, to service his illusions in his familiar way. For Smiley, on the other hand, encounters with communism permit no such easy solutions.

Smiley's embarrassment by 'protestations of anti-communism', and his mild distaste for the 'uncomfortable phrases' in the lexicon of agent-training which 'in the high day of the Cold War culture had turned the Nursery into something close to a moral rearmament centre' (ch. 17), derive to an extent from his characterization as rather withdrawn and gentlemanly, against vulgarity. But the interview with Karla, which he related to Guillam with unusual and painful openness, demonstrates an insecurity in his role as representative of the Western system which has nothing to do with social decorum. Karla, known then only as Gerstmann, had been arrested in India in 1955 and Smiley was sent on what looked like a routine attempt to persuade him to defect. Karla's American network is blown and his Moscow controller is 'busy denouncing him' for his failure:

> ' . . . Karla was the proverbial Cold War orphan . . . I don't think I had ever come across a clearer case for defection.'   (ch. 23)

During the entire interview Karla keeps completely silent and Smiley, tired by travel and anxious about his unsatisfactory marriage, reacts as if he were the one under interrogation; the pressure of Karla's refusing silence and composure (despite his probable imprisonment or death were he to return) causes Smiley to crumble:

> 'I felt I lacked philosophic repose. Lacked philosophy, if you like. My work had been oppressing me much more than I realized; till now. But in that foul cell I really felt aggrieved: I felt that the entire responsibility for fighting the Cold War had landed on my shoulders. Which was tripe, of course . . .   (Ibid.)

Imagining Karla to have a wife, Smiley projects (he 'detests' the term) his predicament and insecurity about Ann on to his antagonist. After a feverish night in which Smiley realizes, 'I wanted him terribly to stay . . . to make him free . . . it was Smiley, not Gerstmann who was stepping out of the conflict that night', the interview resumes. Now knowing that Gerstmann will return, Smiley, against all the odds, tries again:

' . . . I believed, you see, that I had seen something in his face that was superior to mere dogma; not realizing that it was my own reflection. I had convinced myself that Gerstmann ultimately was accessible to ordinary human arguments . . .

I didn't make speeches to him about freedom, whatever that means, or the essential good will of the West: besides they were not favourable days for selling that story, and I was in no clear ideological state myself. I took the line of kinship . . .

"Don't you think it's time to recognize that there is as little worth on your side as there is on mine? Look," I said, "in our trade we have only negative vision. In that sense, neither of us has anywhere to go. Both of us when we were young, subscribed to *great* vision – "

Did he not believe . . . that the political generality was meaningless? That only the particular in life had value for him now? That in the hands of politicians grand designs achieve nothing but new forms of the old misery? And that therefore his life . . . was more important – morally, ethically more important – than the sense of duty, or obligation, or commitment? . . . (Ibid.)

The Smiley of these arguments is not as alienated from 'philosophy' as Leamas and Turner, nor is his lack of commitment to the cause of 'freedom' like the cynicism of de Lisle and Bradfield and the Circus clique he opposed in *Tinker Tailor Soldier Spy*. Despite his protestations to the contrary, Smiley *is* in a 'clear ideological state'. Knowing he has no heart for carrying the burden of fighting the Cold War on his shoulders, he retreats despairingly and defensively into a fall-back position and reveals himself to be a principled liberal and humanist. His rejection of political 'dogma', 'generality' and 'grand design' in favour of a faith in the 'ordinary human', in 'kinship' and in 'life' has a strongly religious quality about it but it is nevertheless a political stance. It is ironic that Smiley (and perhaps even le Carré who called him 'a committed doubter', Bragg, 22 January 1976) do not take it as such. Smiley has not really 'stepped out of the conflict' but has merely vacated one political site to enter another which was there embryonically all along. In other circumstances this Smiley might have been a pacifist; here he is a guilty liberal exposing his despair in the feasibility of both 'freedom' (capitalism) and communism, adhering instead to what proves to be a mistaken assumption that all people at root share his point of view. His liberal alternative is feeble in comparison with the two dominant systems but, just as they do, it too has a programmatic content.

Smiley is given a sufficient level of consciousness for the inadequacies of his real position to become partially apparent to him. At the end of his narrative he leaves Guillam suddenly, his embarrassment and weakness still with him:

Closing the passenger door after him, Guillam had a sudden urge to wish
Smiley goodnight or even good luck, so he leaned across the seat and lowered
the window and drew in his breath to call. But Smiley was gone. He had
never known anyone who could disappear so quickly in a crowd.   (Ibid.)

Smiley has been confronted by a terrifying rigour in Karla – for Smiley
something both admirable and repulsive. Completely impervious to his
appeals Karla 'would rather die than disown the political system to which
he was committed'. Up against this, Smiley's ethos looks inept and
sentimental and it evokes a feeling of self-disgust in him:

'I behaved like a soft fool. The very archetype of a flabby Western liberal.
But I would rather be my kind of fool than his for all that . . .   (Ibid.)

Karla, and later, Polyakov, are both presented as 'fanatics' and le Carré,
like Smiley, towards whose viewpoint he is here sympathetic, can offer no
explanation of fanaticism. It is a further irony in le Carré's fiction that
a sound basis for commitment is always either sought or mourned for its
absence, and yet when genuine commitment appears (invariably in
communism) it is treated as incomprehensible. Commitment becomes
fanaticism, not a strength but a weakness. As Smiley says:

' . . . And if you want a sermon, Karla is not fireproof because he's a fanatic.
And one day, if I have anything to do with it, that lack of moderation will
be his downfall.'   (Ibid.)

Moderation and the other liberal virtues offer no consolation or clarification
and no coherent guide to action. As Smiley waits for Gerald to enter his
trap, his confusion spills out:

He thought about treason and wondered whether there was mindless treason
in the same way, supposedly, that there was mindless violence. It worried
him that he felt so bankrupt; that whatever intellectual or philosophical
precepts he clung to broke down entirely now that he was faced with the
human situation.   (ch. 36)

And when Haydon is exposed he feels not only disgust:

. . . but, despite all that the moment meant to him, a surge of resentment
against the institutions he was supposed to be protecting: 'The social contract
cuts both ways, you know,' said Lacon. The Minister's lolling mendacity,
Lacon's tight-lipped moral complacency, the bludgeoning greed of Percy
Alleline: such men invalidated any contract: why should anyone be loyal
to them?   (Ibid.)

There is no answer to this question. Guillam, who follows in Smiley's
ideological footsteps, is afflicted by a comparable revelation:

His suspicions, his resentments for so long turned outwards on the real
world – on his women, his attempted loves – now swung upon the Circus
and the failed magic which had formed his faith . . . He had thrown away

his gun and was now hurling Haydon from side to side, shaking him like a dog, shouting. Then suddenly there seemed no point. After all, it was only Bill and they had done a lot together. (Ibid.)

The liberal dilemma, so articulately dramatized in the preceding quotations, is treated with real sympathy on the author's part but it is not washed with gushy approbation. Smiley may indeed prefer to be his kind of fool but his final shrug of resignation is void of complacency. Le Carré suggests that the kind of liberalism Smiley possesses leads to an inevitable and unavoidable confusion and it comes without firm recommendation; an escape from a failure of purpose, at best it gives rise to pathos. Although reviewers and critics have written of Smiley as 'tragic', he is in fact awarded none of the transcendent dignity required of a tragic character and any reader who chooses to see him as tragic must ignore Smiley's own political self-deprecation. Pathos, on the other hand, is more legitimately evoked, in that it implies a more distanced recognition, on the reader's part of the inadequaces in Smiley's failed attempts to transcend the political domain. Smiley's appeal to the personal over the political so as to evacuate the latter of its substance is offered to the reader only to be withdrawn – the political content of Smiley and Karla (such as it is) stubbornly remains.

Far away from the Circus and the Ministry there is another institution, an apparently self-contained place unconcerned with political power and issues of 'philosophy' which is nonetheless the breeding-ground for the future Haydons, Prideauxs and Smileys. Thursgood's undistinguished prep school is a foetal microcosm of the adult Circus in which another secret life tries to provide a substitute for a refuge from the outside world of normality. Following his disastrous mission in Czechoslovakia which has left him crippled and compulsorily retired from the Service, Jim Prideaux arrives at Thursgood's as a temporary language teacher. For Prideaux, who has always had 'a rather parentless look' (ch. 29) it is a sort of home from home. Here, the main action's concerns with truths, perspectives, rituals, identities, loyalties and betrayals are played out in full counterpoint.

Beginning wryly with the words 'The truth is', *Tinker Tailor Soldier Spy* introduces the public-school world as a repository of secrets and speculations resonatingly suggestive of a criminality which, though engagingly trivial, has assumed a romantic grandeur. The staff, trained through habit in the arts of interpretation have 'no difficulty in reading the signals' about Prideaux, prior to his appearance there:

He belonged to the same sad bunch as the late Mrs Loveday who had a Persian lamb coat and stood in for junior divinity until her cheques bounced, or the late Mr Maltby, the pianist who had been called from choir practice to help the police with their enquiries, and for all anyone knew was helping them to this day, for Maltby's trunk still lay in the cellar awaiting instructions. Several of the staff, but chiefly Marjoribanks, were in favour of opening that trunk. They said it contained notorious missing treasures: Aprahamian's silver-framed picture of his Lebanese mother, for instance;

Best-Ingram's Swiss army penknife and Matron's watch. But Thursgood
set his creaseless face resolutely against their entreaties. Only five years had
passed since he had inherited the school from his father, but they had taught
him that some things are best locked away.   (ch. 1)

These comic enigmas, all belongong to a parody genre of detective fiction,
are the diversionary, flickering signifiers of some other unwritten novel
and, apart from one further reference to Maltby in an oblique, rumoured
imputation of Prideaux's homosexuality, are not mentioned again. The
connotations of death in 'late', the precious, childish nomenclature of
'Marjoribanks' and the distanced, self-important, authority-figure who has
learned to lock some things away 'for the best' have, on the other hand,
loud echoes elsewhere in the novel. Le Carré succeeds both in suggesting
multiple parallels with the quest for the mole and in giving the school and
its inmates an autonomous existence.

The enigma Prideaux presents to staff and boys alike reflects the enigma
of Haydon, Prideaux's one-time lover to whom he remains magnificently
loyal. Prideaux's name, its troublesome pronunciation and the variety of
replacements offered in its place solidly establish the identity theme:

[Thursgood] brushed away his forelock in self-defence. 'Priddo.' He gave
the spelling 'P-R-I-D' – French was not Thursgood's subject so he consulted
the slip of paper – 'E-A-U-X, first name James . . . '   (Ibid.)

The boys try out a selection of nicknames for him – Trooper, Pirate,
Goulash – but eventually come up with Rhino. Le Carré writes extremely
well about children and the acceptance and success of what seems an only
partially appropriate name is left delightfully unexplained. To the boys,
it evokes his real name, his 'taste for living off the land and his appetite
for physical exercise'; actually, 'Rhino' is a schoolteacher acronym for
habitual truants (Really Here In Name Only) and as such it 'fits' Prideaux
perfectly. In every sense, Prideaux is out-of-place but his strangeness appears
in the school context as an attractive, if sometimes frightening, eccentricity.
Prideaux's 'passionate Englishness', and his popular readings aloud from
'extremely English adventure book[s]: Biggles, Percy Westerman or Jeffrey
Farnol' are complemented by a darker side – his understanding of
criminality, and his disturbing matter-of-fact capability in killing. The
terrifying owl which flutters out of its chimney nest when Prideaux lights
the classroom fire is later found 'neatly dead', its neck 'snapped'. At the
end of the novel, Haydon is to share the owl's fate.

Prideaux does not monopolize the prep-school sections of the novel; the
new boy, Bill Roach, with his glasses and his tears, is given equal place.
Prideaux uses Roach because the boy makes himself so pathetically
available, but uses him kindly; every amiable question he asks, though,
hooks into some hurt or guilt in Roach and, unrecognized by the boy,
Prideaux has constantly to rescue him from a distress bordering on
breakdown:

' . . . Got any friends?'

'No, sir,' said Roach simply, in the listless tone which schoolboys always use for saying 'no', leaving all positive response to their interrogators. Jim however, made no response at all, so that Roach felt an odd stirring of kinship suddenly, and of hope.

'My other name's Bill,' he said. 'I was christened Bill but Mr Thursgood calls me William.'

'Bill, eh. The unpaid Bill. Anyone ever call you that?'

'No, sir.'

'Good name, anyway.'

'Yes, sir.'

'Known a lot of Bills. They've all been good 'uns.'   (Ibid.)

When Smiley is introduced at the beginning of chapter 2 as 'Unlike Jim Prideaux', he is compared instead to Bill Roach. 'Indeed, he might have been the final form for which Bill Roach was the prototype'. Le Carré has even said that Roach is 'not completely unlike' the author himself when he was at school (Bragg, 13 March 1983. I.) and in the naming ritual quoted above there is an obvious suggestion that the Roach–Prideaux relationship makes reference to the Haydon–Prideaux relationship elsewhere. Roach has similarities with Bill too. But the child is a major character in his own right and his fortunes are followed throughout the novel. He has Smiley's personal anxiety, guilt and solitariness and the capacity for loyalty and friendship Haydon pretends to, but Roach is mainly busy negotiating his family traumas and his own debilitating sense of inferiority. Prideaux initiates all the conversations between them and just as Roach and the boys try to identify him, he in turn tries to identify Roach–is he good at football, is he a swat, what is his 'best thing'?:

> Now this was an unfortunate question to ask of Roach just then for it occupied most of his waking hours. Indeed he had recently come to doubt whether he had any purpose on earth at all. In work and play he considered himself seriously inadequate; even the daily routine of the school . . . seemed to be beyond his reach . . . He blamed himself very much for these shortcomings but most of all he blamed himself for the break-up of his parents' marriage, which he should have seen coming and taken steps to prevent. He even wondered whether he was more directly responsible . . . (ch. 1)

Prideaux and Roach never discuss each other's respective problems with family or friends or work and their unequal acknowledgement of each other's disturbance is unstated: the matter of intuition and speculation. Yet both endeavour to support each other without the other's knowledge from those possibly imaginary pressures over which neither has any control. Their relationship, which remains merely assumed, is substitutive, a stand-in for failures elsewhere and is itself, for Roach at least, fragile and worrying:

> All through the summer holidays, as he moved uncomfortably between one household and another, embracing and rejecting, Bill Roach fretted about

Jim . . . he feared that Jim was like himself, without a natural gravity . . .
he had a holy terror that just as he had failed his parents, so he had failed
Jim, largely owing to the disparity in their ages. And that therefore Jim
had moved on and was already looking somewhere else for a companion,
scanning other schools with his pale eyes. He imagined also that, like himself,
Jim had had a great attachment that had failed him, and which he longed
to replace. But here Bill Roach's speculation met a dead end: he had no
idea how adults loved each other.   (Ibid.)

Feeding, and compensating for his guilt by assuming awful responsibilities,
the boy's imagination runs riot, yet nonetheless his speculation about Jim's
'attachment' is right on target. He projects his situation on to Prideaux
and goes through a bizarrely winning sequence of psychological gymnastics
culminating in his self-appointment as Jim's 'guardian':

. . . a regent guardian was how he thought of the appointment; a stand-in
replacing Jim's departed friend, whoever that friend might be.   (Ibid.)

The vocabulary here ('regent', 'guardian', 'stand-in', replacement) is part
of a discourse of substitution, displacement and reversal. It is not only
appropriate to Roach's situation but to Smiley's and Guillam's as well for
they too fall foul of unavoidable transferences.

Le Carré's approach to the psychology of these three characters is deft
and unpretentious; Smiley's thrown-off remark that he detests the terms
'projection' and 'transference' are quite in keeping with the writer's overall
tone in this area. Smiley possesses a developed consciousness of his own
behaviour and when the subject of Ann intervenes, as it intermittently does
in the course of his investigation of the mole, he exercises a remarkably
prepared sense of self-control. The word jealousy is never used in connection
with the Ann–Haydon affair and Smiley acts as if his personal concerns
were completely irrelevant (to the other characters' embarrassment and
surprise) when that relationship arises. For Sam Collins, he even formulates
the facts, sparing Collins the trouble: that on the night of the Czechoslovakia
mission Haydon was at home in bed with his wife. Yet throughout the
entire investigation, Smiley's personal quest intrudes into his thoughts,
thus altering and relocating his ostensible enquiry. Recalling, for instance,
in one of the novel's numerous flashbacks, an earlier interview with Haydon,
he relives his wandering, preoccupied responses:

Smiley, dutifully: Yes, I have forgotten. Yes, I sympathize. No, Ann is
nowhere in my thoughts. We are colleagues after all and men of the world,
we are here to talk about Merlin and Control.   (ch. 18)

Guillam reacts similarly in his encroaching anxiety about Camilla which
grows from nothing to a fully-fledged distrust while he is carrying out his
secret work for Smiley. The more successful he is in stealing confidential
information from under the noses of the Circus clique, the more his guilt
and self-disgust grow, the more he projects his deceit on to Camilla–her flute

lessons are a cover for her infidelity, her teacher must be her former husband:

> She was living a double life. Now whole vistas of deceit opened before him. His friends, his loves, even the Circus itself, joined and re-formed in endless patterns of intrigue. A line of Mendel's came back to him, dropped two nights ago as they drank beer in some glum suburban pub: 'Cheer up, Peter, old son. Jesus Christ only had twelve, you know, and one of them was a double.'   (ch. 21)

The personal and the professional are not divorceable: an unease or disappointment in any one area readily transfers itself into others in a continuum of shifting, unstable exchanges. Le Carré's characters, here as in most of his fiction, are expressed in terms of their substitutive reactions to the strains, disparities and failures they experience in the personal–domestic sphere of marriages, affairs, families and friendships. Le Carré revises the traditional spy-story norm of the individual whose solitariness is assumed, given, by presenting his agents as tied to their ordinary lives: the individual is shown compromised by his inability to evade the psychological pressures any one of his relationships exerts on any other of his equally involving relationships.

The novel's recurrent references to families (and especially parents) are used to indicate a rootlessness or a rejection or a sense of not belonging for most of the characters. Roach's is the most obvious case in point but there is also Prideaux with his 'parentless look' and his invention of a dying mother which he makes his excuse when he goes to avenge himself on Haydon. Haydon himself had 'a loveless childhood'; Bland, Smiley supposes, joined the Secret Service out of 'animosity' towards his working-class and communist father, while Guillam answers Bryant's polite question, 'How's the family, sir?' with 'Fine' although he 'had none' (ch. 11). Lacon, the novel's one family man, makes more of a meal out of a similar enquiry to Smiley:

> 'You never had any, did you?' Lacon piped at once, his head lifted to the sound [of his daughter crying].
>   'I'm sorry?'
>   'Children. You and Ann.'
>   'No.'
>   'Nephews, nieces?'
>   'One nephew.'
>   'On your side?'
>   'Hers.'   (ch. 10)

If Smiley's parents are still alive they are never mentioned; he has relatives only at one remove – Ann's family, which includes Haydon who is her cousin.

Haydon has betrayed, Smiley realizes, as a lover, a colleague, a friend [and] as a patriot (ch. 36). In addition to Smiley himself, Haydon's victims include Ann and Prideaux and, as it turns out, Guillam as well, whose 'model' and 'inspiration' he was and whom he leaves 'orphaned'. Ann, the novel's most clearsighted character, who only appears 'in person' in it at the close, has acknowledged Haydon's betrayal early on and, in another of Smiley's flashbacks, he recalls the time when, without admitting her affair, she 'divorces' him 'from the family, from our lives' (ch. 17). Haydon's disloyalty as friend and lover leaves Prideaux, when he discovers the fact, in an implicitly lethal anger, but Smiley who has 'always known it was Bill', having 'tacitly shared that unexpressed half-knowledge which, like an illness, they hoped would go away if it was never owned to, never diagnosed' (ch. 36), has been left without the possibility of relationship since his introduction in the novel. There are no human substitutes for Smiley:

> . . . and if Jim Prideaux had arisen out of the shadows demanding to know whether he had any friends, he would probably have answered that he preferred to settle for a taxi.   (ch. 2)

At the end of the same chapter Smiley's friendless state is metaphorically emphasized:

> And now it was pouring with rain, Smiley was soaked to the skin and God as a punishment had removed all taxis from the face of London.   (Ibid.)

Le Carré plays thematically on the comparison between the duplicity of the anti-mole investigators and the duplicity of the mole himself and his runners. More important, though, and of more significance in the structuring of the action, another kind of multiplicity is at work: the continual shifts in focus and perspective ensure that personal and professional concerns are made to run at times in parallel, at times divergently, and at times intersectingly. The particular quality of le Carré's fiction is, for this reader, its careful polyphony and the free exchanges in narrative emphasis which constitute its decentred counterpoint. *Tinker Tailor Soldier Spy* has its main plot and its supportive, subsidiary actions but the slippage between them makes that distinction at best imprecise. Characters often seem to occupy some or other periphery, as though they are never quite at the heart of any single situation. Smiley, for instance, has been taken temporarily out of retirement to search for the mole and is obliged to conduct his investigation from diverse locations far from Cambridge Circus, the London headquarters of the new ruling secret service clique which harbours Gerald; his marriage, too, is always seen from some temporal distance and Ann's affair with Bill has been conducted, in the main, in places apart and unfamiliar to him. His assistants and informants, Guillam, Connie, Mendel, Westerby and Tarr are similarly exiled or 'outskirts' characters, and incursion into the secret, central 'safe house' is left until the finale. Prideaux is another Circus exile and casualty – at Thursgood's he is obsessed with looking out and back, over his shoulder, as it were, in anxious anticipation of some unspecified threat from the centre. For Roach, both his parents and Prideaux are centres of attention from which he remains apart: Jim's caravan, sited in the Dip at Thursgood's, exercises a fearful attraction and, through both concern for his charge and simple fascination, he spies on it from the safety of distance.

Consequently, much is made of watching, for purposes either of protection or entrapment. When the boy is first introduced it is explained that, 'Coming from a broken home Roach was a natural watcher' (ch. 1), and he serves Prideaux as lookout:

> 'You're a good watcher, anyway . . . Us singles always are, no one to rely on, what? No one else spotted me . . . Best watcher in the unit, Bill Roach is, I'll bet. Long as he's got his specs on . . . ' (Ibid.)

What Roach sees he is unable to cope with; missing chapel one evening, he observes Jim unwrapping the monkey-wrench that turns into a revolver and pen tops 'that turned into bullets' (ch. 24) – 'the watcher . . . had finally watched too well' – and he tries hopelessly to escape from this guilty knowledge by feigning madness and illness. Children watch helplessly in the novel: what is witnessed triggers off, often inexplicably, powerful, uncontrollable griefs. In an unsettlingly tangential episode quite separate from the preceding action, Jackie Lacon, whose distant crying punctuates the interview between Lacon and Smiley at Lacon's house, watches the men's departure, the chapter ending with the focus unsettlingly on her perception and her upset:

> Middle children weep longer than their brothers and sisters. Over her mother's shoulder, stilling her pains and her injured pride, Jackie Lacon watched the party leave . . . For a moment she really thought there must be something wrong with the fat one, he followed so slowly and so painfully. Then, seeing the handsome man hold the car door for him, he seemed to wake, and hurried forward with a lumpy skip. Unaccountably, this gesture upset her afresh. A storm of sorrow seized her and her mother could not console her. (ch. 10)

Le Carré does not credit the children with any particularly heightened perception and the dubious advantage over adults they have in being able to (or rather induced to) display their emotions openly merely indicates that their mechanisms of control, of turning away or of forgetting are as yet underdeveloped. Whereas Smiley can be 'taken by surprise' by his anger over Haydon and Ann and has dedicated his retirement to 'the profession of forgetting' (ibid), Roach has yet to learn how to anaesthetize himself against feeling: he remembers everything, living up to his nickname. He tries out diverse strategies of evasion:

> He had tried mixing up reality with dreams, in the hope that the event could be converted into something he had imagined; but each morning . . . he saw again . . . (ch. 24)

Yet when Roach eventually sees the man Prideaux is waiting for, he is by now so overcome that what he has seen loses definition and he is incapable of answering questions about the sighting:

' . . . Thin feller?' he asked again, kind but very steady.

But Roach had run out of words. He had no memory any more, no sense of size or perspective; his faculty of selection in the adult world had gone. Big men, small men, old, young, crooked, straight, they were a single army of indistinguishable dangers . . . He saw Jim's eyes on him, he saw the smile go out and felt the merciful touch of one big hand on his arm . . .

Laying his head hopelessly against Bradbury's shoulder, Bill Roach closed his eyes. When he opened them he saw through his tears that Jim was already half way up the staircase.   (ch. 30)

Rain and tears alike distort his already spectacled perception and when, at the end of the novel, he is seen for the last time, he has finally managed to blot out disturbing perceptions and replace them with more consoling illusions. He takes 'the job of dimmer man on the lighting' for the school play and seems happy with Prideaux's recovery from the 'shadow of his mother's death':

The gun, Bill Roach had finally convinced himself, was after all a dream.   (ch. 38)

Le Carré concludes *Tinker Tailor Soldier Spy* with a loosely systematic complex of excursions involving illusion and maturation with the latter including both the shedding of, and the growth into illusion. The plot enigma – the name of the betrayer – is solved but, we learn, it was known all along and merely awaited the recognition of diagnosis. Any gained sense of solace on the reader's part, either in having had his suspicions confirmed, or light unexpectedly thrown on the traitor is challenged by the novel's final recapitulation of its illusion theme. Haydon's name may be known but his identity and true motives, like those of Karla and Ann, remain the objects of speculation, still undefined, resistant to explanation. Social relationships stay, for the most part, opaque. Now facing the revelation concerning their justly named 'Witchcraft' information and its source, 'Merlin', the Circus clique nonetheless seem to have little purchase on its real implications. Esterhase tries to compensate for their defeat by making a gesture of gentlemanly camaraderie to Polyakov but his 'poignant' attempt to relocate and thus salvage that relationship fools only himself:

Esterhase, who would always rather have been a gentleman than a spy, seemed determined to make a gallant occasion of it, and offered his hand, which Polyakov struck petulantly aside. Esterhase looked round forlornly for Smiley, perhaps in the hope of ingratiating himself further with him, then shrugged and flung an arm across Bland's broad shoulder. Soon afterwards they left together.   (ch. 37)

Alleline seems to have come out of it better:

[He] at least had shown a certain bearing. But later Guillam was not sure whether Percy realized, on that first presentation of the facts, quite what the facts were . . .   (Ibid.)

Bill Roach 'matures' by allowing himself to dim his capacity for observation and reinterpret objective vision as dream while Guillam appears to have undergone a reverse process, 'maturing' through learning to see things straight:

> . . . it required an act of will on his own part, and quite a violent one at that, to regard Bill Haydon with much other than affection. Perhaps, as Bill would say, he had finally grown up. Best of all, on the same evening, he climbed the steps to his flat and heard the familiar notes of Camilla's flute echoing in the well. And if Camilla that night lost something of her mystery, at least by morning he had succeeded in freeing her from the toils of doublecross to which he had latterly consigned her.   (Ibid.)

Yet what she has or has not done stays ambiguous; on her preceding appearance she had said to him: 'I am what you think I am' (ch. 32) and had walked out. Smiley walks out of the action to meet Ann at Immingham, where she has frequently received Haydon. Karla called Ann 'the last illusion of the illusionless man' (ch. 38) and Smiley simply repeats both terms to himself. The novel thus ends in ambiguities of illusion, its last phrase, 'after all a dream', ironically negating its opening counterpart, 'The truth is . . . '.

6 Sideshow:
The Honourable Schoolboy

Le Carré has said, quite rightly, that the 'endless debate about the difference between a thriller and a novel . . . really is a very feeble one' (Dean, 5 September 1974. I.) but most of the adverse criticism he has been subjected to in the course of his writing career has depended on the assumption that such a distinction is genuine. Graham Greene's famous defensiveness in calling some of his novels 'entertainments' is a free gift to le Carré's detractors who see him violating the thriller's decorum in his 'ambitious ''literary'' presentation of espionage' (Merry, 1977, p. 212) and even positive reviewers, such as Robert Kee discussing *Smiley's People*, reproduce a certain self-conscious suspicion of their own enthusiasm, as if to suggest that there is something slightly amiss with thrillers that do more than just thrill:

> Le Carré is at least the equal of Graham Greene when he is being 'entertaining', though it is by no means certain that he only intends to entertain. Serpent-tongued insights flicker over the mudlands. (7 February, 1980)

The thriller/novel distinction opposes entertainment to seriousness and considers that a writer occupying the borderland between them must tread carefully indeed to avoid that 'literariness' which is synonymous with pretentiousness. The case against le Carré, put by a variety of critics, including, in addition to Bruce Merry, Clive James, Louis Finger, Richard Ingrams, Kingsley Amis and Christopher Booker, rests invariably on the charge of 'literariness' and both the frequency and the aggression with which it has appeared invite a defence, particularly since even 'pro-' le Carré critics take it partly on board. *The Honourable Schoolboy*, le Carré's most literary fiction, offers itself as an ideal site for refuting the charge.

Jerry Westerby, the novel's hero, is a part-time secret agent, part-time journalist and would-be novelist. Unlike his boss, George Smiley, whose passion for 'the lesser German poets' has remained constant since his first appearance in *Call for the Dead* (1961, p. 8), he has nothing of the don about him. But Westerby is no philistine either. Waiting in Saigon, he reads Ford Madox Ford, Greene, Conrad and T. E. Lawrence as well as 'a truly terrible novel about old Hong Kong' (le Carré, 1977, ch. 17). In Phnom Penh he reads Conrad ('in Phnom Penh he always read Conrad', ch. 15) and also *Candide*: his use of the latter to convey a bribe even earns him a literary nickname, Voltaire. In Battambang he flatters a senior French official's 'excruciating' verses (ch. 16) and the reader recalls that he has patiently humoured his literary agent's critical opinions earlier in the novel. Mencken warns that 'the eastern novel' is full of pitfalls:

> 'Nobody's brought off the eastern novel recently, in my view. Greene managed it, if you can take Greene, which I can't, too much popery. Malraux if you like philosophy, which I don't. Maugham you can *have*, and before that it's back to Conrad . . . '   (ch. 5)

Westerby never gets the chance to write his eastern novel but le Carré does, and *The Honourable Schoolboy* is the result. The prolific literary references that season this story – and, in fact, all his other novels too – attest to a large measure of authorial self-consciousness, but the allusions are never intrusive. They function to suggest the fictionality of the secret world, and that extreme disjuncture between the lonely, contemplative life of the agent and his life of action. Greene uses the same device. His secret agents and newspaper reporters are part-time or ex-literary critics as well. D's pre-war work in *The Confidential Agent* was research into Mediaeval Romance, while Fowler's quotations from nineteenth-century French and English poets in *The Quiet American* are at least as prominent as Westerby's literary memory.

Ever since the older novelist expressed his admiration for *The Spy Who Came in from the Cold*, it has become a mandatory exercise for le Carré's reviewers and critics to compare him with Greene. Such comparisons are invariably instructive, and especially with *The Honourable Schoolboy*, where le Carré enters into a direct dialogue with Greene's Vietnam novel. (I shall discuss this aspect of *The Honourable Schoolboy* later in the present chapter.) But whilst le Carré's detractors accuse him of 'literariness', Greene, perhaps on account of that modest-sounding 'entertainments' distinction, is allowed to enter unhindered into the pantheon of 'serious literature'. It is not le Carré's allusions that bar him entry though; it is his later style and its expansiveness that seem to win him most rebuke.

In an article entitled 'Go Back to the Cold!', an appraisal of *The Honourable Schoolboy* which offers le Carré free advice, Clive James makes a typically pointed demolition attempt on the novel and its author's literary pretension. The review manages admirably to elicit some cheap smiles at le Carré's expense, but James's characteristically entertaining manner projects what are actually substantial, if wrongheaded criticisms of his target. James, incidentally, is solidly 'pro' Greene and has praised Len Deighton's novels. The argument runs like this: until 1968 and *A Small Town in Germany*, le Carré wrote four brief 'tightly controlled efforts whose style, characterization and atmospherics were subordinate to the plot, which was the true hero' (James, 1982, p. 86). These 'merely entertaining' books had a 'more intense life' than their successors which have all demonstrated a chronic 'Elephantiasis'; the latter are over-ambitious and over-praised. *The Honourable Schoolboy*, with its 'coagulated style', adheres to its 'tone of myth-making portent', a 'grandiloquence' masking a 'perfunctory plot':

> The general effect is of inflation . . . the prose style is overblown . . . Whole pages are devoted to inventories of what can be found by way of flora and fauna in Hong Kong, Cambodia, Vietnam and other sectors of the mysterious East . . .
>
> Forever asking questions where he ought to be answering them, the narrator is presumably bent on seasoning mythomania with Jamesian ambiguity: *The Lord of the Rings* meets *The Golden Bowl*. Working on the principle that there can be no legends without lacunae, the otherwise omniscient author, threatened by encroaching comprehensibility, takes refuge in a black cloud of question marks. The ultimate secrets are lost in the mists of time and/or the dusty filing cabinets of the Circus. (James, pp. 88–9)

Adding, for good measure, that the 'myth-mongering' extends to the novel's characterization, James criticizes the 'high-falutin'' discourse of the veteran war-correspondent old Craw, the romanticization of Smiley and the 'legendary codebreaker Connie', (in fact, all of the resurrected and revived Circus personnel), plus the 'abstract', Moriarty-like Karla. Le Carré has been seduced by his character Smiley, 'the author's fantasy about himself' and now, 'the author's fantasy about his beleaguered homeland' (p. 92). Once, le Carré 'was more concerned with stripping down the mystique of his subject than with building it up' but no longer – James rests his case hoping against the odds that le Carré will return to 'his more enviable role as a popular writer' (p. 93).

It is tempting to follow A. Alvarez in dismissing such criticism (James expresses a widespread opinion) as 'tiresome intellectual snobbery' (3 February 1980) but James, firmly gripping the wrong end of the stick is at least holding the right stick. Certainly *The Honourable Schoolboy* is long and expansive and its narrative glories in details at the expense of plot momentum. Describing the composition of *The Spy Who Came in from the Cold*, le Carré has said that he 'applied the discipline of a British civil servant' in cutting and cutting his original quarter-million-word manuscript of that novel (1968. I.) and that early structural economy expected of the standard thriller has by now been fully eschewed in favour of a more relaxed and improvizatory approach. Quitting the extreme generic rigour, the subordination of all 'harmonic' elements to the linear demands of plot, le Carré began, as early as *The Looking-Glass War*, to concentrate on a 'vertical' or 'chordal' method which allowed for fuller characterization, for occasional narrative discursiveness and above all for complex internal dialogues to be produced between parallel thematic strands. In a way, his plots look after themselves; they work like the mechanism of a watch but are not, in general, the main focus of interest in his writing. Le Carré's discipline is of a different order to that of Deighton's terse, fast, colloquial genre writing and, in perhaps more apt comparison, different again from Greene's restrained, cinematic realism. In the description of place, for example, le Carré's later manner gives the narrative voice the opportunity, as it were, to speak in excess of any decorum demanded by plot where his early descriptions out-Greene Greene in their constraint:

> His flat was small and squalid, done in brown paint with photographs of Clovelly. It looked directly on to the grey backs of three stone warehouses, the windows of which were drawn, for aesthetic reasons, in creosote. Above the warehouse there lived an Italian family, quarrelling at night and beating carpets in the morning.   (le Carré, 1963, ch. 3)

Now Greene himself:

> The long city lay spread along the open Atlantic; waves broke over the Avenida de Maceo and misted the windscreens of cars. The pink, grey, yellow pillars of what had once been the aristocratic quarter were eroded like rocks; an ancient coat of arms, smudged and featureless, was set over the doorway of a shabby hotel, and the shutters of a night-club were varnished in bright crude colours to protect them from the wet and salt of the sea. In the west the steel skyscrapers of the new town rose higher than lighthouses into the clear February sky.   (Greene, 1958, part 2, ch. 1)

The context of this extract makes it quite clear that the view is that of the character Wormold, constructed in his perception and in a vocabulary approximating the character's own. Each adjective is, as in the quotation from the early le Carré, simple and unobtrusive. The later le Carré includes many similar passages, especially when description is channelled through character but also present is a more self-consciously 'literary' narrative style, rich in metaphor and more reminiscent of lyric poetry than spy stories:

> There are blocks of flats near the Town and Country Golf Course on the northern fringes of London that are like the superstructure of permanently sinking ships. They lie at the end of long lawns where the flowers are never quite in flower, the husbands man the lifeboats all in a flurry at about eight-thirty in the morning and the women and children spend the day keeping afloat until their menfolk return too tired to sail anywhere. These buildings were built in the thirties and have stayed a grubby white ever since. Their oblong, steelframed windows look on to the lush billows of the links, where week-day women in eyeshades wander like lost souls.   (le Carré, 1977, ch. 10)

The spirit of early Auden inhabits this passage and others like it. In the choice of both metaphor and rhythm there are echoes of 'A Summer Night' and 'In Memory of W. B. Yeats' sounding in every sentence. The tone of sympathetic detachment, the precise generalizations, the surrealist juxtapositions, the quality of disorientation inhering in the normal business of living, the uncertainty of location and the sense of directed aimlessness do more than simply gesture towards Auden. First, there is a very quiet and delicate irony washing over this suburban vignette making it into a mild satire. The narrative voice is gently 'knowing', aware of its own excess, reminding the reader through embellishment that a story is being told and that hard facts in such a story as this one, are hard to come by. Secondly, that phrase 'in the thirties', coupled with the Audenesque devices evokes a 'thirties' atmosphere appropriate both to Smiley, who enters the scene at this point, and to Mr Pelling, whom he is about to visit. As in *Tinker Tailor Soldier Spy*, and like Leclerc and Harting before that, Smiley lives partly in the past of the thirties and forties, the time also, of Karla's rise. In the following chapter, where Connie and di Salis press the elderly Mr Hibbert for information about the brothers Ko, their thirties childhood in his mission school begins his account. The extract from Auden's '1st September 1939', which prefaces the novel with its wry disingenuousness, may well be recalled in Hibbert's story and it keeps the thirties well in mind:

> I and the public know
> What all schoolchildren learn,
> Those to whom evil is done,
> Do evil in return.

Le Carré's legacy from Auden is as large as his inheritance from Greene and he is happy to reproduce at times Auden's way of suggesting opaquely the narrative causes of a situation while at the same time proceeding with a sharp focus on precise local details. The evocation of the thirties is important (it is referred to elsewhere in the novel), but le Carré seems to this writer also to copy Auden's technique of pursuing a narrative line obliquely, tangentially, and of making general and typical what is ostensibly particular and unique. Intricate, and in linear plot terms incidental, description of place and persons is actually neither incidental, nor merely functional, and it is, as often as not, unstraightforward. In the chapter introducing Jerry Westerby, the 'honourable schoolboy' of the novel's title, we are given a characteristic incident which related the arrival of a minor figure, the postmistress of a Tuscan hamlet, who has set off to deliver Smiley's telegram to Westerby:

> Jerry had seen Mama Stefano from a long way off. He had that instinct, there was a part of him that never ceased to watch: a black figure hobbling inexorably up the dust-path like a lame beetle in and out of the ruled shadows of the cedars, up the dry watercourse of slick Franco's olive groves, into their own bit of Italy as he called it, all two hundred square metres of it, but big enough to hit a tethered tennis-ball round a pole on cool evenings when they felt athletic. He had seen very early the blue envelope she was waving, and he had even heard the sound of her mewing carrying crookedly over the other sounds of the valley: the Lambrettas and the bandsaws. And his first gesture, without stopping his typing, was to steal a glance at the

house to make sure the girl had closed the kitchen window to keep out the heat and the insects.   (ch. 2)

The delivery of the telegram and Mama Stefano's report of it structure the whole chapter. The function of this small event has some importance in the plotting (it takes Jerry out of his pastoral inactivity and tears him guiltily away from the orphan) and it helps 'mythologize' Westerby, who is the subject of inflating, gossipy speculation among the villagers, but the incident is used mainly for the purely narrative opportunities it offers. The filmic, photographic quality of careful, inclusive observation is Auden's, as is the consciousness of 'watching', a persistent le Carréan concern. As with Auden, the photography has a surrealist tint: the lame beetle, the tethered tennis-ball, the close-up on the waving blue envelope and the bizarre 'mewing'. Each sentence – after the first which is plain and denotative – moves into strange, off-course qualification. The focus on Mama Stefano follows her arduous climb but leaves the reader more with a sense of the lame beetle negotiating the shadow patterns than of the woman herself. Background becomes foreground in this *gestalt* diagram. The spatial description of Westerby and the orphan's 'own bit of Italy' is similarly made strange as the 'two hundred square metres' (a space that *sounds* expansive) turns out to be only 'big enough to hit a tethered tennis-ball round a pole'.

The waving blue envelope and Mama Stefano's mewing again take the reader away from the literal – the sight of a beetle is now the voice of a cat and the other sounds of the valley mingle with it, giving a generalized impression, suggesting that the oddity of her action is somehow typical and habitual for this place. The last sentence builds up an expectation solely in order to drop it in satisfying anti-climax: the feeling of securing against threat given in 'steal a glance', 'to make sure', and 'closed the kitchen window', all evocative of suspicion and danger, guard against nothing more oppressive than 'the heat and the insects'. Such twists are symptomatic of thirties Auden as is much of the passage's phraseology – 'the ruled shadows of the cedars', 'on cool evenings', the crooked carrying 'of her mewing', 'the other sounds of the valley' and 'the Lambrettas and the bandsaws'.

The anti-generic attentiveness of the writing here, which is a kind of play delighting in inconsequentiality, pretending to be spellbound by the Tuscan postmistress and, in a way, actually being spellbound by her, is not evidence of some parasitic growth on le Carré's early generic style but is intrinsic to his whole approach and was present, at some level, from the start. Details are allowed their own right to leisured and careful appraisal; the incidental, extraneous, trivial, glancing, diversionary and small-scale co-exist alongside the direction of the main plot and its major themes, but not peacefully – they make challenging claims on the reader's attention, slowing down the action and making it diffuse. Often this tendency is difficult to illustrate because it surfaces usually in deft asides, brief and sudden *aperçus*, but it is present as part of the fabric of most of the extracts from his fiction included thus far. The more the narrative voice gives the impression of having its own identity, independent of character perception, the more the tendency flourishes.

What causes James and his companion critics more disquiet than the narrative's discursiveness is, as one reviewer described it, 'a certain knowingness' (West, 10 September 1977) different from the 'literary' excursions already shown. Another voice, part storyteller and part Smiley apologist, makes frequent narratorial interventions commenting on and forwarding the action and also correcting interpretations of it:

> It has been laid at Smiley's door more than once since the curtain was rung down on the Dolphin case that now was the moment when George should have gone back to Sam Collins . . .
>   They are talking simplistic nonsense.   (ch. 10)

> In the scheme of things as they are now conveniently remembered, there is at this point a deceptive condensation of events . . .   (ch. 11)

> It has been whispered once or twice by certain trivial critics of George Smiley that at this juncture he should somehow have seen which way the wind was blowing with Jerry . . .   (ch. 13)

This partisan voice, dismissively rejecting as absurd those hypotheses about Smiley offered by 'trivial critics' asks the reader to accept its judgements wholesale and to take pleasure in its tone of barely maintained patience. Any sense of being fully in the know however, is kept away from the reader who is at this narrator's complete mercy. Le Carré seems to be referring to his idiosyncratic narrator when he says 'I felt I had to make a compact with the reader because it is a long drawn-out story which has three beginnings' (Oakes, 11 September 1977. I.), but though as mere device the intervening voice may be necessary in helping the reader to stay on course, it functions also, as James rightly notices, in contributing to the novel's mythologizing rhetoric.

The Honourable Schoolboy's multiple beginnings (le Carré's three are an underestimate) take up the first three chapters: they indicate various routes into the action and diverse perspectives upon it. Between them, sundry members of the Intelligence fraternity argue over no less than five causes of the Dolphin case, while the narrator, allowing their ignorance, suggests 'a more realistic point of departure' in a Hong Kong Foreign Correspondents Club. Chapter Two introduces Westerby as already described and Chapter Three concentrates on Smiley, relating once more, his personal and professional pasts. Mythologizing is what these openings are all about. The world of the revived Circus is more intelligent than that of the Department in *The Looking-Glass War* and more self-aware, and the Dolphin case has been something of a victory – perhaps, or perhaps not, tarnished a little by being shared with the American Service, but successful nevertheless. Yet where decline and anachronism bred collective fantasies in *The Looking-Glass War* and the disappointments of both betrayal and 'philosophy' bred them in *Tinker Tailor Soldier Spy*, here success, or partial success, breeds them too. Inflation is the method but deflation the aim.

This is the first beginning:

> Afterwards, in the dusty little corners where London's secret servants drink together, there was argument about where the Dolphin case history should really begin. One crowd, led by a blimpish fellow in charge of microphone transcription, went so far as to claim that the fitting date was sixty years ago when 'that arch-cad Bill Haydon' was born into the world under a treacherous star. Haydon's very name struck a chill into them. It does so even today. (ch. 1)

Tone, here, combines three voices:
1   a relaxed and knowingly 'armchair' raconteur manner, establishing a storyteller's contract with the reader ('Afterwards', 'Haydon's very name struck a chill into them. It does so even today.';
2   an amused, satirical voice, patronizing the characters' insularity, and their absurd self-important fantasizing ('dusty little corners', 'secret [not civil] servants', 'crowd', 'blimpish fellow', 'arch-cad');
3   a voice of maybe more than partial complicity with the characters, as though the narrator were one of them, with his own theories to offer, and also perhaps unconsciously subscribing to the myth-making, even seduced by it ('went so far as to claim', 'born into the world under a treacherous star.')

Such a mixture or impurity of tone is sustained throughout the novel, as first one, then another voice gains prominence. It would have been easier, and more in line with convention, for le Carré to opt for a consistent 'single' voice but the equivocation of tone keeps the reader attentive to the activity of legend-making.

The first chapter presents competing myths of origin. With varying degrees of sincerity and credibility, individuals and factions propose, in turn, as 'the true genesis' of the case: Haydon's birth, Smiley's obsession with Karla, the arrival of the British Navy in Hong Kong, Smiley's technical expertise, and Westerby's provocative fieldwork. Each alternative reflects the social class, occupation, age or interest of the proposer and consequently each is placed under instant suspicion. The speakers inflate their pet hypotheses to bolster themselves. The narrative tone allows each a measure of plausibility while simultaneously warning against them all, via connotation and aside. The 'blimpish fellow', to take just the first instance, expresses an archaic national and class pride nourished by nostalgia. In his view, the outcome of Haydon's treachery led to the loss of the Service's independence, letting in 'the Cousins' who, in his words, 'changed the game entirely'. The narration comments that he made his observation 'much as he might have deplored power tennis or bodyline bowling'. Tennis and cricket are here those class recreations that embody a commitment to amateurism and come complete with their own legends and their own betrayals. The narrative aside more than remarks on the blimp faction, it also sets up the theme of amateurism and introduces the first of many sport motifs, both later to be associated with Westerby. When the five alternative theories have been rehearsed, the narrator wryly suggests 'perhaps a more realistic point of departure . . . ' (ch 1) but this enjoys only a slightly higher status than its predecessors, its very specificity ('a certain typhoon Saturday in mid-1974, three o'clock in the afternoon . . . ') is dubious. Each of the points of origin offers a point of entry into the story proper; none is dismissible as pure fantasy (whatever disparagement the narrator throws off) but every one (including the narrator's) is myth-creating too, a more or less sophisticated development of the collective fantasies of the earlier novels, deriving, like theirs, from confusions about the motives, purposes, results, techniques, compromises and betrayals inhering in secret service.

From the start, le Carré's idiosyncratic Intelligence jargon is fully operational. The vocabulary of 'moles', 'sleepers', 'Cousins', 'burrowers', 'fieldmen', 'the Nursery', and 'tradecraft' is soon followed by other terms already familiar from *Tinker Tailor Soldier Spy*: 'handwriting', 'scalphunters', 'lamplighters', 'pavement-artists', 'the Circus', 'the Centre', and the like. Despite being, in the main, 'all made up' by the author (Vaughan, 13 September 1979. I.), they make for a sense of closed-world authenticity and their 'precious' quality and obsessive use suggests some former time when their invention was rooted in the service personnel's self-parody and self-dramatization, strains of which still survive in them. Of course, they imply the glamour of myth-making too. Rather modestly le Carré tells that he has been 'rather gratified to learn that some of my jargon has gone into . . . the language' of the real Intelligence world (ibid.). After an initially detached judgement, 'in their own strange jargon', the terminology is taken by both narrative voices and readers as the natural currency of their world, the myth again exercising its seductive influence.

The mythologizing game is not only played in the Circus and its environs – heavily seasoned with gossip, inflating speculation on Westerby (in Tuscany) and on Smiley (in the Foreign Office), runs rampant:

> Between the villagers of Whitehall and the villagers of Tuscany, there was sometimes surprisingly little to choose.   (ch. 3)

Equally, the patrons of the Hong Kong Foreign Correspondents' Club engage in the pastime. The journalists too have their own self-conscious, group-cementing patois, a hybrid language for expressing competition and comradeship. Addressing his colleagues as 'Your Graces', old Craw parodies some priestly discourse in the club's atmosphere of alternating boredom, sarcasm and hysteria:

> In their tireless pursuit of legends about one another, old Craw was their Ancient Mariner. Craw had shaken more sand out of his shorts, they told

each other, than most of them would ever walk over; and they were right
. . . Craw gave them a sense of history in this rootless place. His style of
speech, which at typhoon times even the hardiest might pardonably find
irksome, was a genuine hangover from the Thirties, when Australia provided
the bulk of journalists in the Orient; and the Vatican, for some reason, the
jargon of their companionship.   (ch. 1)

So 'irked' by Craw's 'putatively mirth-provoking high-falutin'', James
(1982, p. 90) misses the narrative's consciousness of the old man's manner;
in the same way, he ignores that awareness of inflation built into the novel's
closing passages – the post-mortem on the true nature of Smiley's role:

Was there really a conspiracy against Smiley, of the scale that Guillam
supposed? And if so, how was it affected by Westerby's own maverick
intervention? No information is available and even those who trust each
other well are not disposed to discuss the question . . .
   And did Smiley *know* of the conspiracy, deep down? Was he aware of
it, and did he secretly even welcome the solution?   (ch. 22)

The narrative refuses to resolve these questions fully and thus maintains
to the end something of that mythical incomprehensibility accorded Smiley
back in Chapter 3. Guillam recalls an extract from a letter Smiley wrote
to Ann and offers this as a clue to a possible solution. Significantly, the
extract is framed in the narrative with Guillam's literary criticism:

Certainly the style flies a lot higher than anything Guillam would aspire
to for himself.

   I honestly do wonder, without wishing to be morbid, how I reached this
present pass. So far as I can ever remember of my youth, I chose the secret
road because it seemed to lead straightest and furthest toward my country's
goal. The enemy in those days was someone we could point at and read
about in the papers. Today, all I know is that I have learned to interpret
the whole of life in terms of conspiracy. That is the sword I have lived by,
and as I look around me now I see it is the sword I shall die by as well.
These people terrify me but I am one of them. If they stab me in the back,
then at least that is the judgment of my peers.

   As Guillam points out, the letter was essentially from Smiley's blue
period.   (ch. 22)

Guillam's loyalty to Smiley is great enough to allow him some irony against
him, and that irony protects Guillam too. It also distances the movingly
impotent defeatism of Smiley's letter. There is no elucidation as to whether
or not he knew of the likely conspiracy between Enderby, Martello, Lacon
and Collins, and, of course, it doesn't matter. The point is that the characters
make myths about each other and act as if they were characters in myths;
they are given a measure of narratorial approval in so doing. The reader,
confronted continually by this, has a task quite different from the tasks
he or she has been invited to perform in the earlier, more political novels.
Here, the reader is asked to sympathize with characters as fully as possible

and simply to accept in one package, the action's lacunae, its ambiguities, and the frustration and resignation of the three key characters, Smiley, Guillam and Westerby. The 'quest for Karla', Smiley's '*black Grail*' as Ann puts it (ch. 21), the quest for Drake and Nelson Ko (their forenames alluding to a British mythology), together with the suggestion of resurrection myths surrounding the business of Drake's dead son and the return (as if the from the dead) of Nelson and Ricardo, are all offered uncritically to the reader for acceptance. There is no political choice for the reader to make in this, no need to take sides over, say, the rights and wrongs of Westerby's heroically foolish insubordination, his elevation of the personal over the professional, or Smiley's own machinations. No crisis of philosophy is forced into the reader's mind. All judgements on character and on the successes and failures of the Dolphin case, as far as the reader is concerned, are made on individual characters and not on any political implications of their actions.

Certainly the familiar le Carréan issues are present in *The Honourable Schoolboy*: the problem of motive, of what cold warriors are really fighting for, the compromises of alliance, conspiracy, the rituals of bureaucracy and the personal/political division; but the entire narrative's literary-sounding quality of 'knowingness' deliberately makes the familiar issues over-familiar, the tired, incomprehensible and insoluble components of an overall resignation. The novel does not so much illuminate these issues as issues but explores what it is like to live with them and it requires that the reader share some of that experience too. The deflation of mythologizing is not satirical in any strong political sense; it induces a resigned acquiescence on the reader's part, a knowingness similar to that of the narrator and the major characters. In the end, the myths might as well be taken as real because if the old issues cease to prick there is no point in sharpening them. Smiley's letter and Guillam's comments on its literariness express such an incapacity in the face of *issue* that the reader is left simply with sighing and nodding in commiseration.

In no way, however, is the action itself 'tired'. The sense that nothing is quite known or understood, the fact that little seems to turn out as planned and that expectations of all kinds are frustrated as disappointments and reversals are met at every turn, are brilliantly worked-for, giving the action an edgy and bewildering feel. Since, during most of the action, Smiley is a man apart, a figure of enigma, Guillam, his second, holds much of the novel's attention. Eager for knowledge but never in-the-know, committed to the operation but often seen musing distractedly on personal matters and dealing, in teeth-gritting patience, with the mundane and finicky aspects of the case appropriate to his lieutenancy, Guillam is frequently portrayed in a mood of irritation. One of le Carré's particular successes is his careful and exact depiction of 'minor' emotions in situations more akin to normality than crisis – irritation rather than fury, upset rather than despair, surprise rather than revelation, anxiety rather than fear. The presence of Fawn, coffee-bringer, errand-runner and 'silent killer' constantly nags Guillam. In *Tinker Tailor Soldier Spy*, Fawn was a boyish, quiet, almost gentle bodyguard; in *The Honourable Schoolboy*, he still 'flits' in and out of the action and his boyishness is still there, expressed in moments of naive enthusiasm, but the character has developed and is now periodically insolent towards Guillam, in a nastily jaunty way, and Guillam takes especial delight in his occasional error. Rivalry and mutual jealousy are suggested in their early exchanges and their mutually juvenile responses over each other possess a distasteful ulteriority. Although it is never stated, both vie for Smiley's approval and their relationship is one of barely controlled hostility and resentment:

> 'Do you mean she *sent* you here?'
> 'Personal for Chief immediate,' replied Fawn evasively.
> 'I said: "Did she send you here?"' Guillam was seething.
> 'Answer, "no, sir, she did not." You bloody little drama queen, racing round London in your plimsolls! You're out of your mind.'   (ch. 8)

Winning most of the early rounds against Fawn, Guillam loses the later ones in Hong Kong, where Fawn's capacity to wind-up his superior reveals new depths. In a startling passage an incident is recalled, which Guillam has kept from Smiley, where Fawn demonstrated in full a shocking gratuitous viciousness which suddenly and at last makes sense of the tension between them. Fawn is in the passenger seat of the car, his arm resting in the space of his open window. A boy on a Honda draws alongside:

> As they pulled away, the Chinese boy ill-advisedly made a dive for the watch, but Fawn was much too quick for him. Catching hold of the boy's wrist instead, he held on to it, towing him beside the car while the boy struggled vainly to break free. Guillam had driven fifty yards or so before he realized what had happened and he at once stopped the car, which was what Fawn was waiting for. He jumped out before Guillam could stop him, lifted the boy straight off his Honda, led him to the side of the road and broke both his arms for him, then returned smiling to the car. Terrified of a scandal, Guillam drove rapidly from the scene, leaving the boy screaming and staring at his dangling arms.   (ch. 19)

This episode, entirely irrelevant to the main plot, instances well a generalized sense of frustration and confusion, of events and people being out of control. Fawn's sadism is doubly disturbing because it is calculated ('which was what Fawn was waiting for') – his violence may perhaps have been comprehensible had it sprung from a momentary anger. In the same way Guillam's response ('Terrified of a scandal') suggests a repression of his horrified disgust at Fawn's act and a guilt uncalled-for by this situation. Although the event is narrated with deliberate cinematic precision, moving just for an instant into Fawn's perspective ('broke both his arms *for him*'), the effect is of an accelerated, panicky uncontrol.

Anxiety coupled with disappointment sum up Guillam's state on the verge of the resolution of the plot to capture the brothers Ko. Westerby's intervention necessitates Guillam's removal from the scene, with Fawn, to escort Westerby to a place where he can do no more damage, and that just at the time when he feels it urgently necessary to inform Smiley of his evidence of the conspiracy against him:

> He had endured a great deal for this moment. Disgrace and exile to Brixton under Haydon . . . putting up with George's obsessive secretiveness, which Guillam privately considered both humiliating and self-defeating – but at least it had been a journey with a destination, till bloody Westerby, of all people, had robbed him even of that. But to return to London knowing that . . . he was leaving Smiley and the Circus to a bunch of wolves, without even the chance to warn him – to Guillam it was the crowning cruelty of a frustrated career . . . (ch. 20)

Even when, in other spheres, things turn out fortuitously, the sense of incomprehension is equally strong. Lusting after the self-possessed Molly Meakin, Guillam spends time and money in inconclusive attempts to seduce her, until, much later, and resigned to his unsuccess, he drives her home, and is, as usual, invited in for coffee:

> Anticipating the familiar frustrations – 'no-Peter-please-Peter-*dear*-I'm sorry' – Guillam was on the brink of declining, when something in her eye – a certain calm resolution as it seemed to him – caused him to change his mind. Once inside her flat, she closed the door and put it on the chain. Then she led him demurely to her bedroom, where she astonished him with a joyous and refined carnality. (ch. 8)

Completely reversing previous views of her as 'prim', 'a little blue-stocking perhaps, a little inward', but 'capable' (ch. 4'), this incident takes the reader as much off-guard as it does Guillam who, thinking of himself, and behaving, as active is suddenly made passive, without being given any chance for a preparatory period of adjustment. If events have turned out well for Guillam here, it is through no fault of his own. In the main Guillam, Smiley and Westerby experience far less satisfying reversals of expectation; despite the 'success' of the mission, the novel leaves them all with a feeling of business unfinished. Westerby dies, 'his open mouth still calling, his face still siently imploring' (ch. 21); less dramatically, Smiley slips back into the safety of domestic routine and listens either with 'courtesy' or, 'as the deaf do', (ch. 22) to the politicians who call on him to consult about the Circus' future plans.

In an action which does not allow its characters either the knowledge or the distance necessary for political judgment, the moods of resignation and irony are all that are eventually permitted to character and reader alike. On the face of it, *The Honourable Schoolboy* looks as if it will be a powerful contender for the designation 'political novel'. Its locations and the time of its setting are indeed resonant of topical political history. But in all of the novel's political terrain – the Sino–Soviet split, the spy-damaged relations between the British and American secret services, the Hong Kong question, and the South-East Asian complex of Cambodia, Vietnam, Laos and Thailand during the historic events of 1975 – there is an avoidance of issue and an absence of readerly choice. Even le Carré's perennial worry over ends and means, surfacing here in the expedient murder of Westerby, elicits no discussion or commentary in the narrative, no longer needing any, perhaps. Fine reportage of characters experiencing and acting in political situations from the distance of varied estangements take the place, in *The Honourable Schoolboy*, of the political debates of its predecessors. Partly this is due to the narrative's commitment to activity and action in the novel's second section, and also to the very nature of the Dolphin operation where the Circus is on the offensive and outward-looking. Some few and still powerful strains of 'philosophical' introspection survive, notably in Smiley's recruitment pep-talk with Westerby, but now Smiley presents himself as a changed man – a guilty liberal no more, hardened to the Cold War. Speaking of 'will', he seems to have espoused both the clarity and the content of some of Haydon's arguments at the end of *Tinker Tailor Soldier Spy*:

> 'A lot of people haven't these days. The will. Specially in England. A lot of people see *doubt* as legitimate philosophical posture. They think of themselves in the middle, whereas of course really, they're nowhere. No battle was ever won by spectators, was it? We understand that in this service. We're lucky. Our present war began in 1917, with the Bolshevik Revolution. It hasn't changed yet.'   (le Carré, 1977, ch. 5)

Smiley's statement is not offered for anything other than agreement and he turns it, with a little fussy embarrassment, into a profession of faith:

> ' . . . Is that how *you* feel? I don't think we should be afraid of . . . devoting ourselves? Is that old-fashioned of me?'   (Ibid.)

Significantly, his addressee is no opponent (like Haydon), nor an available *confidant* (like Guillam), nor philosophically anxious (like Avery), nor a thought-avoiding cynic (like Leamas). Westerby, like Prideaux before him, has at this point a jolly, dog-like loyalty and in fact the focus of the scene is Westerby's pained discomfiture at George's 'failed priest' bit:

> 'Sport,' he expostulated, with a clumsy laugh, as the colour rose to his face. 'For Heaven's sake. You point me and I'll march. Okay? . . . '   (Ibid.)

The advocacy of devotion and the analogy of secret service with religious service have appeared in all the previous novels, often as matter for comment, but here, the religious dimension eclipses the political. Perhaps, as Westerby guesses, Smiley is publicly airing his private worries, his doubts, in the attempt to negate them, but in the safety of talking to Westerby, there is no question that Smiley will be induced to confront anything. Supportive religious imagery, in this novel, is very much in evidence – from Craw's Vatican-speak, and di Salis's jesuitical intensity, to the mission school past of Reverend Hibbert and the Ko brothers and Drake's double acts of religious devotion at his son's grave and at the headland, awaiting his brother's return. The last chapters of the novel's two sections are entitled, respectively, 'the resurrection of Ricardo' and 'born again'. Duty and devotion stop Smiley thinking politically; Karla no longer substantially represents communism – he is 'a left-over legend':

> who had set out to destroy the temples of his private faith, whatever remained of them: the service that he loved, his friends, his country, his concept of a reasonable balance in human affairs. (Ibid.)

But even most of that, the narrative points out, is unconscious and Smiley has as little rational comprehension of what his quest is about as Guillam and Westerby:

> Never had Smiley gone into battle knowing so little and expecting so much. He felt lured, and he felt pursued. Yet when he tired, and drew back for a moment, and considered the logic of what he was about, it almost eluded him . . . He blinked around him and knew there was nothing for him where he stood. Yet he advanced without the ultimate conviction. (Ibid.)

While *The Honourable Schoolboy* is firmly le Carréan, building securely on theme and character established in *Tinker Tailor Soldier Spy*, some of its inspiration undoubtedly lies with that other South-East Asian novel, or 'entertainment', it recollects: Greene's *The Quiet American*, which appeared just over twenty years earlier in 1955. When he was working on his novel, le Carré evidently had Greene very much in mind. He told James Cameron that he intended to avoid a Vietnamese setting as Greene had 'defined that for all time in *The Quiet American*'; he added, 'It stands up brilliantly still' (8 September 1974. I.). In the end he overturned this decision, including Vietnam as part of a larger South-East Asian canvas. Although Greene's shadow is clearly visible in *The Honourable Schoolboy*, le Carré turns the debt to his own advantage by debating the older novel. At first, it looks as though le Carré is simply paying homage – his 'foreword' strongly resembles Greene's dedicatory letter prefacing *The Quiet American*; both remark on significant borrowings and departures from fact and make acknowledgement in similar terms to friends and helpers still resident in the places their novels portray. Many more correspondences follow. Both novels have journalist 'heroes' who are both induced to make a principled moral stand which involves vacating a prior position. Both stands involve a betrayal and express a new-found and new type of loyalty. In each case, the act leads directly to death.

Le Carré constructs Westerby as something of an amalgam of Greene's Fowler and Pyle and places him in predicaments analagous to theirs. Fowler's self-centredness, adultery, guilt and jealousy and Pyle's crude, self-rationalizing and successful sexual rivalry (together with the concomitant business of desertion and exchange) are reproduced in Westerby. Guilty over his double desertion of his daughter and the Orphan, Westerby recalls Fowler; transforming himself into the romantic rescuer of Lizzie from Drake

Ko, he evokes Alden Pyle. The themes of 'honour', 'innocence' and 'immaturity', adapted from Greene, reappear in le Carré's novel. On frequent occasions Greene's first-person narrator, Fowler, describes Pyle as a 'schoolboy', or 'boyish', acting 'with the caution of a hero in a boy's adventure story' or 'in a kind of schoolboy dream' (1955, part 3, ch. 2). Le Carré's loud Englishman, named 'schoolboy' by the Tuscan villagers, speaks a public-school jargon and his bluff, sporty outwardness makes him seem, as T. J. Binyon notices, 'a throwback, in some respects, to an earlier type of hero'. The critic adds:

> . . . the novel itself assimilates – rather than rejects – the former tradition when it implicitly compares Jerry with Kim, or allows Smiley to call himself Mr Standfast when interviewing Lizzie's abandoned husband. (9 September 1977)

Both Greene and le Carré explore what transpires when a character derived in part from Kipling or Buchan is put into situations where boyish honour and innocence will have destructive consequences. Yet where for Greene, Pyle's sinister naive honour is condemned as a sick delusion, profitable only in illuminating the untenability of Fowler's culpable disengagement, le Carré avoids moralizing on Westerby's turn.

The Quiet American incorporates much political allusion. To cite the obvious instance, Pyle is reputedly based on Colonel Lansdale, Chief of the American Military Advisory and Assistance Group in fifties Vietnam, who promoted Ngo Dinh Diem as the head of a wished-for 'third force' to counter both the French and the Communists (Maclear, 1982, p. 65). And Fowler's principled betrayal of Pyle to the Communists is offered to the reader as an act of political commitment. However, Greene's novel, despite its authentic political and historical background detail, in fact occludes the political as much as it can, preferring to concentrate on internal moral dilemmas, far removed from political statement, programme or choice. Readers who found *The Quiet American* anti-American mistook, at the very least, Greene's emphasis. The issues he discusses, love *versus* honour and commitment *versus* abstention, have little to do with politics. Greene's sympathies are clearly with Fowler when he disparages Pyle's genuinely political commitment on the basis that every political philosophy kills people who 'just aren't interested' in either democracy or communism and simply 'want enough rice' (part 2, ch. 3). The force of this opinion remains unchanged, even when Fowler has betrayed Pyle to the rebels, as commitment here, as in many other places in Greene's fiction, is defined in religious terms, centred on the individual looking inwards and finding the need to relate to some transcendent other, an unearthly confessor. Fowler's last words in the novel, 'I wished there existed someone to whom I could say that I was sorry' (part 4, ch. 3), illustrate well that the 'political' choice he makes is hardly more than a narrative mechanism. It is the *'engagé' act* of conspiring in Pyle's assassination that stimulates Greene: it stems from shocking self-realization and is devoid of programmatic content. In

one moment of truth, hidden in a paddy field, Fowler hears the cries of
a wounded soldier in the watchtower he and Pyle have just escaped from
at the onset of a Vietminh attack; he learns to take guilt upon himself:

> I was responsible for that voice crying in the dark: I had prided myself on
> detachment, on not belonging to this war, but those wounds had been
> inflicted by me just as though I had used the sten, as Pyle had wanted to
> do . . . I wanted to join him . . . to share his pain. (part 2, ch. 2)

As I have already suggested, *The Honourable Schoolboy* is less political than
its thriller predecessors. Certainly, it contains a wealth of political and social
documentation with, one supposes, an authenticity equal to Greene's. The
careful differentiation between the portrayal of the Khmer Rouge, the North
Vietnamese Army, the Pathet Lao and the private armies of the Thai
warlords or the diverse roles of various American characters are cases in
point. But political choice is downplayed. Westerby alone makes a choice
and it is rather like Fowler's, at least superficially, yet le Carré ensures
that the political issues inherent in it are left insubstantial. Le Carré
concentrates on Westerby's *experience* of his indiscipline, allowing the reader
to sympathize with his confusion rather than take up its political causes.
Where Fowler undergoes a grand moral self-revelation, Westerby's
'honourable' act clarifies nothing – for himself or others – and the Circus's
view of his intervention as a blundering idiocy remains unrefuted.

Until he is shaken into disillusionment by the deaths of Frost and his
friend Luke, Westerby has hardly thought about the Western cause; his
loyalty has been to the club-like Circus fraternity, a personal loyalty centred
on Smiley. Now forced to face the competing claims on his honour and
loyalty – the Circus or Lizzie – he chooses the second alternative but le Carré
goes to considerable lengths to make his change of heart unlike Fowler's.
Westerby steps backward from commitment into frustrated confusion, not
forward into the knowledge of some greater truth. Increasingly worried
about 'truth', he is reminded of an extract from a poem by Donne, learned
at school: 'On a huge hill/Cragged and steep, Truth stands . . . ' (ch. 21),
but any such truth as Fowler arrives at eludes him. His act of
insubordination is presented as bloody-minded, angry, emotional and
impulsive, and what justifications he gives for it, in the imaginary dialogues
he conducts with Smiley, smack of hurt and a rather less grandiose guilt
that Fowler's. His rationale for his turnabout retains a sentimental and
self-pitying quality:

> He'd mention that to George one day, if they ever, over a glass, should
> get back to that sticky little matter of just why we climb the mountain. He'd
> make a point there – nothing aggressive, not rocking the boat you
> understand, sport – about the selfless and devoted way in which we sacrifice
> other people . . .
>
> . . . he thought: trouble is, sport, the paying is actually done by the other
> poor sods.

. . . he tried to imagine what they would do with Nelson: stateless, homeless,
a fish to be devoured or thrown back into the sea at will.

And what will Drake do with Lizzie – he wondered – *while that little drama
unfolds? Which particular scrapheap is she headed for this time?* (ch. 20)

Westerby is right, of course, but he is stating the obvious, the already-
known, and the fact that it strikes him only now, makes him pathetic and
deflates his almost tantrum-like realizations. Moreover, what he offers in
a spirit of altruism is clearly not quite that: Westerby is bemoaning his
own 'sacrifice', 'paying', 'homelessness' and his own 'scrapheap'
destination.

With this action, le Carré implicitly combats Greene's religious moralism
which can leave Fowler wiser and sadder, but human at last. Westerby,
equally subjective, becomes a poor little victim where Fowler attains an
almost martyred dignity. And where Pyle at least dies for a belief, grotesque
and reactionary as it is, killed to contain the murderous National Democratic
'third force' he is striving to build, Westerby is killed as an interfering
irritant. Throughout the final part of the novel, he is shown acting with
a cool, thoughtless technique interrupted by moments of breathlessness and
panic, bordering on the absurd. Lizzie calls him 'Galahad' when he turns
up at her apartment and when, later, on the boat to Po Toi, he begins,
ludicrously, to believe that some butane cylinders are about to explode,
she has to calm him with maternal kisses. Le Carré allows his ironically
'honourable' act of schoolboy adventurism no transcendent moral dignity:
a futile gesture on the part of someone who should have known better,
it kills him and fails to prevent the Kos' capture. Again, frustration is the
driving force and deflation the aim. If *The Quiet American* subordinates the
political issue of imperialist presence in Vietnam to a 'fourth force' of
confession and acceptance of guilt, *The Honourable Schoolboy* also displaces
the political, but this time, the vacancy is exposed, and no resolution,
religious or tragic or otherwise, is put in its place. In the last chapter, Sam
Collins brings the news of Westerby's death back to London, suitably
doctoring its circumstances, and the Circus personnel are led to regard
it as 'operational' and 'noble' (ch. 22). The Hong Kong Club's newsmen
are left only with gossip and rumours as to the whereabouts of Westerby
and Luke:

. . . the two men had been seen hunting together during the Hue collapse –
or was it Da Nang? – and drinking together in Saigon. Another had them
sitting side by side on the waterfront at Manila.
    'Holding hands?' the dwarf asked.
    'Worse', was the reply. (Ibid.)

Far from Fowler's discovery of 'the truth', here, the activity of myth-making
continues unabated.

There is not a trace of mythologizing, however, in *The Honourable
Schoolboy's* realism of place. Where Greene gives a stage-like, focused action,

concentrating mainly on Saigon and its environs and defining place on a severe scale of urban-provincial-rural *loci*, le Carré's action is expansive and de-centred. Greene's small-scale selectivity causes him to ignore possible supportive locations – there is no mention of the siege of Dien Bien Phu, nor of the activity in Laos contemporary with his fictional action and his cast of Vietnam characters is correspondingly limited, each one representing a social and/or moral type: the mysterious young mistress, the battle- and world-weary officer, the priest-like policeman, the cynical reporter and so on. Place is always strictly subordinate to character. In contrast, le Carré's geography is heady and vast. Like *The Quiet American*, *The Honourable Schoolboy* is set at a time of crisis and transition – the siege of Phnom Penh and the imminent collapse of Saigon are both represented – but le Carré's focus never stays still for long. The war against Karla and Moscow Centre is to be fought over a human target on the Chinese mainland, the point of entry to whom is found in Hong Kong and yet, in turn, investigation there necessitates further search in Thailand, Cambodia, Vietnam and Laos, each place directing the quest elsewhere. Part Two charts Westerby's disorientating journey beginning in Hong Kong and taking in Bangkok, Phnom Penh, Battambang, Phnom Penh again, Saigon, Xuan Loc, Saigon again, Vientiane, the Thai interior, Vientiane again, and finally back to Hong Kong and its surrounding islands. Each of these locations is precisely differentiated. Airports and flights figure prominently, giving a sense of confusion and whirl in the interim times between locations. Greene's more static approach takes the reader straight to the next setting in sharp scene-changes.

It might have been expected that Vietnam would occupy more of le Carré's action but Westerby's stay there fills no more than three of the novel's five hundred-odd pages. That expectation is deliberately avoided. If anywhere is concentrated upon besides Hong Kong it is Cambodia. A book on that country's recent history (which le Carré recommends) is entitled *Sideshow* and its author's foreword explains the choice of title in a way which, by analogy, illuminates le Carré's interest in Part Two of his novel:

> During the early seventies Cambodia was often referred to as a 'sideshow'. Journalists who covered the war there used the term with irony; in Washington some officials employed it almost as a matter of policy. It was apt enough. The main arena was Vietnam, and it was there that attention was concentrated. Cambodia was always off-stage, away from the light. Many of the decisions regarding the country were made in secret, others were presented inaccurately; inquiry was discouraged and exactly what was happening remained obscure. (Shawcross, 1980, p. 11)

Le Carré achieves a constant 'sideshow' effect in Part Two which is aided by frequent interruptive cutting back to London. The places on Westerby's journey and the characters peopling them are given a remarkable diversionary dynamic of their own, extrinsic to him and his quest for

Ricardo. Events and scenes take place around and despite him, sometimes striking him as bizarre, sometimes merely observed, sometimes barely noticed. He is conscious of his own intrusiveness at times, and at times, of his own irrelevance. Much of what he sees remains largely undigested. When, for example, he meets Major Masters at a Thai airbase with its own 'separate spook encampment', complete with its own 'compound and aerial masts' and 'little black-painted small planes' (ch. 18) he notices detail with the distance of a reporter, and that distance is suddenly enlarged when Masters sarcastically taunts his Englishness in a misplaced attempt to come to terms with the recent news of the undignified evacuation of the US Embassy in Saigon. The sense that both characters occupy quite different worlds and have utterly different concerns is immense. Westerby is out-of-place; the exchange with Masters leaves him cold. He muses distractedly for a moment on the American defeat:

> This is how they tried to win, Jerry thought: from inside soundproof rooms
> . . . This is how they lost. He drank, feeling nothing.   (Ibid.)

His thoughts veer off to Lizzie and Luke and Ricardo, unaware of the Major's presence for a time. The effect is of displacement, as it is throughout most of this section of the novel.

Earlier, in Phnom Penh, he observes his surroundings and feels more pointedly extraneous:

> There was no traffic but between the sentry posts the refugees had made up their own night villages in a long column down the pavement . . . On an ox-cart, a girl lay with a boy, children Cat's age when he last had seen her in the flesh. But from the hundreds of them not one sound came, and after he had gone a distance he actually turned and peered to make sure they were there . . . He was irrelevant here, yet somehow he had contributed to the disaster.   (ch. 15)

'Irrelevant' detail and a sense of the bizarre take over in the battle locations. When Keller, the veteran war correspondent takes Westerby and Lorraine (who was 'taking a swing through the war zones for her group of mid-Western dailies', ch. 15) to the front, they drive past a unit of Khmer Rouge, waiting to ambush a more important target behind them. The concentration is as much on the girl's fascination with their 'black pajamas' as on the threat of the situation, and, once past, the incident is left alone. Westerby is excited, but there is none of Fowler's 'I hate war' reactions to battle in le Carré's treatment – events are simply given their head.

No major character is in his or her right place in *The Honourable Schoolboy*. Either expatriate, in transit, in hiding, in exile, or separated in some other way, characters are shown not really belonging to their environments. This is most vividly imaged in multiple references to parted families, and the consequent search for substitute parents, brothers, and children brings into

play a motif already familiar from *Tinker Tailor Soldier Spy*. Westerby's
'Orphan' girlfriend reminds him 'vaguely' of his daughter Cat, 'but only
vaguely because he hadn't seen Cat for ten years, which was when his first
marriage fell in' (ch. 2). He is recalled to London by the codeword *'Guardian'*
and rumour has it that he has gone back to claim his inheritance from his
dead father, whose reputation seems always to precede Westerby's arrival
anywhere. Back at the Circus, Westerby muses on Guillam's relationship
with Smiley:

> Father and son? That kind of relationship? Brawn to brain? More exact,
> perhaps, would be a son to his adopted father, which in the trade is held
> to be the strongest tie of all.   (ch. 5)

And if Smiley is Guillam's substitute father, Drake Ko is Westerby's.
Consulting Ko's file, he is reminded 'of old Sambo' (ch. 7), his father's
nickname, and when he first sees Drake and his wife at a Hong Kong
racetrack, Mrs Ko sets off the same train of association:

> For a second Jerry was reminded of old Pet in her prime. Just the way Pet
> looked, thought Jerry, when Sambo's pride came in a good eighteenth. Just
> the way she stood, and coped with failure.   (Ibid.)

Westerby's ultimate transfer of loyalty from Smiley, 'old George' who
epitomizes the service 'he loved' (ch. 18), to Drake is prefigured when he
observes Ko at one of his regular visits to the grave of his son, Nelson,
dead at ten years of age:

> . . . he had an overwhelming feeling – only for a moment, but dangerous
> at any time – of completeness, as if he had met a family, only to discover
> it was his own. He had a feeling of arrival.   (ch. 7)

The feeling is momentary but it keeps recurring. Much later, in Lizzie's
flat he looks into Ko's 'den . . . fascinated despite himself, seeing the man
in everything, and his kinship with old Sambo' (ch. 20).

There is no portentousness in le Carré's handling of the 'crossed' family
theme – the narrative even allows space for gentle parody of it. When Smiley
visits Lizzie's ex-husband Peter Worthington, the latter's self-deluding
psychotherapeutic rationalism is amusedly patronized. Elizabeth, Smiley
is told, 'couldn't bear to say *Peter*. She loved me as a *concept*' (ch. 10) and
'couldn't bear the chains of "Mummy"'. Peter has it all workd out:

> ' . . . You have to understand basic human behavioural psychology. She
> was a text-book case. She couldn't wait to get rid of her father's name. One
> very good reason why she married me was to have a *new* father and a *new*
> name.'   (Ibid.)

Smiley listens patiently as the diagnosis continues, heavily indebted as it
is, to the Transactional Analysis of Eric Berne and Thomas Harris:

> ' . . . Her mother just wanted Elizabeth to be admired. As a substitute for
> herself, of course. It's perfectly natural, psychologically. Read Berne. Read

anyone. That's just *her* way of defining *her* individuality. Through her daughter. One must respect that those things happen. I understand all that, now. She's okay, I'm okay, the world's okay, Ian's okay, then suddenly she's off.'   (Ibid.)

Smiley, of course, is playing his own game during all this, and the conversation at this point is lightly humorous, but the theme of ulterior play, harking back to the fames of *The Looking-Glass War* and the 'crossed' transactions concerning parents, children, spouses, friends and lovers familiar in all of le Carré's fiction, has its serious side. Le Carré deepens and intensifies the parent-adult-child terminology of Transactional Analysis by using it not only in the metaphorical sense Berne and Harris prefer, but as instancing the practices of substitutive relationships which contain the residue of real relationships that existed formerly in now parted families. Worthington's absurd list of 'okays', parodying the title of Harris's book *I'm OK – You're OK* (1973), is taken up with quiet authorial glee when Westerby is later seen playing 'complicated games with the name of KO' (ch. 11), a man whose separation from his brother, son and parents has left him the reverse of OK. Yet in spite of the authorial self-consciousness here, Ko's predicament is presented as genuinely disturbing. Divorce, separation and estrangement are the norm in *The Honourable Schoolboy*. Smiley has 'dismissed his wife' (ch. 3) and even identifies with Worthington ('you never knew your Elizabeth, Smiley thought, . . . and I never knew my Ann.' ch. 10). Lizzie has left first her husband and then Ricardo for Drake who has been, so Mrs Pelling reports, 'a real father to her' (ibid.). Drake required that Lizzie change her name to Leise – the name of the orphan boys' adopted mother – and old Craw remarks in his lecture to Circus trainees how his agent Phoebe found a replacement for her dead father in the Western Cause. Charlie Marshall, to cite one last example, lives in revering, loving fear of his father, the General, who 'hate me very bad, okay?' (ch. 16) and Marshall finds his substitute in opium. The sense of loss and not-belonging remains a constant in the novel and gives it an elegiac feel.

7   The Sandman: *Smiley's People*

'Why did Valdimir call him the Sandman?' Smiley asked, knowing the answer already.

'It was his joke. A German fairy tale Vladi picked up in Estonia from one of his Kraut forebears. "Karla is our Sandman. Anyone who comes too close to him has a way of falling asleep." . . . '   (le Carré, 1980, ch. 15)

The Sandman is the dreaded father at whose hands castration is expected.   (Freud, 1955, p. 232)

With *Smiley's People*, le Carré continues the de-politicizing trend of *The Honourable Schoolboy*; in fact he takes it much further. Where the second novel of the trilogy downplayed political choice, *Smiley's People*, the third and final part of *The Quest for Karla*, excludes even the acute, topical historical observation of its predecessor. On the face of it this is not instantly apparent: from the KGB-style assassinations of White *émigrés*, the allusions to labour camps, Soviet political psychiatry and the return to the Berlin Wall crossing of the novel's finale, to the tensions between government and secret service and the assiduous descriptions of bureaucratic malfunctioning and ineptitude, the novel displays an ostensibly political world. Given its publication date, 1980, a time of recently renewed Cold War, *Smiley's People* with its striking imagery of white versus black, good against evil, might initially look like a literary salvo contributing to the upsurge of growing war fervour. However le Carré is never so crude – his imagery serves other than political purposes and he goes to considerable trouble to de-specify the political situation his narrative depicts. In direct contradiction to the history contemporary with the novel's late seventies setting, le Carré portrays a new Labour government committed to a policy of *détente* following a previous Conservative administration. The new government's instruction to cut back on Secret Service spending, to rule 'certain categories of clandestine operation . . . *ipso facto* out of bounds' and its moves towards 'open hearings' (ch. 4), all so distressful to Lacon and the Circus chiefs,

127

reflect, of course, what Nigel West has called 'the Labour Party's innate distrust of all intelligence organizations' (1982, p. 176). But le Carré seems to be employing this commonplace in order both to satirize Lacon's hysteria and to establish the themes of personal nostalgia and isolation associated throughout the novel with Smiley, whose anger at what he sees as the outrageous interference of the 'Wise Men', turns into a bitter *personal* lament at the injustice done to a former collaborator and friend. The chapter conveying the news of changed Circus policy culminates in the crescendo of his elegy to the murdered agent Vladimir, whose value Smiley alone honours. The debilitating injunctions of the 'Wise Men', so prominently surrounding Smiley's return to the Circus pay-roll early in the novel, are set up only to be later circumvented. In that process their intrinsic political content ceases to hold any real significance and they eventually come to serve at most as circumstantial plot details. The political substance of *Smiley's People* is small, and its historical reference points are general and unspecific. The novel's interest lies instead in the peculiar psychology of its principal character, and Smiley's mental and emotional states are mainly explored through the fantastic imagery of legend, folk- or fairy-tale, forms far removed from those of political discourse.

For the first time in the trilogy, Karla is associated with a new name – 'the Sandman' – and the Sandman motif generates a considerable connotative power. Hans Andersen's tale of the benevolent, child-loving, story-telling Sandman seems to be le Carré's obvious source. Andersen's soporific character is anything but a threatening presence yet in the last of the stories he tells little Hjalmar he speaks of his brother, 'the other Sandman who is called Death' (1979, p. 187). This strange introduction of 'the double' finds many echoes in le Carré's novel where Smiley and his Sandman prove to enjoy a similarly intimate connection. However, Andersen's version of the legend is subordinate, in *Smiley's People*, to its equally well-known incarnation in Hoffmann's *Tales*. Hoffmann's story of the Sandman firmly centres its attention on the wayward psychology of its leading character, Nathaniel, and it has itself been the object of distinguished psychological study.

In an article entitled 'The Uncanny' which he published in 1919, Freud addressed himself to Hoffmann's tale. It provided him with key material for his investigations into the nature and cause of uncanny feelings in literature and real life. Freud observes that 'the uncanny is that class of the frightening which leads back to what is known of old and long familiar' (1955, p. 220), and suggests that in Hoffmann's story the most important source of the uncanny sensation which is aroused there is 'the theme of the "Sand-Man" who tears out children's eyes' (p. 227). In *Smiley's People*, Vladimir has named Karla the Sandman, and although the latter is not instantly recognizable as a reincarnation of Hoffmann's figure because le Carré's allusions are unobtrusively disguised, the parallel soon becomes clear. The following resumé, paraphrased from Freud's own summary of the story, should begin to identify the extent of le Carré's borrowings from that place:

The tale begins with the childhood recollections of the student Nathaniel who cannot banish the memories associated with the mysterious and terrifying death of his beloved father. On occasion his mother would send the children to bed early, warning them that 'the Sandman was coming'; and each time Nathaniel heard the heavy tread of a visitor. When questioned, his mother denied the existence of the Sandman but Nathaniel's nurse told him the Sandman was a wicked man who throws handfuls of sand in the eyes of naughty children and then collects their bleeding eyes to feed his own grotesque offspring. One evening the boy hides in his father's study and recognizes the visitor as the lawyer Coppelius. The men are working at a brazier with glowing flames and, on hearing Coppelius call out 'Eyes here!', Nathaniel screams. Coppelius seizes him and is on the point of dropping red-hot coals into his eyes when his father's pleas save him. In the course of another of the Sandman's visits, his father is killed by an explosion and Coppelius disappears.

Now a student, Nathaniel believes he recognizes the Sandman in the itinerant optician Coppola who offers to sell him barometers and 'fine eyes!' The proferred eyes turn out to be harmless spectacles and Nathaniel, much calmed, buys a pocket spyglass from him. Here, the animated doll action begins as Nathaniel looks into Professor Spalanzani's house and spies his beautiful but motionless daughter. He falls in love with her. But Olympia is an automaton whose eyes have been put in by Coppola the Sandman. When Nathaniel surprises them Spalanzani picks up Olympia's bleeding eyes and throws them at him. Eventually recovered both from his fit of madness and a long illness, Nathaniel returns to his former fiancée and, on her suggestion, one day they climb the Town Hall tower. From the top, Nathaniel looks through Coppola's telescope and falls into a new attack of madness, trying to throw the girl off the tower. Among the people below is the lawyer Coppelius. Seeing him, Nathaniel shrieks 'Fine eyes – fine eyes!' and flings himself over the parapet. The Sandman vanishes and the story ends.   (Freud, 1955, paraphrased from pp. 227–30)

Freud explains that the fear of blindness has a sexual cause, being 'often enough a substitute for the dread of being castrated' (p. 231), and that in the story Hoffmann brings 'the anxiety about eyes into . . . intimate connection with the father's death'. The Sandman (Coppelius and Coppola in the tale) threatens eyes, sells spectacles, kills the father and 'always' appears 'as a disturber of love'. The pervasive employment in the tale of 'the phenomenon of the "double"', which appears in every shape and degree of development' (p. 234) signifies ' a doubling, dividing and interchanging of the self' but its uncanniness derives from the double 'being a creation dating back to a very early mental stage' (p. 236) which, recalled or re-encountered in the present, becomes 'a thing of terror', 'the uncanny harbinger of death'. Freud finds the dominant cause of the uncanny sensation related to this factor of recurrence and the larger part of his article is concerned with 'involuntary repetition' (p. 237) and the 'compulsion to repeat' (p. 238). *The Sandman* is structured around precisely such figures of repetition.

It would be uncanny indeed if le Carré had not either or both Hoffmann's tale or Freud's analysis of it in mind while writing *Smiley's People*. The novel is saturated with pertinent allusions and recapitulations of those Hoffmannesque features Freud scrutinizes. Le Carré's use of the material of *The Sandman* is not rigorously systematic; rather, that material serves as a pool of motifs and effects to be dipped into whenever the already-established logic of situation and character allows. What exact parallels there are remain localized. Although Freud does not comment on this feature, the beginning of *The Sandman* comprises an exchange of letters detailing Nathaniel's family history and his renewed disturbing encounter with the Sandman; Ostrakova's letters in *Smiley's People* perform a similar function. The old woman's encounter with the 'stranger' which opens le Carré's novel is immediately recognizable as just the kind of uncanny event, both strange and familiar, that Freud describes:

> Then suddenly aware of being watched, she wheeled round and peered upward at the heavily built man towering behind her.
>
> He was the only other person waiting, and indeed, at that moment, the only other person in the street. She had never spoken to him, yet his face was already familiar to her: so big, so uncertain, so sweaty. She had seen it yesterday, she had seen it the day before, and for all she knew, the day before that as well . . . (le Carré, 1980, ch. 1)

The reader has yet to learn that the 'stranger' is the agent of Karla, the Sandman, and that he threatens her with death. The 'magician' who comes to rescue her appears in the following chapter in a complementary uncanny incident, although this time, *he* is the disturber, the figure of threat. The 'boy', Willem, has been sent by the General (Vladimir) on a clandestine mission to collect secret information and is seen on a Hamburg steamer, anxiously awaiting the transfer:

> At the same instant exactly, he realized he was being watched. The woman at the railing still had her back to him and he noticed again that she had very pretty hips and legs. But her sexy little companion in the black overcoat had turned all the way round to face him, and his expression put an end to all the good feeling he had just experienced. Only once had he seen a face like that, and that was when his father lay dying in their first English home . . .
>
> All through the drive back . . . the boy saw that face before him in the wet road, wondering as the hours passed whether it was something he had merely imagined in the emotion of the handover . . . I was overstrung, he told himself. At a crucial moment, an unknown man turned round and looked at me and I hung an entire history on him, even imagining he was my dying father. (ch. 2)

The concern with faces and eyes, with dead fathers, and with erotic feelings (the latter hitherto unusual in le Carré's political thrillers) are foregrounded in *Smiley's People* just as in Hoffmann's tale.

When Smiley sees the dead body of Vladimir, his first request is to look at the murdered man's face – there is virtually nothing left of it – and the reader later learns that the old man has been shot point-blank with a soft-nosed bullet; such an assassination is typical of 'Moscow Centre', and thus of Karla. When Nathaniel discovers his father's body in *The Sandman* he finds the face 'blackened' and 'hideously distorted' (Hoffmann 1982, p. 93). Throughout the trilogy Smiley's parentage remains unspecified but if he has any father-figure, it is Vladimir; his obituary speech for the General expresses an uncharacteristic passion and reverence, much to the irritation and embarrassment of its auditors. Vladimir is the godfather to Willem and Stella's child and the death of his own father in one of Stalin's purges was the first in a train of horrifying events which culminated in his transfer of loyalty from the USSR to the British. Willem's heroic father is also dead and his memory lingers; when Stella tries to give Smiley the brush-off she insists somewhat unconvincingly that her husband has 'got over his dad being a martyr' (ch. 9). And Glikman is dead – Ostrakova's lover, and the father of their lost child Alexandra.

Where the death of the father accounts for one of le Carré's borrowings from Hoffmann, the unusual attention he pays to sexuality indicates another. The sexual lives of most of the novel's characters are included – Ostrakova, Vladimir, Willem, Tatiana, Connie, Grigoriev, and even Smiley himself. Ostrakova is attracted to her 'magician' and falls in love with him:

> He had rekindled her, and there was enough of the alley cat in him to remind her of Glikman and other men as well; she had never been particularly continent. (ch.6)

Vladimir's sexual appetite is part of his myth and Ostrakova plays at being one of his former lovers in her search for him. Willem sees men and women in sexual terms, speculating on their capacity and enjoyment in bed; he is also shown fantasizing about sleeping with Stella on his return from Hamburg. Connie's relationship with Hilary is strikingly sexual in its overtones. Smiley dwells momentarily on their 'brass double bedstead' (ch. 14), and when he mistakes a gesture of hers and moves to kiss her, she teases him, 'not *that*, you sex maniac'. For the first time Smiley is presented as a sexual being, whether lying alone in his half of his bed or 'politely' bantering with Vladimir's neighbour about being 'fancied' (ch. 7). The brothel scene and the erotic photograph of Kirov, Leipzig and Vladimir, naked with prostitutes, focuses this theme in terms of the main thriller action, as does the sexual blackmailing of Grigoriev by both Karla and Smiley in the later part of the novel.

Although most evident in the presentation of Tatiana, connections between sexuality and eyes and seeing are made throughout *Smiley's People*. Characters' eyes, spectacles, voyeurism and related images frequently appear. Ostrakova thinks lovingly of her 'magician' whose 'merry eyes' seem to contain 'a dash of magic' (ch. 1), and part of her security precautions include the installation in her apartment door of a 'fish-eye peep-hole' (ch. 18). When Willem is on his mission he recalls the General's warning to *'avoid eye contact'* (ch. 2), and Smiley's legendary habit of polishing his spectacles with his tie, familiar from the two previous novels, again figures prominently in the narrative. And alongside Hoffmann's 'eyes' motifs are equally pointed Hoffmannesque references to fire and burning. In the following extract, le Carré's narrator is allowed to indulge in an amusing extra-diegetic whimsicality on Smiley's fire-lighting, alluding *en route*, to *The Sandman*:

> And for those who like a heavy symbol, it is a matter of history that the fire, despite the fire-lighters, was all but out, since the coal consisted in great measure of damp slag, and that George Smiley had to puff at the flames to prevent it from dying, crouched on all fours for the task. Thus it might have occurred to him – though it didn't . . . that the action was exactly contrary to Lacon's jangling order to douse the flames and not to fan them. (ch. 12)

The jokey obtrusiveness of this narrative self-reflection is untypical. Perhaps it refers obliquely to the later 'burning' (blackmailing) of Grigoricv and also, possibly, to the cigarettes–matches–lighter matrix which connects Smiley with Ann, Valdimir and Karla. But more directly le Carré seems to have in mind the scene in *The Sandman* where Nathaniel witnesses Coppelius and his father at their bizarre work around the glowing brazier:

> as my old father bent down to the fire, he looked quite different! . . . He looked like Coppelius. (Hoffmann, 1982, p. 91)

Just for emphasis, le Carré prefaces Smiley's fire-lighting with a reference to his kitchen timer 'which ticked and grumbled like something from *Coppélia'*, Delibes's ballet of the girl who impersonates a doll, which of course also has its source in Hoffmann's tale.

In Freud's analysis, the figures of Nathaniel's father and Coppelius:

> represent the two opposites into which the father-image is split by his ambivalence; whereas the one threatens to blind him . . . the other, the 'good' father, intercedes for his sight. The part of the complex which is most strongly represssed, the death-wish against the 'bad' father, finds expression in the death of the 'good' father, and Coppelius is made answerable for it. (Freud, 1955, p. 232n.)

So, the divided image of the father is itself a defensive projection by the ego, pushing 'that material outward as something foreign to itself' (p. 236), creating the figure of the double as the 'thing of terror'. Le Carré uses this aspect of *The Sandman* to explore the opposite-identity complex in Smiley whose own double is Karla, the death-bringing, love-disturbing shadow-presence. Where in Hoffmann the Sandman is a metamorphic figure and one upon whom diverse interpretations are projected (the mother, the nurse, Clara and Nathaniel each offer competing views), in *Smiley's People* a similar real-unreal opposition is associated with him. At times Karla is the 'devil' or a 'priest' from some modern-day Inquisition and, in concert with these fantasies, Smiley uses his pseudonym 'Mr Angel' in one of his enquiries. The Sandman's agent Kirov seems, as far as Ostrakova is concerned, 'a giant' while his pursuer, Leipzig, appears to her as 'a magician', 'a little hobgoblin', 'a midget'. Valdimir himself suggests the wise-old-man archetype; his adherence to 'Moscow Rules' gives his speech the tantalizing quality of fairytale riddles:

> *I have two proofs . . . Tell Max that it concerns the Sandman . . . The Sandman is making a legend for a girl . . . Because the object is unique in the whole world . . . It is a treasure without a counterpart . . .* (chs. 5–15 *passim*)

Clearly such formulations suggest the unreality of Karla and his world of mysteries but at the same time Karla stands as murderer, as Haydon's recruiter and thus, too, as the corrupter behind Ann's most distressing infidelity.

Smiley sees himself as Karla's antithesis; he has done so ever since the traumatic encounter between the two men first described in *Tinker Tailor Soldier Spy*, where Karla's 'otherness', his incomprehensible fanaticism, resists Smiley's hardest attempts to apeal to something common and shared between them. *Smiley's People* charts the process by which this duality is proved incorrect. In the crucial conversation between Smiley and Connie, roughly half-way through the novel, she repeats at his request the story of the origin of Karla's Sandman name, and rehearses the old rumour of Karla's domestic past – that he had a daughter by a 'mistress' who betrayed him. Her account ends with an observation which so disturbs Smiley that he is forced to his feet in anger:

> That hag was Karla's shrine, George. And she betrayed him. Twin cities, we used to say you were, you and Karla, two halves of the same apple. George, darling, don't! Please!'
> She had stopped, and he realized that she was staring up at him in fear, that her face was somehow beneath his own; he was standing, glaring down at her. Hilary was against the wall, calling 'Stop, stop!' He was standing over her, incensed by her cheap and unjust comparison, knowing that neither Karla's methods nor Karla's absolutism were his own. He heard himself say *'No, Connie!'* and discovered that he had lifted his hands to the level of his chest, palms downward and rigid, as if he were pressing something into the ground. (ch. 15)

Smiley's wish to repress such knowledge is progressively diminished as Karla's 'humanity' is brought increasingly into play. Karla is to be induced to sacrifice his beliefs and his career in order to save the daughter who replicates many of her mother's characteristics. What the political Karla loses in plausibility by this movement, the psychological Smiley gains, as he is brought to acknowledge their shared identity:

> There are two Karlas, he reasoned, remembering again the stoic face . . .
> There is Karla the professional, so self-possessed . . . the old spy, the
> pragmatist . . .
>   And there is the other Karla, Karla of the human heart after all, of the
> one great love, the Karla flawed by humanity. (ch. 17)

From seeing Karla as double, he has then to see him as *his* double. In the
final scene of the novel where Karla crosses over to the West the process
is completed:

> an unholy vertigo seized him as the very evil he had fought against seemed
> to reach out and possess him and claim him despite his striving, calling him
> a traitor also; mocking him, yet at the same time applauding his betrayal.
> On Karla has descended the curse of Smiley's compassion; on Smiley
> the curse of Karla's fanaticism. I have destroyed him with the weapons
> I abhorred and they are his. We have crossed each other's frontiers, we are
> the no-men of this no-man's-land. (ch. 27)

Instead of the hero being defeated by the Sandman as in Hoffmann, here
the Sandman is himself defeated – and de-mystified. Nonetheless Smiley's
victory is compromised by other factors and its uncertain nature will be
considered later in this chapter.

The theme of the Karla–Smiley identity is complemented neatly in the
character of Tatiana. She is Karla's daughter, a young woman who has
been guilty of anti-Soviet behaviour and who is at present an inmate of
a special clinic in Berne run by the 'interdenominational Christian
theosophist' sisters, her very worldly warders. It is left unclear as to whether
she is a sane dissident, taking after her mother who was 'Soft on revolution
. . . Wanting the State to wither away' (ch. 15), or if her schizophrenia
is genuine. Whichever is the case, Karla is secretly attempting to find her
permanent residence in the West. It seems he loves her – she is so like her
mother – but she is also an embarrassment to him; she knows that 'Daddy
had had Mummy killed for showing insufficient faith in the historical
process' as Connie cynically explains. Tatiana lives in surreal incarceration,
sometimes acting as a wilfully naughty child and, left alone, occupying
herself with erotic fantasies. Le Carré reproduces in her classic schizophrenic
symptoms – pretence, the sense of imprisonment and the experience of a
'divided self' in which a private 'real' self hides behind a false 'compliant'
self. As R. D. Laing describes, schizophrenics habitually 'pretend' (1965,
p. 164) and le Carré uses the ambiguity inherent in the condition to increase
uncertainty about the real and the false in Tatiana's understanding of her
family history. More important, Tatiana's 'schizophrenia' contributes to
the novel's interest in doubles and division in the self. She represents an
internationalization of this theme.

Tatiana has two names – Tatiana-Alexandra – the first is her 'own', the
second her publicly assigned designation. To her, all other people seem
similarly double. Thus Mother Felicity becomes 'Felicity-Felicity' in the
language of her 'self-imposed role as child' (ch. 22):

> Which was funny because her real name was not Felicity at all; Felicity was
> what she had chosen for the other nuns. Her real name, she had told
> Alexandra as a secret, was Nadezhda, meaning 'Hope'. (Ibid.)

This implicitly takes up the doubling evident in her father's name (Smiley's
life-long opponent is 'known through Centre only by his workname Karla.
This is a woman's name . . . ' ch. 19). Karla's man Grigoriev visits her
each week, calling himself Uncle Anton:

> He was the first left-handed man she had known and sometimes, watching
> him write, she wondered whether he was a mirror image, with the real
> version of him sitting in the car behind Andreas Gertsch's barn. She thought
> what a wonderful way that would be of handling what Dr Ruedi called the
> 'divided nature' – to send one half away on a bicycle while the other half
> stayed put in the car with the red-headed woman who drove him. Felicity-
> Felicity, if you lend me your pop-pop bicycle, I will send the bad part of
> me away on it. (ch. 23)

This is not to say that Laing is here substituted for Hoffmann and Freud;
on the contary Tatiana speedily returns the reader to *The Sandman*. In accord
with her internal, introverted division she has the characteristics *both* of
Nathaniel and of the Sandman. As with Hoffmann's boy, it is ambiguous
whether she is fantasizing about the past or if she is remembering real
traumatic events. With Nathaniel, she shares the memory of a beloved
parent's death, although here, it is not a dead father but a dead mother,
apparently murdered by a father. She too is apprehensive about the
intrusions of a curious, bespectacled visitor. Like Nathaniel, she is terrified
by her nurse's threats of a grotesque punishment for her disobedient acts;
where Nathaniel's nurse tries, with only partial success, to make him believe
that the Sandman carries off naughty children's eyes 'to the half moon
to feed his children' (Freud, p. 228), Felicity warns of a like retribution
in being transported to Untersee:

> . . . Untersee became Alexandra's worst terror, a threat that silenced her
> at any time, even her naughtiest: 'If you are bad you will go to Untersee,
> Sasha. If you tease Dr Ruedi, pull up your skirt, and cross your legs at him,
> Mother Felicity will have to send you to Untersee. Hush, or they'll send
> you to Untersee.' (ch. 22)

But Tatiana is also Nathaniel's opposite and is associated with features
of the Sandman. She too threatens the destruction of eyes and, an arsonist,
recalls the Sandman's connection with fire. And, unlike the repressed
Nathaniel, her sexuality is blatant:

> Do you know I was once a whore called Tatiana? That I can do no wrong?
> That I can set fire to things, even myself . . . ? (ch. 22)

> . . . she prayed to any God that would have her that Uncle Anton might
> be run over or have a heart attack, or, best of all cease to exist . . . She

thought of his rimless spectacles and in her imagination she drove them into
his head and out the other side, taking his eyes with them, so that instead
of his soggy gaze to stare at, she would see straight through him to the world
outside.   (ch. 23)

From the foregoing, it might have been expected that le Carré would also
have incorporated in his novel allusions to the animated doll, Olympia,
which Professor Spalanzani has constructed and whose eyes Coppola has
supplied, but Tatiana carries enough weight of allusion as it stands and
this Hoffmannesque motif is left virtually unreferenced.

For Freud, the determining source of the 'uncanny' effect in *The Sandman*
is not to be found in the living doll device and the 'intellectual uncertainty'
(p. 230) which attends it and nor is it located in the figure of the double
per se. Freud isolates the factor of 'unintended recurrence of the same
situation' or 'involuntary repetition' (p. 237) as the authentic cause of the
sensation and he offers as an explanatory instance from his own life an
anecdote recalling 'one hot summer afternoon' in an Italian provincial town
where, while walking, he found himself in the prostitutes' quarter:

> Nothing but painted women were to be seen at the windows of the small
> houses, and I hastened to leave the narrow street at the next turning. But
> after having wandered about for a time . . . I suddenly found myself back
> in the same street, where my presence was now beginning to excite attention.
> I hurried away once more, only to arrive by another *detour* at the same place
> yet a third time. Now, however, a feeling overcame me which I can only
> describe as uncanny . . .   (Ibid.)

A substantial part of the material of *Smiley's People* is re-deployed from its
predecessors and a resulting sense of repetition and recommencement affects
the reader over and again. Although le Carré's recurrences are *not* in the
main 'uncanny' in Freud's sense of the term, their very presence is striking
and curious. What is odd is that the repetitions are so specific and so
insistent; they seem to ask for a response far more pointed than those evoked
by the standard generic recommencements in which, for example, the evil
antagonist is reintroduced to be outwitted once more. Nor is the return to
the familiar settings of London, Oxford and Berlin particularly remarkable
in this respect for most of the novel's locations are new. The reappearance of
characters from *Tinker Tailor Soldier Spy* and *The Honourable Schoolboy* is slightly
more relevant here but that feature is largely accepted by the reader as a
given of the Smiley series and it invites only barely attended-to gestures of
recognition on the reader's part. A sensation akin to *déjà vu* is however
compelled by the recycling of specific incidents which have been more or
less fully described beforehand. When *Smiley's People* first appeared, even
pro-le Carré critics admitted to their irritation with this device, adding to
their otherwise enthusiastic reviews reservations concerning the reintro-
duction of Smiley's unfaithful but beautiful spouse, acting as predictably
as ever. A. Alvarez confesses that 'There are, in fact, times when I find
myself wishing le Carré would marry Ann off to some appropriate creep'

(Alvarez, 3 February, 1980), while John Coleman complains of 'that tiresome running business of Lady Ann . . . One is relieved to see Smiley . . . seems to have ditched her for good this time round' (Coleman, 3 February 1980). Not only does *Smiley's People* insistently recall the permanently temporary separation of Smiley and Ann for the Nth time since *Call for the Dead*; its counterpart – the Haydon affair – is again rehearsed and, for the third time, Smiley's interview with Karla in that Delhi jail, is reintroduced for yet further consideration.

For first-time readers, of course, such material serves necessary informative functions while for devotees or fans it may offer the pleasure of familiarity, the comfort of acknowledging the already-known. However, it is not necessary to know of Freud's repetition hypothesis to deduce that le Carré's recurrences are expressive of a kind of pathology in the character of Smiley which is a principal subject of investigation in the novel. Smiley, the obsessive, relives his traumatic encounter with Karla because he cannot come to terms with Karla's difference, his otherness; Smiley's incomprehension of Karla's 'fanatic', 'awesome . . . completeness' remains to torture him. And, as suggested above, the otherness in Karla he allegedly seeks to understand, proves to be its opposite in the end; what Smiley actually resists is the suspicion that he and Karla are identical. Together with Karla, Haydon and Ann comprise Smiley's 'unfinished business' which surfaces whenever his mind wanders from the matter at hand. It is to be a compelling irony of the novel that the capitulation of Karla and Ann which finally allows him to control both characters completes that business which by its very intractability has sustained him throughout his later life. Although there are many references in the novel to Smiley ageing, it seems unlikely that le Carré is dramatizing Smiley's compulsive repetition in terms of the death wish Freud associates it with; le Carré's use of the device acts rather as a more general invitation to read Smiley 'psychologically'.

Smiley's People strikes a fine balance between the sense of stubborn repetition in its redeployed incidents and the capacity of these incidents to yield new meanings. Each time, for instance, the Karla interview intervenes, the narrative focus and perspective are slightly changed as the event is inspected yet again. When Guillam is told about it in *Tinker Tailor Soldier Spy*, Smiley relates the episode with a painful, confessional, rationalizing articulacy, concentrating on his subjective responses as he experienced them at the time; in *The Honourable Schoolboy*, a narrative voice recounts the incident in a weary, long-distance, dream-like tone which demonstrates Smiley pushing the experience away from him:

> And it was true that now and then the memory of that encounter, of Karla's unshaven face and watchful, inward eyes, came at him like an accusing spectre out of the murk of his little room, while he slept fitfully on his bunk.
> But hatred was not really an emotion he could sustain for any length of time, unless it was the obverse side of love. (le Carré, 1977, ch. 5)

In *Smiley's People*, the treatment is at greater length and this time concentrates on Smiley reliving or re-enacting the event. Now, the narrative yields new information, the peripheral, circumstantial details of Smiley's journey to meet 'Gerstmann'. A disengaged expansiveness here contrasts with the version in *Tinker Tailor Soldier Spy* which there took Smiley, 'travelled to death', straight into the 'appalling' heat of the cell in the Delhi jail (le Carré, 1974, ch. 22) and in the revised account offered in *Smiley's People* there is new material. Here Smiley's memory is allowed freer range:

> . . . he relived the rattling, honking jeep-ride to the jail, the laughing children hanging to the tailboard; he saw the ox-carts and the eternal Indian crowds, the shanties on the brown river bank. He caught the smells of dung and ever-smouldering fires – . . . (le Carré, 1980, ch. 12)

The interview proper appears now in the form of creative summary, its key components highlighted to the point of distortion as the sub-text of Smiley's conduct is pulled into foreground. Smiley re-runs the event, quickening some parts and slowing others, and his refabrication repeats the desperate plea to Karla as if it had *then* been voiced with the ritualized urgency it now assumes:

> Join us, Smiley had said to him across the iron table.
> Join us and we will give you life.
> Go home and they will give you death.
> His hands were sweating – Smiley's in the prison. The heat was dreadful.
> Have a cigarette, Smiley had said – here, use my lighter.   (Ibid.)

Where the original version of the incident dramatized confusion and panic and concentrated on Smiley's inept tactics, the second account in *The Honourable Schoolboy* featured a haunting, nagging self-accusatory quality. In this latest rehearsal, Smiley's touching, naive openness expresses the incident with the pathos of defeatism. Le Carré is fascinated by his character's continued compulsive attempt to face and digest one resistant experience on which he is hooked. The effort involved in the repeated encounter with the experience serves, however, to keep it unpalatable and its disruptive effects simply increase. The more intransigently the experience forces itself back into the character's consciousness, the more diffuse it becomes.

In his review of the novel, John Coleman suggests that 'Smiley is defined . . . by what other people say about him' more than by those recurrent physical attributions ('fat, spectacles constantly cleaned on the end of his tie, expensive, ill-fitting clothes') which 'come out of a theatrical trunk' (3 February 1980). Coleman notes also that Ann, 'a lay-figure', is used as 'part of the structuring of Smiley's character or of the Smiley-character'. One could add that Karla is too. Just as with the redeployed incidents, there is a continued reiteration of Smiley characteristics, the external reference points of the man, which have remained virtually the same since *Call for the Dead*. He is still toad-like, 'breathtakingly ordinary' in appearance, the solitary taxi-traveller, blinking, quiet and courteous. In the 'Brief

History of George Smiley' which introduced him he was described thus:

> . . . without school, parents, regiment or trade, without wealth or poverty, [he] travelled without labels in the guard's van of the social express, and soon became lost luggage, destined, when the divorce had come and gone, to remain unclaimed on the dusty shelf of yesterday's news. (le Carré, 1961, ch. 1)

Nearly twenty years later, little has changed:

> He sat without expectation. He sat like an old man at a country railway station, watching the express go by. But watching all the same. And remembering old journeys. (le Carré, 1980, ch. 4)

As Coleman remarks, reactions to him remain the same:

> . . . friends and enemies alike conspire to praise him to the skies. On Hampstead Heath, a police superintendent solemnly registers his 'legendary features'; and in book after book the same refrain crops up . . . And so it goes, wonderfully leaving him to his significant pauses, his stunning, hesitant interrogations, while the world quite talks its head off around him, at him. (3 February 1980)

Yet Smiley is more than a collection of adjectives describing his external appearance and more than a series of metaphors suggesting his lack-of-belonging. And, as already noted, he is other than these legendary features' ascribed to him, and is also experienced as a character in excess of that admirable ingenuity which is given as natural to him: it is a role he expertly plays, his ingenuity invariably suggesting a consciousness behind it, and separate from it. In each novel of the trilogy, the Smiley stereotype or caricature is set against an alternative Smiley 'personality'. He is often an external figure and, true to the thriller genre, eccentric but the narrative of *Smiley's People* investigates with the most assiduous detail so far those features of him which are, in a sense, psychologically and behaviourally typical. Smiley's 'people' are the component parts of Smiley and those individuals – Ann, Karla, and Vladimir – with and against whom he defines himself. Narratorial explanations or analyses are absent; behaviour is simply observed and recorded. The 'private' Smiley is conveyed through his repetitions.

Until Smiley and Ann are seen directly facing each other for the first time (about three quarters into this novel), the trilogy has concerned itself solely with his memories of her infidelities, in particular, her affair with Haydon. Until *Smiley's People*, Ann has appeared 'in person' just twice before, each time observed from a distance by a waiting or watching Smiley. She is frequently referred to by others who mythologize her much as they do Smiley. She is the 'beautiful' Ann, Smiley's unlikely partner, and the periodic 'How's Ann?' formula with which Smiley is so often greeted, to his unstated annoyance, runs like a leitmotif through the trilogy. Mostly, the intrusive memories of her form randomly, extraneously; intermittent recollections season the present narrative too:

I need you, thought Smiley watching [Lacon] gyrate. *I love you, I hate you, I need you.* Such apocalyptic statements reminded him of Ann when she had run out of money or love. The heart of the sentence is the subject, he thought. It is not the verb, least of all the object. It is the ego, demanding its feed. (le Carré, 1980, ch. 4)

Duty to *what*? Smiley wondered, with that part of himself which sometimes seemed to be a spectator to the rest. Loyalty to *whom*? 'There is no loyalty without betrayal,' Ann liked to tell him in their youth when he had ventured to protest at her infidelities.   (ch. 5)

Elvira returned, this time with an empty ashtray, and as she put it on the table Smiley felt a surge of tension like the sudden working of a drug. He experienced it driving sometimes, waiting for a crash that didn't happen. And he experienced it with Ann, watching her return from some supposedly innocuous engagement and knowing – simply knowing – it was not.   (ch. 10)

Such interruptions retain their earlier displacing effect yet their content does not say a great deal about either character; it is not as if the relationship develops or is substantially explained through them. Simply the fact of their (by now) expected appearance attests to the division between Smiley and Ann and to their tide-like partings and reconciliations. It is the arresting function of the recollections, their capacity to bring Smiley up short and hold him there, always mildly amazed by their obstinate quiddity, which takes the reader's main attention. Until he is shown talking with her in *Smiley's People* Ann, for Smiley, is always the same, always 'other' and always surprising. He uses the recollections to moralize, privately, against her, but that project never quite succeeds; she stays, like Karla, unmanageable and unfixable. 'Their long puzzled marriage' seems to have no dynamic; it is just *there*, a relationship of rejecting and half-forgiving conducted in botched communications:

they were a mystery to each other, and the most banal conversation could take strange, uncontrollable directions.   (le Carré, 1974, ch. 17)

Smiley's obsession with her infidelity is completely non-analytic and there is no material on the motivations behind her behaviour. Until her direct appearance in *Smiley's People*, she is a mediated fantasy presence, and, curiously perhaps, le Carré neglects to take up what looks like an ideal opportunity to explore further dimensions of the Smiley-personality through the latter's responses to her. Smiley manifests only his compulsive response of jealousy, pain and incomprehension. The private Smiley, emotionally confused and 'blocked', undergoes no psychological change, presenting himself to the reader who desires an impression of development in realist characters as discomfortingly static. His stasis, however, derives from the psychological state he embodies and not from any malfunctioning in the author's approach to characterization. Le Carré provides Smiley's stasis as pathological.

On his own in their Chelsea house, Smiley is surrounded by reminders of Ann – her grandmother clock, her indoor clothes-line, her 'things' in her desk, her magnifying glass, the Mahler record she gave him, her telephone – all questioning his tenancy. The phone rings – it is Ann – and an uneasy, silence-punctuated dialogue ensues, 'They began their conversation as strangers, much as they began their love-making' (ch. 12). Their exchange is not a game but it is full of deflections. The conversation reveals nothing new about their relationship; it merely illustrates, for the first time directly, its unsatisfactory nature. The writing of the scene betrays what seems a deliberate recalcitrance, a refusal to penetrate in depth either character's remarks or thoughts, a refusal to psychoanalyse. It stays with the familiar 'hurts', 'the list of lovers . . . Bill Haydon' and with Ann's (implied) plea 'to be together again'. The stubbornness of Smiley's habitual response to her jars as does the writing's seeming complicity with him:

> to forget Bill Haydon, the Circus traitor, whose shadow still fell across her face each time he reached for her, whose memory he carried in him like a constant pain. (ch. 12)

On it goes, with only bare traces of an independent narrative voice which refuses to warn the reader to stand back from Smiley's jealousy and sense of victimization, and offers no pointer to the fact that this time Ann is reaching for Smiley, the reverse of his diagnosis. The writing's recalcitrance shows in its apparent contentment to remain with the outer responses or with Smiley's standardized reflections – the conversation is kept on the *superficial* and disturbingly powerful surface level of similar transactions in real-life. Ann wishes Smiley to forgive, Smiley wishes her to suffer, and the narrative respects their wishes by reporting them without explanation:

> 'Where are you?' he asked.
> 'Hilda's.'
> 'I thought you were in Cornwall.'
> Hilda was a divorced woman of some speed. She lived in Kensington, not twenty minutes' walk away.
> 'So where's Hilda?' he asked when he had come to terms with this intelligence.
> 'Out.'
> 'All night?'
> 'I expect so, knowing Hilda. Unless she brings him back.'
> 'Well then I suppose you must entertain yourself as well as you can without her,' he said, but as he spoke he heard her whisper, 'George'.
> A profound and vehement fear seized hold of Smiley's heart . . . He knew – he was barely at the threshold – yet he still knew that he had been given, in late age, a chance to return to the rained-off contests of his life and play them after all. If that was so, then no Ann, no false peace, no tainted witness to his actions, should disturb his lonely quest . . .
> 'You mustn't,' he said. 'Ann? Listen. You mustn't come here. It has nothing to do with choice. It's to do with practicalities . . . (Ibid.)

Smiley's questions seem designed to punish Ann, taking satisfaction in her evening loneliness. The implied criticism of Hilda's 'fastness' is really directed at Ann. What is given as a momentous change in Smiley – recognition that he must be single-minded in his pursuit of Karla – is not that at all. His explanation, not 'choice' but 'practicalities', is an outright evasion which rejects her through its obfuscation. He enjoys this opportunity to keep her at bay because formerly most of the rejecting and leaving has been her prerogative. The 'profound and vehement fear' is the fear of emotional proximity which he is unable to handle, and always has been. Missing completely the irony in the realization that 'he had been given . . . a chance to return to the rained-off contests of his life' – Ann's call is an identical chance – he rationalizes his own punitiveness. Earlier in the conversation she has criticized Lacon's wife for leaving him, thus reversing the reaction expected of her, and Smiley, with another reversal, has appeared to condone the desertion. Now that Ann is no longer the unattainable object he wants her to be, Smiley dismisses her, putting down the phone as she pleads for meeting. The coded ulteriority of this scene is remarkably achieved, and it begins to transfer the reader's sympathies from Smiley towards Ann. Perception of their relationship changes completely; Smiley is no longer pathetic victim but cruel rejecter, former impressions of his possessing some self-awareness are severely qualified, and Ann becomes a solid figure at last. The pattern of this conversation involves the reader in a double-take; its new perspective challenges former understandings of the relationship and invites its re-evaluation. That this is accomplished through an encounter which evidently rehearses long-established practices ingeniously undermines any sense of Smiley as a developing personality.

Eventually, for the first and last time, Smiley and Ann meet face to face. The encounter takes place as a conclusion to the English action; afterwards the preparation in Berne for the finale in Berlin takes over, leaving Ann, one supposes, back in her Cornish family home, rejected for good. The Cornish setting, and Ann's background there, are treated expansively and Ann is at last placed in context. The reader is instantly reminded of the cliff-top walk related in flashback in *Tinker Tailor Soldier Spy* when Ann told him she had 'divorced' Haydon. A pathological misreader of signals then as now, Smiley took away only a warped comprehension of her announcement, resenting her inability or refusal to name Bill as her lover:

> He understood only: go back to the Circus, finish your business. It was one of a dozen ways she had of saying the same thing.   (le Carré, 1974, ch. 17)

Smiley's appearance at the house surprises everyone, including the reader. His ostensible purpose is to explain his impending absence and instruct Ann that she should not visit their London home for the time being. As soon as she greets him the recurrent comes into play:

She kissed him on the mouth, putting her fingers along the back of his neck to guide him, and Haydon's shadow fell between them like a sword. (le Carré, 1980, ch. 20)

Smiley takes refuge behind 'Haydon's shadow' and keeps her apart by neglecting to spell out the logical reason – her safety – why she should avoid Bywater Street. The ambiguity of his message allows her to think that the prohibition stems from him not wanting her which, of course, ultimately it does:

'Let me try it differently,' she proposed when they had walked a distance. 'If Bywater Street had been *in* bounds, would you have suggested that I *did* go there? Or are you telling me it's out of bounds for good?'

She stopped and gazed at him, and held him away from her, trying to read his answer. She whispered, 'For godness' sake,' and he could see the doubt, the pride, the hope in her face all at once, and wondered what she saw in his, because he himself had no knowledge of what he felt, except that he belonged nowhere near her . . . He loved her, he was indifferent to her, he observed her with the curse of detachment, but she was leaving him. If I do not know myself, he thought, how can I tell who you are? He saw the lines of age and pain and striving that their life together had put there. She was all he wanted, she was nothing, she reminded him of someone he had once known a long time ago; she was remote to him, he knew her entirely.   (ch. 20)

The Smiley presented here stands completely outside his generic persona – the winning, pudgy, charming, brilliant old eccentric. There is something chilling about him now. Even though, as ever, his perception of her provides the main focus, glimpses of an alternative perspective emerge; the real Ann comes through – not the beautiful goddess but someone herself lined and troubled. Smiley wants the concentration to be on his suffering alone – as usual – but that is not the case here for the encounter includes more than Smiley's selective, censored view of her which has until now omitted everything he needs not to acknowledge. The key statement, the key to the private Smiley that, 'he himself had no knowledge of what he felt' is meticulously demonstrated in the contradictory formulations of feeling which comprise the bulk of the extract. Their effect is giddying; their inauthenticity suggested glancingly in the self-deception of 'but she was leaving him'. Smiley retains his fantasy of knowing 'her entirely' but what he knows entirely is only his fantasy of her. His own emotional confusion disturbs him but so does his fear of resolving it and so he punishes Ann by coming to see her in order to reject her. Afterwards, when walking alone he thinks to himself, 'I am a thief of the spirit . . . Faithless, I am pursuing another man's convictions' (ibid.), and the despondency of that partial awareness is both self-tormenting and consoling.

Le Carré refuses to subject Smiley to any therapeutic learning process. Ann's ability to begin to understand Smiley's neurosis and to question him gently about his behaviour, induce only more extreme pathological reactions as Smiley retreats, a little burned perhaps, into the safe compulsion of the quest for Karla. Unable to cope with the demands of the present when they concern his feelings, Smiley takes refuge in distortive memories and the fantasy goals of the future. Although he sees himself as apart from the institution he is working for, it is his real home; itself embodying a pathological concern with retrospection and prediction. However, where for the Department there will be an authentic payoff in Karla's capture, for Smiley, finally confronting that very prospect as imminent, the realization comes that he wants anything but a defeated Karla. The realization is sudden and arresting but Smiley only expresses an understanding of part of its cause; that concerning his identification with his life-long opponent. Where Ann was a goddess and adultress prior to their Cornish meeting, Karla has been the demon 'Sandman', a black 'priest', Moriarty to Smiley's Holmes but these fantasy constructs are also in their turn belied by the reality:

> One small man, in a worker's half-length coat, with a worker's satchel slung across his little chest, walking neither fast nor slowly but walking like a man who walked a lot. One small man, his body a fraction too long for his legs, hatless despite the snow. That is all that happens, Smiley thought; one little man walks across a bridge.
> 'Is it him?' Guillam whispered. 'George, tell me! Is it Karla?'.
> *Don't come,* thought Smiley. *Shoot*, Smiley thought, talking to Karla's people, not to his own. (ch. 27)

Karla's safe crossing of the border signifies for everyone else Smiley's victory, the crowning achievement of his career, whereas it actually evaporates in an instant his *raison d'être*. He alone hears 'the ring of something metal falling on to the icy cobble' and Karla's mark of defeat in dropping the cigarette-lighter that has betokened the Smiley–Karla–Ann complex offers Smiley no satisfaction:

> It lay at the halo's very edge, tilted slightly, glinting like fool's gold on the cobble. He thought of picking it up, but somehow there seemed no point and no one else appeared to have seen it. (Ibid.)

In relinquishing the lighter, Karla hands himself over to his opponent and, as it were, returns Ann to him. These are the two objectives Smiley has believed he wanted accomplished whilst actually desiring neither. The narrative's mandatory recognition and reversal are, for Smiley, empty. The externalized objects of his obsession – the Sandman and Ann's metonymic lighter – have had their former significance removed in a matter of moments, and now that their sustaining function has ceased, Smiley is left with nothing but a hollow victory. The knowledge that he is 'cursed' with the same 'fanaticism' as Karla changes nothing; he rejects the 'triumph' of the capture, refusing to accept that it belongs to him:.

> He recited in his despair a whole list of crimes – the tortures, the killings, the endless ring of corruption – to lay upon the frail shoulders of this one

pedestrian on the bridge, but they would not stay there: he did not want these spoils, won by these methods. (Ibid.)

The Sandman is merely 'a pedestrian', and this de-mystification brings with it a collapse of the novel's obsessive good/evil imagery, now the arc-light's 'halo' is 'empty'. The inflating moral language of religion and fairytale which pervades the earlier part of the novel is discarded. But Smiley's recognition of realities, like his final rejection of Ann, leaves his condition essentially the same. He is shown taking a last look at the bridge, 'as if to establish whether anything had changed, but clearly it had not', and the novel's closing passage returns Smiley to his public, stereotype persona performing that endearing, habitual, involuntary gesture which confirms the point:

> From long habit, Smiley had taken off his spectacles and was absently polishing them on the fat end of his tie, even though he had to delve for it among the folds of his tweed coat.
> 'George, you won,' said Guillam as they walked slowly towards the car.
> 'Did I?' said Smiley. 'Yes. Yes, well I suppose I did.' (Ibid.)

The ending of the novel consigns him, once more, to regret and confusion. Le Carré's characterization of Smiley as spymaster, accomplished though that is, takes second place to the authenticity and consistency of his depiction of Smiley as neurotic.

8 Taking Sides:
The Little Drummer Girl

'I settled for the irreconcilability of the problem.' (le Carré on *The Little Drummer Girl*. Bragg, 27 March 1983. I.)

The success of Alec Guinness's characterization of George Smiley in the televised adaptations of *Tinker Tailor Soldier Spy* and *Smiley's People* induced le Carré to 'defect' from his most famous character and let the Smiley series rest – as a trilogy. In his interview with Melvyn Bragg, he explained that Guinness 'took the character away from me', and that Smiley's entry into 'the public domain' made writing him 'very difficult' (Bragg, 13 March 1983. I.)

Yet it would be an injustice to *The Quest for Karla* to view it simply as a compendium of three novels about Smiley which had been designated a trilogy by virtue of nothing more than the author's *post facto* recognition that Smiley was no longer his own. As I have suggested, the trilogy's movement from political to personal is a highly organized process, and it is not easy to see how le Carré could have recovered his more political interests in any future Smiley novels. With or without Guinness's admirable theft, the ending of *Smiley's People* leaves the impression that Smiley's story is now complete. Le Carré told Bragg almost as much himself:

'I'd like to stay as close as I can to contemporary reality. By the end of the Smiley books I'd gone too far into a private world.' (Ibid.)

The contemporary reality he chose for his next novel was the vexing problem of the Near-East. With *The Little Drummer Girl*, le Carré returns to his earlier practice of confronting characters and readers with political choices. Now departing from the overt manifestations of the Cold War, le Carré looks to its principal surrogate theatre but concentrates primarily on the more autonomous and specific issues of nationalism and nationality implied in the conflict between Israelis and Palestinians. The larger antagonism of imperialism against 'communism' remains quietly in the wings, a minor offstage point of reference. The characteristic le Carréan themes of public and private betrayal, of the liberal dilemma, of the multiple causes of commitment and motivation, are all retained – so too is the continuing investigation of the morality of espionage. To these are added a presentation of the ethics and effects of both individual and state terrorism.

The new character, through whose experience these issues are focused, is far removed from the introspective, obsessively private Smiley. Charlie – the little drummer girl – an English actress in her mid-twenties, could hardly differ more from George Smiley. Where the old man invariably manages to avoid the definitions projected on to him by others, Charlie is nothing if not a public character, defining herself by being on show for others. The novel permits her virtually no private life to speak of. It charts the complete invasion of what little privacy she possesses, an invasion which presses on to take over her personality. Charlie is particularly open to such treatment because, an actor to the core, she exhibits her feelings and attitudes as if only their display validates her. An expert Israeli intelligence unit writes, lights, directs and stage-manages Charlie's recruitment to their side, casting her as their agent in spite of, *and because of*, her previous immersion in the real-life roles of the radical. For the first time in her life, Charlie is forced into making choices that will have concrete effects in the real world (defined here as the taking and saving of lives). Like her, the reader is faced with the competing nationalisms of 'Israel' and 'Palestine' and like her, the reader is taken to attempt to evaluate both claims.

The novel of le Carré's which most resembles *The Little Drummer Girl* is *A Small Town in Germany*: the resemblance lies in the attention to history. Both invoke and discover a larger history through the analysis of a limited and contemporary present. In *A Small Town in Germany*, one week in Bonn proves to be the reverberation and culmination of an action that began thirty or so years beforehand in the more resonant context of World War Two: in *The Little Drummer Girl*, the search for a Palestinian-led terrorist group in Europe at a time when an Israeli assault into the Lebanon seems imminent, calls up the forty-odd-year fortunes of the two nationalities involved. Le Carré's desire to stay close to contemporary reality with his new novel immediately comes up against a problem which he ingeniously incorporates into its action. The problem is that, for most Western readers, the Near-East question seems remote by comparison with either the two Cold Wars or the Nazi past, which are so firmly scored in Western consciousness as to require virtually no pedagogical description. Significantly, the characters of *A Small Town in Germany* seek to block out their knowledge of the past for reasons of political contingency and it is that grotesque project that the novel's 'heroes' challenge. But it is a great irony that the history of the Near-East is comparatively vague for Western readers and is accordingly in need of explication in le Carré's novel, even though its roots lie firmly in exactly the same historical circumstances that *A Small Town in Germany* intersects.

The Little Drummer Girl requests that its readers recall this history, and the novel supplements and reinforces what it assumes to be a hazy knowledge with further information and definition provided by characters speaking for both sides. It quickly becomes useful to the reader, even necessary,

to be aware, for example, that Zionism became a mass movement primarily
as a result of the German events of the early thirties, and that, at the end
of the war, it was British camps in Cyprus that forcibly prevented the
survivors of the Nazi persecution emigrating to join their fellow Jews already
settled as a nation in all but name in the territory of Palestine. Frequent
speeches in the novel, from both Israeli and Palestinian characters refer
to the Western responsibility for the problem and to those Western reactions
to it which assume no responsibility at all. 'Western', for le Carré, is a
national rather than a class designation, as if he sees that the entire
populations of Britain, the United States and Germany, should participate
in collective self-recrimination. Certainly, Western governments were
heavily involved. British forces attempted to stop further emigration into
Palestine because of the costs of maintaining a substantial army there to
'police' the mutually fearful groupings. This policy was only to be reversed
because the problem of what then to do with 100,000 dispersed Jews
remained, and neither President Truman nor Prime Minister Attlee wanted
to offer them homes in either the USA or Britain. Attlee's single remaining
option was to withdraw completely from the Mandate of Palestine. The
political vacuum that was instantly created led to the Arab–Israel War of
1948 in which the Palestinian Arabs were the only outright losers. The
leaders of Egypt, Syria, Iraq and what was to become Jordan fought for
their own political and territorial ambitions, some secretly compromising
with Israeli leaders, and a new diaspora began – that of the Palestinian Arab
population.

Apart from the necessity of giving the reader sufficient historical
information to invite a more than stereotyped understanding of the political
motivations of both sides, le Carré's main narrative difficulty is to find
a way of presenting the issue through Western eyes while retaining both
a sense of spectating as a foreigner and a sense of Western 'conscience',
of complicity in the problem. The character of Charlie provides the solution.
As an English actress, recruited to play a fictional part, she participates
from a distance; as a confused and guilt-ridden radical-liberal, she has mixed
feelings of sympathy for both sides and, whatever her former abstract
romanticized loyalties, she will swing in the direction of the side that is
able at any point to exert the most powerful moral pressure upon her.
Although she is in many ways an idiosyncratic character, she also is
required, in the first instance, to 'stand for' a more generalized perception:

> It had to be a Westerner . . . I mind first my own feelings about it which
> are simply that there is a terrible historical irony in the fact that, because
> very properly and far too late, the Jews engaged our Western conscience,
> we gave them a country which was not ours to give, and we, in fact, obliged
> the Palestinians to pay the price for the Western conscience. It was not the
> Palestinians who persecuted the Jews – it was us . . . us Brits for not letting
> them in, it was the Americans for not letting them in, it was a whole mucky
> Western conspiracy, of which the Germans were the spearhead. (Bragg,
> 27 March 1983. I.)

> But Israel was a confused abstraction for her, engaging both her
> protectiveness and her hostility. She had never supposed for one second that
> it would ever get up and come to face her in the flesh.   (le Carré, 1983, ch. 6)

Charlie feels guilt for the treatment of both Jews and Palestinians and the
narrative forces her into a position where she has the opportunity to partake
of both experiences in reality. Israel and Palestine alike 'get up and come
to face her in reality' in the course of the novel. Yet the sense of distance
remains. Le Carré employs a metaphor which has many functions in the
narrative but which, above all, signifies the semi-reality of the events of
the Near-East for a Western audience: 'the theatre of the real' (ch. 12 and
passim), suggests simultaneous engagement and detachment, identification
and separation, and the paradox of the very notion of a 'theatre of the
real' gives the historical referentiality of this novel an uneasy elusiveness
that is absent from the history of *A Small Town in Germany*. Charlie's role
as an Israeli secret agent is the most demanding part she has ever played
and it causes an all-out assault on her hitherto inchoate mixture of leftist
perceptions and opinions.

Not since Liz in *The Spy Who Came in from the Cold* had le Carré portrayed
an open, professing leftist: Karla, Haydon and Nelson Ko inhabit a different
realm altogether – a secret world of resistant, opaque commitment which
refuses dissection, however many attempts are made on it. The poor,
imprisoned Tatiana in *Smiley's People* was possibly, like her mother, a
victimized leftist but, of course, her status is completely ambiguous – perhaps
instead she was a would-be counter-revolutionary, or merely an adolescent
rebel, or genuinely unbalanced. Tatiana bears some faint resemblance to
Liz and Charlie, but she too belongs to a different order. Like Liz, Charlie
is a young woman who is idealistic and unworked-out. Like Liz, she steps
through the looking glass into a grotesque and dangerous reality which
threatens to destroy her as the price of the knowledge it gives. Like Liz,
Charlie falls in love with a man who is her political antithesis and rescues
him morally: Leamas refuses to cross back over the Wall and, here, Gadi
turns his back on Israeli Intelligence. It would be wrong to see le Carré's
attraction to the figure of a young female radical who has the capacity to
save but who is almost culpably ignorant as cut-and-dried gender
stereotyping. Charlie and Liz are, in many respects, socially recognizable
and if they are contrasted with the comparatively rigid fanatic or inspired
men around them, they also stand in opposition to equally powerful women.
Where Liz has to face the imposing female Tribunal President, Charlie
is brought up against Rachel and Rose (on the Israeli side) and Helga and
Fatmeh (on the Palestinian side). These women are finely differentiated
characters, each with her own carefully drawn personality. Rachel is sexy,
unpretentious and homely, quite calm and matter-of-fact with Charlie, even
when she describes the acute distress she experienced as a Jewish child in
'the unhappiest place on earth' (ch. 7) – not a city ghetto but plain, provincial
Macclesfield. Rose, the South African, is, by comparison, quiet, efficient

and, herself torn between two competing loyalties, acts out a more distanced sympathy. The German terrorist Helga, intelligent, urgent, calculating, barely suppressing a suspiciously manic streak, contrasts, in her turn, with Fatmeh (the sister of Salim and Khalil) who possesses a radiant strength and is simply bewildered by Charlie's involvement in her struggle and with her people. All these female characters nonetheless challenge and patronize – either explicitly or implicitly – Charlie's naiveté and insecurity from positions of uncompromising commitment. What le Carré needs most in his central character is a plausibly confused sense of conscience and a correspondingly plausible flexibility.

In terms of their political beliefs though, Liz and Charlie part ways. They are both, it is true, somewhere at the left end of a scale of liberalism: both wish more to 'do good' than fight in the class struggle and both find themselves disturbed with the kinds of political discourse and behaviour which their decent moral impulses push them into contact with. But Liz's membership of the British Communist Party of the early sixties is more readily convincing than Charlie's rather more chaotic collection of sympathies. Liz represents the petit-bourgeois social milieu from which the Communist Party draws (in real life) a portion of its membership and if she dislikes selling papers outside factory gates and is saddened by the self-bolstering white lies of her comrades, her enthusiasm for Peace Work and her desire for community accord completely with one familiar image of Communist Party membership. Her sense of history and her problems with the discipline of 'democratic centralism', her idealism and her charm, are all consistent with each other in psychological terms and if, like Charlie, she seeks to disregard or rationalize the contradictions involved in her allegiance, unlike with Charlie, the terms of her allegiance are clear.

Charlie's politics, on the other hand, are far more amorphous, her political sympathies more multiple and more contradictory and it might look initially as if le Carré had not been quite certain himself what kind of political sector he wished Charlie to stand for. In some of her activities she seems too involved to be faddish, at other times too faddish to have ever become involved in the first place. As a pro-Palestinian actress she calls to mind the Workers Revolutionary Party and her nickname, 'Charlie the Red' . . . 'in deference to the colour of her hair and to her somewhat crazy radical stances' (ch. 3), points the reader in a similar direction. Perhaps 'Charlie the *Rad*' is more apposite however, for her reading matter (mostly *unread*), Guevara, Debray, Marcuse and Fanon, together with her allegedly 'liberated' life-style suggests more the politics of the late-sixties New Left than ostensible Trotskyism. The weekend schools for revolutionaries on Colonialism and Imperialism which she has attended with her companion Al, look like an amalgam of public Solidarity meetings, 'Trotskyist' educationals, free-love gatherings and urban guerilla training camps. Superimposed on top of these are her feminism, her pacifism and her relationship with the anarchist Al, who, ironically, humiliates her with extreme chauvinism in public and private alike. When her theatrical agent,

Ned Quilley, is probed by the Israeli team on the subject of her political past, le Carré's satire becomes obvious:

> As to her politics or whatever one wished to call them, he said . . . Charlie had been a passionate opponent of apartheid – 'Well, one can't fault that, can one?' (though they seemed to think one could) – a militant pacifist, a Sufist, a nuclear marcher, an anti-vivisectionist, and until she went back to smoking again, a champion of campaigns to eliminate tobacco from theatres and on the public underground.   (ch. 4)

Le Carré is undoubtedly taking pleasure in Charlie's fifty-seven varieties of radicalism (and this the reader happily shares) but, at the same time he manages to keep the balance between a satire verging on caricature and a sense that Charlie is both genuinely impelled to protest injustices and that her indiscriminate, changeable, contradictory positions originate in a credible political confusion. Le Carré told Bragg that 'She has loyalty in her pocket like loose change and [the Israelis] tell her how to spend it' (13 March 1981, I.). She is particularly open to such manipulation because the contradictions and confusions in her 'loyalty' make perfect material for her captors to work upon. In an appropriate comparison, le Carré speaks of Charlie's recruitment as resembling Patty Hearst's conversion, 'from, one assumes, a spoilt little millionairess into a radical fighter' (ibid.), and the analogy is judicious. What Patty Hearst accepted in the short-lived Symbionese Liberation Army was, almost incredibly, precisely such a mélange of political attitudes and tactics that Charlie is on the verge of espousing in her pre-Israeli life. The bizarre SLA group combined terrorism, a New Left rhetoric and rebellious mysticism, describing their programme as an intention to destroy 'all forms of racism, sexism, ageism, capitalism, fascism, individualism, possessiveness, and competetiveness' (quoted *New York Times* 23 February 74), positions rather close to Charlie's own. And their professed mentors, Fanon, Debray, Mao, Cleaver and Reich, are remarkably similar to hers too. The SLA is usefully recalled here not simply because its composite politics resemble Charlie's, nor because it provides a real-life source for her but, more important, because it exemplifies a dynamic of radical-liberalism which has been taken to its extreme, to its logical conclusion. The *The Little Drummer Girl* deals with terrorism as an extension of more conventional political positions (on the liberal-left and the right) and le Carré's satire on Charlie's political promiscuity is part of the novel's more serious investigation of this phenomenon. As in previous novels, the ideology of liberalism is again placed under le Carré's microscope for analysis. The liberalism in question here is the kind that has rejected the possibility of peaceful, reformist solutions to social injustices but has not taken account of orthodox Marxist alternatives.

Charlie herself has little time for political categories; she sees herself as *'subversive'* as though that were sufficient explanation alone. The entry of Joseph-Gadi into her life begins the dissection of her incoherences.

Immediately, Gadi exposes her declaration as pretentious:

> 'But whom are you subverting, Charlie?' he protested earnestly. 'You strike
> me as a most orthodox person, actually.'   (ch. 3)

Wisely, she backs away from the accusation. Her fellow actors, the 'family'
on holiday with her, are as naive as she is in their understanding of her.
Pauly explains to Joseph that Charlie's anti-man mood:

> wasn't personal . . . it was political – her bloody mother was a sort of witless
> conformist, and her father was this incredible crook, he said.   (Ibid.)

Unconsciously refuting his own analysis and in the process recapitulating
Charlie's fiction about her past, Pauly opens himself to Joseph's almost
gleeful, benign contempt. Joseph is in a different league altogether and
so too is his boss, Kurtz, whose later interrogation of Charlie cuts through
her lies, her rationalizations, her postures and her illogicalities with a
composed, insistent clarity:

> ' . . . The whole system is crap! It's fixed, it's corrupt, it's paternalistic, it's – '
>   'Then why don't you destroy it?' Kurtz enquired perfectly pleasantly.
> 'Why don't you blow it up and shoot every policeman who tries to stop
> you, and for that matter every policeman who doesn't. Why don't you blow
> up colonialists and imperialists wherever you find them? Where's your
> vaunted integrity suddenly? What's gone wrong?'
>   'I don't want to blow anything up! I want peace! I want people to be
> free!' she insisted, scurrying desperately for her one safe tenet.
>   But Kurtz seemed not to hear her: 'You disappoint me, Charlie. All of
> a sudden you lack consistency . . .'   (ch. 7)

Taking up Gadi's earlier remark about Charlie's orthodoxy, Kurtz locates
her (to her intense irritation) in a general tradition of dissent, beginning
with what he calls the 'classic anarchism' of 'the eighteenth century':

> 'Namely, a revulsion against regimentation. Namely, a conviction that
> government is evil, *ergo* the nation state is evil, an awareness that the two
> together contradict the natural growth and freedom of the individual. You
> add to this certain modern postures. Such as a revulsion against boredom,
> against prosperity, against what I believe is known as the air-conditioned
> misery of Western capitalism. And you remind yourself of the genuine misery
> of three-quarters of the earth's population. Yes, Charlie? You want to quarrel
> with that? Or shall we take the "Oh balls" for granted this time?'   (Ibid.)

Kurtz insists that individual terrorism is implicit in her position. The Israelis
have picked Charlie out because she is stuck at that point where her concern
for the oppressed is in conflict with the terrorist methods the oppressed
have had recourse to. Her attendance at the revolutionaries' weekend schools
where meetings have been addressed by Bolivian, Irish and Palestinian
nationalists has been in part due to her tag-along relationship with Al but
it is not politically accidental nevertheless. She tries to cover up the extent

of her involvement in these meetings but Kurtz not only has photocopies of the cheques she donated, he also knows the content of her own verbal contributions to the discussions that took place. Her evasions stem from embarrassment and the desire for privacy but also from a rather guilty recognition that in supporting the Liberation Movements she has betrayed her pacifism. She is kept on the hook of the contradiction which is where Kurtz – and le Carré – want her.

Charlie is made to submit to the indignity of having her attitudes exposed but the process does not end there; Kurtz goes on to explain her 'ingenious fiction', her concocted family history, as the product of her guilt over her privileged upbringing. His gently devastating psychoanalysis is as patronizing and irrefutable as his political surgery:

> 'We're your friends, Charlie. Do you think we would ever blame you
> for such a thing? Do you think we do not understand that your politics
> are the externalisation of a search for dimensions and responses not supplied
> to you when you most needed them? We're your *friends*, Charlie . . .'
> (Ibid.)

Conversion is not Kurtz's objective. He wants Charlie's confusions out in the open but unresolved in order that she will play her part as a double agent with a conviction that derives from the fact that her initial sympathies for the Palestinians have been left intact. She has to be recruited to *both* sides and this is accomplished not by winning her politically to the Zionist position but by putting an overwhelming pressure upon her which answers needs in her nature. Charlie is only partly an Israeli victim: she invites their attention by wanting to belong to any family that will have her. As Julie Diamond puts it in her review article, 'She woos her captors; she participates in the theft of herself' (1984, p. 36). Just as Charlie's composite politics contribute to her transformation into an Israeli agent, her personal impulses – choosing to fall in love, wanting to play a star role, seeking a home, needing a discipline – all make her a willing victim:

> They wanted her. They knew her through and through: they knew her
> fragility and her plurality. And they still wanted her. They had stolen her
> in order to rescue her. After all her drifting, their straight line. After all
> her guilt and concealment, their acceptance. After all her words, their action,
> their abstemiousness, their clear-eyed zeal, their authenticity, their true
> allegiance, to fill the emptiness that had yawned and screamed inside her
> like a bored demon ever since she could remember. She was a featherweight,
> caught in a swirling storm, but suddenly, to her amazed relief, theirs was
> the commanding wind.   (Ibid.)

There is no substantial political content in this reaction; she has no more political commitment and understanding than she had beforehand – her 'conversion' is religious, she feels saved. In the character of Charlie, le Carré condenses those other, non-political impulses that might typically propel the individual into political action.

Charlie finds provisional definition through the roles she adopts and le Carré neatly makes full use of her being an actress. Ned Quilley tries to shake off the intrusive questions of Kurtz and Litvak about Charlie's politics by stating what he knows to be a self-evident truth:

> 'Dash it all, she's an *actress*! Don't take her so seriously. Actors don't have *opinions*, my dear chap, still less do actresses. They have moods. Fads. Poses. Twenty-four-hour passions. There's a lot wrong with the world, dammit. Actors are absolute suckers for dramatic solutions . . .'   (ch. 4)

Quilley's dismissive platitudes might well have served a more generic writer than le Carré as sufficient explanation for Charlie's subsequent behaviour but the narrative of *The Little Drummer Girl* takes the idea much further, allowing a sophisticated cross-reference between Charlie's dramatic roles and the parts she has to play in the novel's reality. Clearly le Carré has in mind Brecht's *Mother Courage and her Children* which furnishes many parallels for his novel. Implicitly Charlie is compared with dumb Kattrin, Brecht's abused innocent who drums out her rooftop warning to save the children of a threatened town at the climax of the play. Kattrin's act, ambiguously motivated in a mixture of sentimentality and compassion is also a political expression of non-political feelings. Brecht ensures Kattrin's act assumes heroic dimensions as she suffers death for her pains, but all the same, it is a heroism which changes nothing. The meaninglessness of the Thirty Years War, its indistinguishable Protestant and Catholic armies, and the futility of taking sides in such a conflict, all reverberate in the situations Charlie faces in *The Little Drummer Girl*. But le Carré chooses not to pursue his Brecht parallel openly, avoiding the obvious temptation to have had Charlie play Kattrin (or Courage herself) in her theatrical career. Instead, le Carré fixes on Shaw and Shakespeare for comparison.

In his interview with Bragg, le Carré described the relationship between Charlie and Gadi as 'Pygmalion', and Shaw's *Saint Joan* is heavily featured in the novel. The seduction of Charlie begins while she is starring in this role as a member of a small-time repertory group. 'Michel' (Gadi) sees her performance and seems to fall for her. Like Eliza Doolittle, Joan undergoes a remarkable transfiguration, and Charlie suggests both Liza in being coached into change and Joan in being 'called'. Again, all these female characters are innocents. Gadi tells Charlie that *Saint Joan* is 'one of my favourite plays. I am sure that not a year passes without my rereading the Introduction . . . ' (ch. 3), and in the Israeli script 'Michel' identifies Charlie with Shaw's heroine:

> '. . . She was a true revolutionary, who lit the flame of freedom for the exploited peoples of the world. She turned slaves into heroes. That is the sum of his critical analysis. The voice of God addressing her is no more than her own revolutionary conscience urging her to resist the colonialist . . .'   (ch. 10)

'Michel's' critical analysis is less than finely tuned but his persistent identification of Charlie with Joan certainly appeals to Charlie's ideas about herself. In the 'Introduction' that 'Michel' is so fond of, Shaw writes of Joan's 'unbounded and quite unconcealed contempt for official opinion, judgment and authority' (1926, p. vi) and describes her 'Feminist' genius 'in the traditional masculine departments' of 'soldiering and politics' (p. x). Perhaps le Carré is stretching the comparison a little too far in giving his heroine what Gadi thinks is 'a boy's name' (ch. 3) but some of Joan's other characteristics, her 'innocence' and preference for simple, direct, world-shaking solutions based on the force of conviction alone, make for a close parallel:

> She thought political changes much easier than they are, and, like Mahomet in his innocence of any world but the tribal world, wrote letters to kings calling on them to make millenial rearrangements. Consequently it was only in enterprises that were really simple and compassable by swift physical force . . . that she was successful. (Shaw, 1926, xxvi)

But of course Charlie is not Joan, her convictions are poses, her genius is not in leading but in being manipulated, and her motives are not singular but multiple – even her sexuality contrasts with Joan's chastity. In the theatre of the real she is to act as Joan's antithesis. Long before she meets Khalil she daydreams the headlines which sum up her difference: '"FAMOUS FANTASIST MEETS REALITY." "JOAN OF ARC BURNS PALESTINIAN ACTIVIST."' (ch. 10). She is the little drummer girl to Joan's General and her victories involve her not in principled martyrdom but squalid betrayal.

Yet Charlie's forthcoming role as Rosalind in *As You Like It* is nearer the mark. This time Gadi (playing 'Joseph' playing 'Michel') shows a sounder critical sense:

> 'She is so many people under one hat, I would say. Watching her unfold throughout the play, one has the impression of a person occupied by a whole regiment of contrasting characters. She is good, she is wise, she is forfeit somehow, she sees too much, she has even a sense of social duty. I would say that you were well cast for this part, Charlie.' (ch. 3)

It is with Rosalind in mind that Charlie's masculine name finds a more productive function. Rosalind's temporary disguise as a military man – 'a swashing and martial outside,/As many other mannish cowards have' (Shakespeare, 1975, I, iii, 116–7) – gives her a new freedom to remain in greater control of experience and it allows her also to re-evaluate her strengths and weaknesses and to try out new definitions of her identity. Gadi is right when he describes her occupation by 'a whole regiment of contrasting characters' – her flexibility, like Charlie's, is both creative in giving her the space she needs, and limiting, because authentic solutions lie in the discovery of a lasting personality beyond disguise and the provisional identities and roles it offers. And just as in *As you Like It* the assumption of disguise brings with it the risk of putting on an image which is self-glamorizing, and, in the terms of the play, 'affected', so Charlie runs a similar risk, a risk perhaps even more dangerous for her in that from the start she has been guilty of affectation – her faddish, romantic, pretentious politics provide a far more feeble base from which to depart into self-discovery. Like Rosalind, Charlie is 'forfeit somehow', forced into choice, induced (albeit with some willingness) to give herself over to forces outside her in order to face what she is. For Charlie too, role-playing eventually breaks down as a legitimate mode of behaviour and at the end of *The Little Drummer Girl*, she is seen quitting the stage in mid-performance as the female lead in a 'lousy' modern domestic farce. Charlie's conclusion is not a comic one like Rosalind's and nor does it suggest any tragic release; all she learns is that her former self is 'dead' and that, in 'the theatre of the real . . . the bodies didn't get up and walk away' (ch. 27). She walks out of the novel, arm in arm with Gadi, 'Locked together . . . awkwardly . . . ', in a sour parody of the celebratory weddings and dancing of Shakespeare's romantic comedy.

Kurtz's selection of Charlie as his double agent is explained as deriving from the fact that she can be made to see the Israelis and the Palestinians as equally attractive alternatives. The equilibrium in her sympathies is never seen in perfect balance – she inclines, in turn, towards one or the other, falling for the side which is exerting the most pressure at any given moment. This device obviously aids le Carré in presenting the two sides as equally deserving of the reader's political interest in addition to what it enables the reader to learn of Charlie's psychology. When 'Michel' tells her of his background and beliefs, she has to be shown as capable of being won over by his passion even though 'Michel' is Gadi, the Israeli agent, impersonating Salim, creating him. For Kurtz's purposes, she must seem as much as possible to have been converted by Salim and for le Carré's, the more convincingly Gadi plays 'Michel's' part, the more the voice of the Palestinian cause can engage in debate the Israeli counter-position. Le Carré's narrative is extremely successful in ensuring that the reader, with Charlie, periodically 'forgets' that Michel's voice is an Israeli fiction.

If for no other reason than the sake of plausibility, the device of Charlie's double focus needs a complementary mechanism in the character of Gadi. At the very least, he must be a good actor, and so he is, but le Carré invents a similarly see-sawing ambivalence in Gadi to explain, *politically*, his expertise in the role of Michel. In formal terms, then, the characters of Charlie and Gadi are made to parallel each other. Kurtz chooses Gadi as Charlie's co-star, coach and director-on-location because his sympathies, mirroring hers, are in the process of moving away from loyal Zionism and more in the direction of understanding his Palestinian adversaries. The process is not one of gradual evolution: Gadi also intermittently tilts towards and away from the Israeli position. He is a *sabra* (born in Israel), who has chosen to live abroad, retiring from military service and separating from his wife Frankie in Jersualem. Kurtz wants him for the team, 'Because he is in the middle ground . . . Because he has the reluctance that can make the bridge . . . ' (ch. 2). The narrative gives Gadi little space for introspection but there are telling moments when he is caught thinking about himself. Following a telephone conversation with Kurtz, he catches sight of his reflection in the mirror and the image is acutely distasteful:

Who the hell are you? . . . *What do you feel?* He drew closer to the mirror. I *feel* as if I am looking at a dead friend, hoping he will come alive. I *feel* as if I am searching for my old hopes in someone else, without success. I *feel* that I am an actor, as you are, surrounding myself with versions of my identity because the original somehow went missing along the road. But in truth I feel nothing . . .   (ch. 10)

On the road Charlie is taking, she meets Gadi coming back. The motif of the mirror reappears in slightly altered form when, at the beginning of Part Two, Charlie decides (erroneously, as it happens), that she understands herself and the world, that she has been given access to a knowledge which makes things coherent and substantial:

Then slowly, as time dragged by, her fear of exposure gave way to an affectionate disrespect for the innocents around her who failed to see what was shoved under their noses every day. They are where I came from, she thought. They are me before I walked through the looking-glass.   (ch. 16)

Her new sense of identity is in reality just a more powerful 'version', and, as such, it corresponds with Gadi's fractured sense of self.

As Gadi–Joseph enters increasingly into the part of Michel, he more and more loses grasp of who he is. The character of Michel takes over, but not completely, and his dialogue reveals a barely noticed slippage of character in which the boundaries separating Gadi from Joseph and Joseph from Michel lose definition:

''' . . . Do it for my great brother. Are your vows meaningless? Were you merely mouthing Western hypocrisies when you professed yourself a revolutionary?''' He paused once more. 'Do it because if you don't, your life will be even emptier than it was before I picked you up at the beach.'
'You mean the theatre,' she corrected him.
He barely bothered with her. He remained standing with his back to her, his gaze still upon the Mercedes. He was Joseph again . . .   (ch. 12)

His various identities allow him to take 'refuge' in whichever is the easiest role whenever one of Charlie's remarks or questions comes too close. All the same, he reveals his real family background to her and, just before she is about to embark on the last and most dangerous part of her mission which will take her to Khalil, he tries to dissuade her from continuing. As Kurtz knows, Joseph's acknowledgment of his concern for her will have the reverse of its intended effect. Towards the end of the novel, Gadi has free time while Charlie is ensconced in the Palestinian refugee camp and he makes a strange, wandering pilgrimage – to his father's grave in Tel Aviv, to Hebron-El Khalil where he chats to admiring Israeli soldiers and, 'in Arabic', to a shopkeeper; from there, he visits the village 'where Michel's family had lived until '67' (ch. 22) and on through Arab towns and Israeli settlements on the Lebanese border. He works for a couple of days on his old kibbutz, where he is regarded 'as if he were some kind of prophet' and listens to questions he cannot answer about Israel's future. He is seen alone, in the evening, at the camp perimeter, with 'a light side and a dark side because of the setting sun' and, the following day, he walks round Jerusalem, watching the 'decent American' tourists, and, finally:

> he spent a whole afternoon in the Holocaust Museum, worrying over the photographs of children who would have been his age if they had lived. (Ibid.)

Kurtz angrily recalls him to work, cutting short his leave. Gadi's affecting journey of conscience illustrates well the ambivalent politics which are fundamental to the novel. *The Little Drummer Girl*'s major point-of-view is Charlie's but the ambiguity of Gadi's vision neatly interlocks with her 'ambivalent perception'; 'I was determined,' says le Carré, 'to balance the story as perfectly as I knew how' (Bragg, 27 March 1983. I.).

The balance between Charlie and Gadi co-exists alongside that between Kurtz, the Israeli counter-terrorist and his quarry, Khalil. Of course, le Carré is much taken with the notion of the identity of opposites and, here, Kurtz and Khalil share more than their recourse to the means of terrorism. Both men enjoy a reputation of majestic success and both are aware of their own personal charisma; both are fully committed to their respective causes and it is a new departure for le Carré to explore the motives of characters who could well have been presented as Karla-like fanatics, with empathy and straightforwardness. What commitment means in the world of action is not a simple matter, however, and both characters know that, in the theatre of the real, the complexities of duplicity, role-playing, disguise and the reactions elicited best by illusion, are part and parcel of the business of their attaining their clear political goals. For both, the ambiguity suggested in acting – the dual sense of acting as 'doing' and acting as a performance – necessitates a way of proceeding which attempts to 'direct' both events and responses to them. Kurtz prepares Charlie for her most demanding role to date, and acts out his own part in that preparation, while Khalil too consciously emphasizes the parallel between the terrorist act and the effects normally produced in the theatre. 'Are you nervous in the theatre?' he asks Charlie just prior to her first mission to plant one of his infamously crude bombs; she replies, 'Yes,' and he comments:

> 'It is the same. Terror is theatre. We inspire, we frighten, we awaken indignation, anger, love. We enlighten. The theatre also. The guerilla is the great actor of the world.' (ch. 25)

The main action of *The Little Drummer Girl* concludes with the theatrical invasion of Khalil's 'safe house' by a gun-blazing Israeli, the heroic rescuer of countless melodramas who enters on cue, at the last climactic minute, in accordance with Kurtz's shooting script.

The brutality of both commanders is handled so as to move the reader's sympathies away from Kurtz and towards Khalil during the course of the novel. In a nice opposition, Khalil is at first presented as the director of an inhuman villainy with Kurtz as his comparatively humane counterpart. Through the reader's growing acquaintance with Khalil, that feeling is reversed, with Kurtz as villain and Khalil as his eventually martyred victim. At the outset, Kurtz's motives are given as those of a man who loves not only Israel and survival, but 'peace' and 'moderation' as well (ch. 2). For some time, the novel invites its readers to accept his use of small-scale terrorist methods as preferable (!) to the impulses towards cataclysmic state terror which are again becoming realized in the policy of the government which employs him:

> If we don't take the enemy from inside his own camp, those clowns in the Knesset and Defence will blow up the whole of civilization in their hunt for him. (ch. 2)

The reader is asked to concur with him, and Kurtz's traditionalism, individualism and his aura of intelligence and culture, work to support the reader's view of him as an authentically principled, decent, 'moderate', and therefore, attractive, character:

> He was not a sabra; he lacked the élitist background from the kibbutzim, the universities and the crack regiments that, to his dismay, increasingly supplied the narrowing aristocracy of his service. He was out of tune with their polygraphs, their computers and their ever-growing faith in American-style power-plays, applied psychology and crisis management. He loved the diaspora and made it his speciality at a time when most Israelis were zealously and self-consciously refurbishing their identity as Orientals.   (Ibid.)

Only after Charlie has witnessed the sight of the drugged, pathetic Salim, denuded of dignity by his Israeli captors, does the reader begin to pull back from Kurtz. The double murder at the end of Part One, prefaced by Kurtz's grossly functional phone call to his wife Elli, ('He wanted to hear Israel talking to him live' ch. 15), speeds up the process of the reader's growing revulsion. That process is completed and confirmed in Kurtz's later interview with the British Intelligence 'Commander', Picton, who summons him for an explanation of Israeli activities on Picton's home soil. The British Commander had been an officer serving in the postwar Mandate when the British had hanged a 'handful' of Jews and 'Arabs galore', and he reminds Kurtz of another 'amiable young field security officer' at whose hands he had received 'beatings' during his own imprisonment (ch. 18). With distaste and accuracy, Picton draws attention to the Hagannah terrorist past of Kurtz and his boss, Gavron, taking Kurtz's confident denial for what it really is. Because Picton was himself a counter-terrorist, and acted, it is implied, with the cruelty that role requires, he is the only character able to see through, and dismiss, Kurtz's otherwise winning charm:

> But a nice man, that Picton, all the same, thought Kurtz . . . A little rough
> maybe . . . But in the end as fair as most men. A fine practitioner too. A
> fine mind inside the violence. Misha Gavron always said he'd learned a lot
> from him.   (ch. 18)

The effect of Kurtz's granite generosity is chilling and it places him as an
individual who is as much an instrument of the Zionist state as its tanks
and planes. The ruling Herut Party ('those clowns in the Knesset') may
have originated in the marginally more right-wing Irgun terrorist group
but, in the end, Hagannah and Irgun, Kurtz and the state, are
indistinguishable, whatever Kurtz's protestations to the contrary.

Where Kurtz's violence and policy are made to seem repugnant, Khalil's,
on the other hand, become almost justifiable; what was formerly portrayed
as indiscriminate terror is eventually provided with a grisly but nonetheless
moral motivation:

> 'The Zionists kill for fear and for hate,' he announced. 'Palestinians for
> love and justice. Remember this difference. It is important.' The glance
> again, swift and commanding. 'You will remember this when you are afraid?
> You will say to yourself "for justice"? If you do, you will no longer be
> afraid.'   (ch. 25)

> 'I am not anti-Semitic, you know that?' . . .
>   'Anti-Semitism, this is a strictly Christian invention'   (Ibid.)

Coupled with the description of his torture by brother Arabs and Syrians,
Khalil's perspective on his oppressed people succeeds in winning over the
reader with Charlie, emotionally and morally, to his side. This is further
reinforced by Charlie's own experience of the habitual bombing raids on
Palestinian camps, and her feelings of admiration and warmth for the
Palestinians she meets there. The novel ensures, however, that at a political
level, over and above individual feeling, the reader is eventually *not*
permitted to opt for the programme of one side in preference to the other.
The presentation of Kurtz and Khalil comprises a movement by which
the reader's sympathies are turned but the political issues remain stubbornly
unresolved and unresolvable, thus challenging the reader's final attraction
to the Palestinian leader and repulsion from his Israeli antagonist.

The Little Drummer Girl was completed by July 1982 (the date of its
foreword), only one month after the bombing of Beirut and the Israeli
invasion of the Lebanon. Le Carré had gone to Beirut at the beginning
of 1982, where he had talked with Yasir Arafat and visited a Palestinian
camp before going on to Jerusalem. An article he wrote for *The Observer*
in June of that year reports on his visit and it is of historical interest that
some of the remarks attributed to 'Michel' and his novel's other Palestinian
characters are transcriptions of comments from the real Palestinians
(including Arafat) he met during his trip. Presumably the same is true of
the Israeli characters. The novel's foreword movingly thanks the 'Many
Palestinians and Israelis' who helped the author and it also serves as a brief

obituary to some of the former. While this acknowledgment is elegantly balanced, expressing gratitude to members of both nationalities, le Carré's piece for *The Observer* concludes with a scathing denunciation of the recent invasion. Menachem Begin, Ariel Sharon and their Herut Party then in government had argued that their military action had been taken in retaliation for the PLO shelling of Northern Israel and for the attempt on the life of Shlomo Argor, the Israeli ambassador to London. Le Carré points out that the terrorist shooting could not have been the work of the PLO because the 'hit list' recovered soon afterwards included the name of the PLO's own London representative on it. Le Carré implies that the shooting provided Begin with a long-awaited excuse. A companion article by Patrick Seale in the same edition of *The Observer* was headlined, 'Blitzkrieg shifts power balance' and le Carré joined other voices in comparing Begin's genocidal attack on Lebanon's Palestinian population with Hitler's racialist atrocities. His piece ends without a trace of ambiguity:

> The attack was a monstrosity, launched on speciously assembled grounds against a people who, on the Israelis' own admission, constitute no serious military threat. It is as if we British had lost our temper with the IRA and decided to punish the entire Irish people once and for all – convincing ourselves at the same time that when we had done so, we would hear no more of their troubles.
>
> Too many Israelis, in their claustrophobia, have persuaded themselves that every Palestinian man and woman and child is by definition a military target, and that Israel will not be safe until the pack of them are swept away. It is the most savage irony that Begin and his generals cannot see how close they are to inflicting upon another people the disgraceful criteria once inflicted upon themselves. It is worse still that they have so far taken the Americans with them. (le Carré, 13 June 1982)

The narrative voice of *The Little Drummer Girl* differs considerably from the tone of le Carré's polemic in his *Observer* article. Whether it is recounting the effects of the suitcase bomb at the home of the Israeli Labour Attache in Bad Godesberg (the incident which opens the novel) or the 'unexplained explosion west of Munich' (Kurtz's murder of the terrorists Salim and Larsen, which closes Part One), or, in Part Two, the mopping-up of the remainder of Khalil's European group and the eradication of refugee camps in the build-up to the Israeli invasion, the tone of the narration is chillingly restrained. When the narration is indirectly giving Charlie's perception – as in the account of the aerial bombing of the camp she stays in – her subjective reactions are reproduced in full:

> Another pair of planes followed – or was it the first pair making a second run? – the oil lamp swung, and her vision righted itself as a stick of bombs approached in careful crescendo. She felt the first two like blows on her body – no, not again, not again, oh please. The third was the loudest and killed her outright, the fourth and fifth told her she was alive after all. (ch. 21)

But when the narration is independent of the consciousness of the main characters it takes on a divorced, 'knowing' distance, permitting itself to weigh the speculative and digressional aspects of an event equally with what normally would constitute its principal components. Where explanations seem unnecessary they are given, where a particularly horrifying incident seems to demand the narrator's acknowledgment of that horror, none is forthcoming. Often there is a throwaway matter-of-factness to descriptions or, again, a disturbing faux-naiveté. Such techniques give a cool pathos to parts of the narrative, suggesting either that the narrator does not fully understand the moral significance of one or other outrage, or that the narrator is being condescending towards a reader who he believes needs to have even the obvious patiently explained. Here are some examples, from the beginning and the end of the novel:

> Of the non-Jews who died, one was the Italians' Sicilian cook, another their Filipino chauffeur. Of the four injured, one was the wife of the Israeli Labour Attaché, in whose house the bomb had exploded. She lost a leg. The dead Israeli was their small son Gabriel. But the intended victim, it was afterwards concluded, was neither of these people, but rather an uncle of the Labour Attaché's injured wife who . . . (ch. 1)

> The rest of the apartment was airy but, like the Olympic Village, awfully down-at-heel. Northward the windows gave a grimy view of the road to Dachau, where a great many Jews had died in the concentration camp . . . (ch. 2)

> A succession of other, less interesting deaths passed virtually unnoticed, as did the Israeli bombing of an ancient desert fortress on the Syrian border, which Jerusalem sources claimed was being used as a Palestinian training base for foreign terrorists. As to the four-hundred-pound bomb that exploded on a hill-top outside Beirut, destroying a luxurious summer villa and killing its occupants – which included both Tayeh and Fatmeh – it was about as impenetrable as any other act of terror in that tragic region. (ch. 27)

The clenched narrative irony in these accounts is retained for the description of the eventual Israeli drive into the Lebanon, which, unknown to Charlie, kills off those of her Palestinian contacts who have survived the previous raids. Here, though, the ironical tone is barely sustained:

> And in the late spring at last . . . the long-awaited Israeli push into Lebanon occurred, ending the present phase of hostilities or, according to where you stood, heralding the next one. The refugee camps that had played host to Charlie were sanitized, which meant roughly that bulldozers were brought in to bury the bodies and complete what the tanks and artillery bombing raids had started . . . (Ibid.)

In real-life, the 'Lebanese Forces' of Saad Haddad and the Damuri Brigade, units controlled by the Israeli authorities, concluded that next short phase with the massacre of Palestinian refugees at the camps of Sabra and Shatila, less than three months later.

Given *The Little Drummer Girl*'s acute topicality, it was to be expected that the novel's reviewers would discover in it the author's own political leanings, a task made seemingly easy by his *Observer* piece. David Pryce-Jones castigates what he sees as le Carré's 'clear-cut' attitude of hostility towards the Israelis (16 April 1983) but, in the following issue of *The Spectator*, Auberon Waugh rebukes Jones for misreading, claiming instead that it shows little evidence of political partiality and, anyway, is really about Charlie, 'a silly mixed-up, promiscuous English actress, a compulsive liar and fantasist . . . ' and is 'not about the political issues involved' (23 April 1983). Other reviewers divided into those seeing the novel as no more than romance and those – the majority opinion – who commended le Carré's balance between, in Julian Symons' words, 'the two violent idealisms' (27 March 1983). Probably the most substantial review, Julie Diamond's article in *Race and Class*, looked critically at the novel's political ambiguity or 'neutrality' as deriving from le Carré's avoidance of evaluating the political positions he reproduces. Diamond concludes that, 'in its choice of moral values', *The Little Drummer Girl* is 'uncompromising' but that its programmatic evasiveness, its choice of *'no choice'*, is itself expressive of 'a position, indeed, an ideological one' (1984, p. 40).

When the terms 'balance' and 'neutrality' are applied to political alternatives it is true that they may indeed suggest the kind of judiciousness which complacently absents itself from the immediacies of a given situation in what may be perceived as a more or less wilful refusal to take the responsibility of choosing. Being resigned to the neutral viewpoint may well imply a more general politics of resignation and acquiescence which, denying the possibility of making a legitimate choice between two equally understandable positions, takes refuge in the complexity, and ends in a submissive acceptance of the status quo. Alternatively, a position of 'no choice' may imply that any choice is simplistic and that a shrugged acknowledgment of confusion is at least the more honest and honourable, if utterly ineffectual, preference. I have argued elsewhere in this book against the assumption that a political novel must propangandize for a preferred line in order to qualify as political, and have also demonstrated that balance and ambiguity are never consoling in le Carré's fiction but are invariably precarious and disturbing, always open to criticism, yet neither of these observations is of overriding importance with respect to *The Little Drummer Girl*. This novel takes its form and engineers its responses directly from the specific political situation it images; its sense of 'balance' and 'neutrality' originate less in the author's 'ideology' than in the objective situation which is his subject.

The horizontal, in le Carré's political 'balance', is never achieved. The narrative is, by turns, fiercely partisan and its see-sawing effect is giddying. Through Charlie's swaying loyalties, the reader is kept on the minute-to-minute arguments which confront her, and t'e narrative's detail in articulating the conflicting attitudes betweer and within the Israeli and Palestinian groups prevent its readers, unless so confirmed in their judgements on the question outside the novel, from coming down ultimately in favour of any of its offered political positions. This prevention occurs in spite of the fact that readers are permitted to form localized political, (but mainly), emotional and moral sympathies for the respective groups at different times. For example, whatever the reader may feel about Kurtz manipulating Charlie or working from a carefully prepared script or avoiding outright some of her stronger objections, his justification of Israel's right to survive has an undeniable force as a political argument independent of the character who voices it:

> May Israel survive or must all of us here pack up our belongings and go back to our former countries and start over again? Maybe you would prefer us to take a piece of Central Africa? Or Uruguay? Not Egypt, thank you, we tried it once and it wasn't a success. Or shall we redisperse ourselves over the ghettos of Europe and Asia while we wait for the next pogrom? What do you say, Charlie?'   (ch. 6)

The rhetorical persuasiveness of his statements is well-rehearsed and its pleading-patronizing sarcasm produces some anxiety in the reader but there is no doubt that Kurtz's position is deeply felt and, moreover, expresses a truth. There are flaws and gaps in Kurtz's arguments; when Charlie challenges his claim to be acting on behalf of 'Innocent people' he avoids answering her and she takes it up later with Gadi when he repeats the sentiment:

> 'I'd like to write a book actually, on the guilt of all those innocent bystanders you go on about. I'd start with your Lebanese bombings and fan out from there.'
>
> Seated or not, he came back faster and harder than she had bargained for. 'That book has been done, Charlie, and it is called the Holocaust.' (ch. 14)

Gadi's statement too, avoids her particular objection, but, again its force is unquestionable, winning the reader, for the moment, to the Israeli side.

Yet the fact of the Holocaust cuts two ways and le Carré includes alternative Israeli voices which, with similar force, acknowledge that the Jewish oppressed have now turned oppressor. That it is Israeli characters, civilians threatened both by Zionists and Palestinian nationalists, who make this point, gives the scene in which Kurtz calls on Professor and Mrs Minkel a narrative weight that more than compensates for its brevity. The Minkels represent liberal Israeli opinion, canvassing for Arab civil rights and withdrawal from Gaza and the West Bank. Kurtz and the Professor reach a stalemate over the latter's small-state theory of compromise and coexistence; Kurtz has merely to articulate the Palestinian objection to the Professor's advocacy of what they deem 'the Bantustan solution' to arrest the discussion but the Professor is in no way thrown by an objection he has lived long with, and they part in mutual distaste, the argument unresolved. Mrs Minkel's intervention in the middle of their conversation, however, has a moral power that stays with the reader, even if the political conclusions she draws from it are not better than Kurtz's:

> But Mrs Minkel was clearly a lady who was used to making her point. 'We couldn't stop the Nazis, now we can't stop ourselves. We get our own country, what do we do? Forty years later, we invent a new lost tribe. Idiocy! And if *we* don't say it, the world will. The world says it already . . . ' (ch. 23)

The reader may lean on Mrs Minkel's analysis, agreeing wholeheartedly with it, while the intractable political sediment continues to collect wearisomely around it.

Against the Israeli memory of the Holocaust is the Palestinian memory of Deir Yasseen, the history of which begins Charlie's fictional recruitment to their cause. That the event is related by a Zionist impersonating an Arab nationalist in convincing empathy, is considerably disorientating:

> 'Once more I shall answer as if I saw it happen yesterday with my own eyes. In the small Arab village of Deir Yasseen on April 9, 1948, two hundred and fifty-four villagers – old men, women and children – were butchered by Zionist terror squads while the young men were working in the fields . . . Within days, nearly half a million Palestinians had fled their country . . .' (ch. 10)

'Michel's' account continues through the 1967 war and on into his own Jordanian exile and Fatah training. Pausing for a moment, out of role, Gadi coaches Charlie on her reaction, 'Overawed. Amazed. By his romanticism, his beauty, his fascination', and criticizes 'Michel's' rhetoric:

> 'He has a jargon-ridden vocabulary and an impressive store of rhetorical phrases, questionable statistics, and tortuous quotations. Despite this, he communicates the excitement of a young and passionate mind, and an expanding one.' (Ibid.)

But just as the novel's political arguments may be separated from the specific business of action and character, so too they also survive their rhetorical formulation – whether in the language of Arabs or Israelis. When, for example, Charlie tries (rather unconvincingly) to deny the effects upon her of Salim's speech at the weekend school she says, sharply, 'I was not enraptured! I thought you were way over the top, and I had a damn good mind to tell you so!' (ibid.), but the 'jargon' of Salim – Michel, 'over the top' as it is, never allows the reader to dismiss its content:

> 'Yet who has the simple courage to tell out loud the cruellest joke in history: that thirty years of Israel have turned the Palestinians into the new Jews of the earth? You know how the Zionists described my country before they seized it? "A land without a people for a people without a land". *We did not exist!* In their minds, the Zionists had already committed genocide; all that remained for them was the fact.' (Ibid.)

The narrative technique of *The Little Drummer Girl* offers Charlie and the novel's readers many opportunities for political partisanship, but each and every alignment is compromised and negated when the next convincing claim is made on the reader's complicity. Le Carré is scrupulously careful to refrain from endorsing any one of either nationality's programmes for 'solving' the problem of the Near East. Like Charlie, the reader is given no chance to stand back to come to a rational overview; both sides have to be experienced in the here-and-now with Charlie and the reader subject to powerful, immediate pressures. Only when the see-saw ride is over, with Charlie left completely numbed, is the reader faced with the impossibility of choice. The fundamental political questions asked by the novel's committed characters remain open and unanswered – should the state of Israel have been formed in the first place; should the Israeli people be fought until they are defeated and their state then dismantled; is the West Bank solution really impossible; should the Palestinians be regarded as the victims of history and left to their unfortunate fate; is Israeli restraint possible and if so, what would it achieve; the victory of which side would represent the lesser evil? Ultimately, the novel sees these questions as admitting of no equitable answers: there is indeed, in Diamond's words, *'no choice'* preferred. But the latter is not the same as a position of 'neutrality' – le Carré abstains from nothing in refusing to take a side because taking a side involves the chooser in the invidious act of preferring one nationality over another. The novel intermittently choruses one overriding observation: that nationalism *per se* has inherent in it an ultimate capacity for genocide. Significantly, le Carré's *Observer* article makes the comparison between Palestine–Israel and the issue of Northern Ireland and the analogy is apt: in both cases the right of national self-determination is unrealizable because two opposed communities (in Ireland) and two (or more) opposed nationalities (in the Near-East) occupy one and the same area of land. *The Little Drummer Girl* records the knowledge that genocidal acts and the fear of genocide invalidate any even-handed nationalist 'solution' to the Palestinian problem; it implies that an outright victory for one side bespeaks the oppression of the other, and that the national antagonisms are so great that a Minkel-style compromise is likely to fail. Le Carré has selected the material for his novel from one of the few situations in the world where the interpenetration of peoples in a single geographical space gives any nationalist 'solutions' a particular venom and a particular inoperability. Thus, to canvass for either side is to compound the problem by accepting as good coin its actually 'irreconcilable' terms; to make no choice, on the other hand, does not derive from an 'ideological' inability or unwillingness to choose, it simply reflects the facts of this specific *nationalist* conflict. Le Carré reproduces the process by which that knowledge is arrived at in the narrative strategies of his novel. If *The Little Drummer Girl* does express a political ideology, it is perhaps in its silence on any programme that is other than nationalist but le Carré is no Marxist, nor even a politician, and his project ceases with accurate, empirical reflection alone.

Afterword

It feels distinctly odd to attempt a general concluding statement on a writer who is still presumably in mid-career – even allowing for the fact that such a conclusion could be at best provisional. But more than that, the thought of concluding seems singularly inappropriate in the case of John le Carré because the very notion carries with it an implication of development – an expectation of something like growth – which, I have suggested, is noticeably absent in the last twenty years of le Carré's work. This is not to say that his fiction lacks variety, nor that it is changeless. And almost self-evidently, the comparative lengths of his novels from *The Spy Who Came in from the Cold* to *The Little Drummer Girl* attest to a 'progression' from a generic sparseness towards a later expansiveness or inclusiveness. Yet it would be highly dubious to deduce that changes in the novels' structural organization and styles make for anything other than a formal 'development'. In terms of *issue* le Carré's political fictions comprise a serialized repetition – albeit a repetition with precise variations. I use the word repetition here with no intention of tapping its depreciatory sense because repetition as such is inherent in le Carré's subject matter and is also a conscious component of his method. Though repetition is most marked in his trilogy, and especially in *Smiley's People*, it is clearly recognizable in his work as a whole. Returning to obstinately recurrent states or situations and again either seeking to evade or actually to face their claims and challenges constitutes more than just a 'theme' in le Carré's writing.

Liberalism's instability constantly and implicitly demands of its adherents that they confront the issue of taking sides – whenever, that is, coherent alternative positions intrude upon their perception of things. Fearing the definition and cost that taking sides entails, the liberal is most comfortable in attempting to choose all the possible alternatives – both West *and* East, neutrality *and* commitment, rigour *and* flabbiness, work *and* home, the public *and* the personal. Seeking to live (impossibly) with the contradictions in inert balance, the liberal is quickly and drastically sent spinning out of control in response to any pressure exerted by any more single-minded and grounded force. Le Carré's narratives reproduce this phenomenon and their stubborn repetitions demonstrate simply the authenticity of the writer's grasp of it.

Certainly there is a risk involved in the writer's reworkings of these disturbing repetitions. The danger lies in what must be the great temptation to reduce and abstract problems of choice by downplaying the specific content of each particular option and employing different social/historical contexts merely as convenient forms in which to focus on generalized, 'essential' questions of individual morality. It is arguably Graham Greene's tendency to concentrate too readily on what is too easily presented as some transcendent realm of the personal. Le Carré, however, ensures that the issue of taking sides is never abstracted from those concrete situations which ask for concrete choices. The differences between competing political positions are retained objectively – as alternatives existing independently of individual perceivers.

The sense of objectivity is primarily provided by the topical situations which are given in all of le Carré's political novels – perhaps with the single exception of *Smiley's People*. Of course the selection of topical subjects springs in part from the writer's commonsensical concern to maintain and foster a market for his work. He spoke of having had 'so much luck' (Bragg, 27 March 1983. I.) in the coincidence of the BBC dramatizations of *Tinker Tailor Soldier Spy* and *Smiley's People* being broadcast during the press furore over a run of allegations concerning spies in high places. Le Carré's hard-headed topicality both reflects and feeds popular enthusiasms – however short-lived they may prove but it also serves to anchor his own longstanding concerns within immediately comprehensible and already 'live' contexts. The Berlin Wall, spy-flights, the generation of the thirties, the celebrated double-agents, the English Establishment, Neo-Nazism, the South-East Asian wars, the ending of Empire, the Near-East question – all of these are used to reformulate the liberal dilemma but with each the immediacy of the social issue is sufficiently powerful to make the recasting and recognition of same-ness sharp and arresting: le Carré's liberal voices retain their distinctiveness, their diverse emphases. And equally, each of these objective issues is described and discussed in its own right as a matter of general concern.

It is a sign of le Carré's capacity to hone in on particular political events that he continues to be judged as a commentator who is persuasive enough to direct mass opinion. I have argued that the quality of le Carré's insight is expressed in his avoidance of canvassing a line but, for whatever reasons and according to whatever misreadings of his novels, he is nevertheless seen as an effective ideologist. And moreover he continues to be seen – at least in a society more consciously political than our own – as an ideologist who has undergone radical changes in his political orientation. A recent piece by Alan Rusbridger of *The Guardian* reports on le Carré's new-found favour in the Soviet Union which seems to evidence this perception of him:

> There is a big demand in Moscow for copies of *Literaturnaya Gazeta* which, to the astonishment of most Russians, has started to serialize the latest work

of John le Carré. *The Little Drummer Girl* is admittedly sympathetic enough to the Palestinian cause to meet official approval. On the other hand, the Lit Gaz is the journal which once described le Carré as 'the evil genius of the British spymasters' and 'one of the West's most lavishly paid Cold War propagandists' . . . (16 May 1985)

Evidently le Carré's objective of making his Western liberal readership self-critical seems barely relevant here. But his changed fortune in the USSR invites many speculations. Perhaps the Stalinist censors feel able to relax their hold a little – perhaps the editorial board of *Literaturnaya Gazeta* is now controlled by a liberal wing? Maybe the Near-East situation has become so massively complicated by sectoral and communalist antagonisms that the Israeli–PLO conflict as it appeared back in 1983 now seems positively historic in its apparent simplicity and is thus safe for public consumption? Or is le Carré's first Soviet reviewer, V. Voinov (or one of his confederates), still demonstrating and publicizing his literary enthusiasms? Whatever determined the revision of le Carré's 'official' status it can clearly have had no basis in a right-minded appraisal of *The Little Drummer Girl*'s refusal to settle for a partisan viewpoint. In fact, John le Carré refuses to foreclose on each and every issue he engages with. For that reason, reading him – if he is to be read as he deserves – must continue to be an unfinished business.

List of References

ALVAREZ, A. 'Half-angels versus half-devils'. *The Observer*, 3 February 1980.

ANDERSEN, H. (1977) *The Sandman*. in *The Complete Fairy Tales and Stories*. Translated E. C. Haugaard. Victor Gollancz.

ATKINS, J. (1984) *The British Spy Novel: Styles in Treachery*. John Calder.

AUDEN, W. H. (1977) *The English Auden: Poems, Essays, and Dramatic Writings 1927–1939*. Edited E. Mendelson. Faber and Faber.

BENNETT, T. (1982) 'James Bond as popular hero'. *Politics, Ideology and Popular Culture 2*. Course Unit 21, U203, 5–25. The Open University Press.

BERNE, E. (1967) *Games People Play: the Psychology of Human Relationships*. Penguin Books.

BINYON, T. J. 'A Gentleman Among Players'. *Times Literary Supplement*, 9 September 1977.

BOOKER, C. (1969) *The Neophiliacs: a study of the revolution in English life in the Fifties and Sixties*. Collins.

BOYLE, A. (1980) *The Climate of Treason*. Coronet Books.

BRAGG, M. 'The Things a Spy Can Do = John Le Carré Talking'. *The Listener*, 22 January 1976. I.

'A Talk with John le Carré'. *The New York Times Book Review*, 13 March 1983. I.

The South Bank Show. London Weekend Television. 27 March 1983 (Unpublished broadcast). I.

BRECHT, B. (1964) *Brecht on Theatre: the Development of an Aesthetic*. Edited and translated J. Willett. Hill and Wang.

(1975) *Mother Courage and her Children: a Chronicle of the Thirty Years War*. Translated E. Bentley. Eyre Methuen.

BROMLEY, R. (1978) 'Natural Boundaries: the Social Function of Popular Fiction', *Red Letters*, 7, 34–40.

CAMERON, J. 'The case of the hot writer'. *The New York Times Magazine*, 8 September 1974. I.

CARROLL, L. (1970) *Alice Through the Looking-Glass* in *The Annotated Alice*. Edited M. Gardner. Penguin Books.

CAUTE, D. 'It Was a Man'. *New Statesman*, 8 February 1980.

COCKBURN, C. *The New York Times*, 23 November 1979.

COLEMAN, J. 'A Crafty le Carré: Smiley springs the trap'. *The Sunday Times*, 3 February 1980.

DEAN, M. 'John le Carré: the writer who came in from the cold'. *The Listener*, 5 September 1974. I.

DEIGHTON, L. (1962) *The Ipcress File*. Hodder and Stoughton.

DIAMOND, J. (1984) 'Spies in the Promised Land: a review article'. *Race & Class*, 24, (4), 35–40.

EAGLETON, T. (1983) *Literary Theory: an Introduction*. Basil Blackwell.

FREUD, S. (1955) 'The Uncanny' in vol. 17, *Standard Edition of the Complete Psychological Works*. 24 vols. 1953–1974. Edited J. B. Strachey. The Hogarth Press.

GREENE, G. (1939) *The Confidential Agent*. William Heinemann.

(1955) *The Quiet American*. William Heinemann.

(1958) *Our Man in Havanna*. William Heinemann.

GROSS, M. 'The Secret World of John le Carré'. *The Observer*, 3 February 1980. I.

HALPERIN, J. (1980) 'Between Two Worlds: the Novels of John le Carré'. *South Atlantic Quarterly*, 79, 17–37.

HAMILTON, I. (1973) *A Poetry Chronicle: Essays and Reviews*. Faber and Faber.

HARRIS, T. A. (1973) *I'm OK – You're OK*. Pan Books.

HEWISON, R. (1981) *In Anger: Culture in the Cold War 1945–60*. Weidenfeld and Nicolson.

HICKS, G. 'Spies Without a Sense of Mission'. *Saturday Review*, 48, 24 July 1965.

HOFFMANN, E. T. (1982) *The Sandman* in *Tales of Hoffmann*. Translated R. J. Hollingdale. Penguin Books.

JAMES, C. (1982) *From the Land of Shadows*. Jonathan Cape.

KEE, R. 'Dangerous Mudlands'. *The Listener*, 7 February 1980.

LAING, R. D. (1965) *The Divided Self: an Existential Study in Sanity and Madness*. Penguin Books.

LE CARRÉ, J. (1961) *Call for the Dead*. Victor Gollancz.

(1962) *A Murder of Quality*. Victor Gollancz.

(1963) *The Spy Who Came in from the Cold*. Victor Gollancz.

(1965) *The Looking-Glass War*. William Heinemann.

(1966) 'To Russia, with Greetings: an open letter to the Moscow *Literary Gazette*'. *Encounter*, 26, 3–6.

(1968) *A Small Town in Germany*. William Heinemann.

(1968) 'Spies'. Tape 1949. Bibliothèque Sonore, Faculté des Lettres, Nancy 54000. I. (Unpublished US broadcast)

(1971) *The Naive and Sentimental Lover*. Hodder and Stoughton.

(1974) *Tinker Tailor Soldier Spy*. Hodder and Stoughton.

(1977) *The Honourable Schoolboy*. Hodder and Stoughton.

(1980) *Smiley's People*. Hodder and Stoughton.

'Siege'. *The Observer*, 1 June 1980.

'Memories of a Vanished Land'. *The Observer*, 13 June 1982.

(1983) *The Little Drummer Girl*. Hodder and Stoughton.

MACLEAR, M. (1982) *Vietnam: the Ten Thousand Day War*. Thames Methuen.

MERRY, B. (1977) *Anatomy of the Spy-Thriller*. Gill and Macmillan.

NEUSE, S. (1982) 'Bureaucratic Malaise in the Modern Spy Novel: Deighton, Greene and le Carré'. *Public Administration*, 60, 293–306.

OAKES, P. 'Hard Cash and le Carré'. *The Sunday Times*, 11 September 1977. I.

PAGE, B., LEITCH, D., and KNIGHTLEY, P. (1968) *Philby: the Spy Who Betrayed a Generation*. Introduction J. le Carré. André Deutsch.

PALMER, J. (1973) 'Thrillers: the Deviant Behind the Consensus' in I. Taylor and L. Raylor (eds), *Politics and Deviance*. Penguin Books.

PHILBY, K. (1969) *My Silent War*. Introduction G. Greene. Granada.

PRYCE-JONES, D. 'Drumming Up Hatred'. *The Spectator* 16 April 1983.

RUSBRIDGER, A. *The Guardian*, 16 May 1985.

SEALE, P. 'Blitzkrieg shifts power balance'. *The Observer* 1 June 1980.

SHAKESPEARE, W. (1975) *As You Like It*. Edited A. Latham. The Arden Shakespeare. Methuen.

SHAW, B. (1926) *Saint Joan: a Chronicle Play in Six Scenes and an Epilogue*. Constable.

SHAWCROSS, W. (1980) *Sideshow: Kissinger, Nixon and the Destruction of Cambodia*. Fontana.

SLAUGHTER, C. (1980) *Marxism, Ideology and Literature*. Macmillan.

SYMONS, J. (1972) *Bloody Murder: from the Detective Story to the Crime Novel: a History*. Faber and Faber.

'A book to be buried with'. *The Sunday Times*, 27 March 1983.

TREPPER, L. (1979) *The Great Game: the Story of the Red Orchestra*. Sphere Books.

TURNER, E. S. 'Chancery Creeps'. *The Listener*, 31 October 1968.

VAUGHAN, P. 'Le Carré's Circus: lamplighters, moles and others of that ilk'. *The Listener*, 13 September 1979. I.

VOINOV, V. 'John le Carré: Spy Tamer'. *Literaturnaya Gazeta*, 16 October 1965.

WAUGH, A. 'Oversensitive'. *The Spectator*, 23 April 1983.

WEST, N. (1982) *A Matter of Trust: MI5 1945–72*. Weidenfeld and Nicolson.

WEST, R. 'Local Colour'. *The Spectator*, 10 September 1977.

WORPOLE, K. (1983) *Dockers and Detectives*. Verso.

Index